EDUCATIONAL
MEASUREMENT
AND
TESTING

EDUCATIONAL
MEASUREMENT
AND
TESTING

William Wiersma

Stephen G. Jurs

The University of Toledo

Allyn and Bacon, Inc.
Boston   London   Sydney   Toronto

To
Dean GEORGE E. DICKSON

administrator, researcher,
scholar, teacher,
and friend

Series Editor: Jeffery W. Johnston
Production Administrator: Jane Schulman
Editorial/Production Services: B & W Hutchinsons, Orleans, Massachusetts
Cover Coordinator: Christy Rosso
Cover Designer: Virginia Mason

Library of Congress Cataloging in Publication Data

Wiersma, William.
    Educational measurement and testing.

    Includes bibliographies and index.
    1. Educational tests and measurements. 2. Examinations—Study guides. I. Jurs, Stephen G. II. Title.

LB3051.W493 1985   371.2'6   84-20352
ISBN: 0-205-08364-1

Printed in the United States of America.

10 9 8 7 6 5 4 3 2 1   90 89 88 87 86 85

Overview

Contents   xi

Preface   xxi

Contents

Preface

Educational Measurement and Testing has been designed as a textbook for an introductory course, whether the course is offered on the undergraduate or graduate level. The book may be used for the measurement component in an undergraduate course or instructional block that covers a variety of topics, including measurement and/or testing. Classroom teachers or anyone else concerned about constructing tests can use the book as a reference.

This introductory text covers basic concepts and procedures of educational measurement, test construction, and test usage. The contents include adequate theory for understanding educational measurement and emphasize the practical application of measurement and testing procedures. The statistical concepts required for measurement are discussed, along with the concepts of validity and reliability. However, there is no statistical prerequisite for the use of this book. Several chapters are devoted to the construction of test items, and measurement in the psychomotor and affective domains is covered, as well. The concluding chapter deals with current testing issues.

Several features of the book are designed to enhance its use as a learning device and a teaching tool. Important points are summarized and displayed prominently throughout the content. Key terms and concepts introduced in a chapter are highlighted in the text and listed at the end of that chapter, pinpointing major ideas and facilitating review; these terms are then defined in the Glossary of Key Terms and Concepts.

At the end of each chapter is also a set of review items that the reader may use to check understanding of chapter content; answers to the review items are provided in appendix 2. In addition, exercises are included for all chapters; solutions to selected exercises are given in appendix 3.

Two glossaries are provided for the reader's convenience. One glossary contains commonly used measurement terms, as mentioned above; the other contains statistical symbols and formulas.

This book, as a text, provides considerable flexibility for the instructor and the reader. The sequence in which topics are considered may be rearranged to meet the needs of the students or the preference of the instructor. For example, the chapter "Current Issues" (chapter 14) could be considered first, if such an overview is desired early in the instruction.

A mastery of the content of the book will provide the reader with a basic understanding of educational measurement and testing. And since the content emphasis is upon concepts and procedures used by classroom teachers, prospective teachers or practicing teachers, along with other educators who work in the school setting, will find the text helpful.

Special acknowledgment goes to Professor Herbert J. Klausmeier of the University of Wisconsin for his permission to reproduce content from *Evaluation of Instruction in IGE,* a book in the Leadership Series in Individually Guided Education, of which Professor Klausmeier was the Series Editor.

We also wish to acknowledge Harry Bluhm (University of Utah), Juan Franco (New Mexico State University), and Marie Llabre (University of Miami), who reviewed our work in its early stages.

W. W.
S. J.

1

Introduction: The Logic of Testing

Introduction

Any professional educator—teacher, principal, or guidance counselor—is concerned with **measurement** and testing. **Tests** are measurement devices that provide information about students, and possibly others, although in the educational enterprise, the emphasis is certainly on students. There are diagnostic tests, achievement tests, aptitude tests, ability tests, and the list could go on. There are tests purchased from commercial publishers, as well as teacher-constructed tests. Why do the schools engage in all this testing?

The specific reasons for testing are many and varied—probably about as many as there are specific tests. But generally, tests are used to provide information about student characteristics and performance—information that probably cannot be obtained in other ways, at least not as efficiently and effectively. There is considerable controversy about the extent of testing and the use of test results in today's schools. Some argue that there is too much testing and that some very important decisions are based on test results of questionable value. There may be some merit to this argument, and even the strongest supporters of testing readily admit that tests are not perfect. But educational tests and other measurement devices are a useful and essential part of teaching and learning. Tests are undoubtedly here to stay.

Educators have varying levels of expertise about the nature and use of tests. For example, guidance counselors are generally more knowledgeable about aptitude tests than are teachers, since guidance counselors use results from such tests in advising students about career choices. Classroom teachers assess students on performance in academic and skills areas, almost on a continuing basis; knowledge about measurement and testing is thus necessary for the teacher. Overall, since testing runs through all of education, it is important that all educators have a basic knowledge of measurement and testing.

Education is a diversified profession that has many specialties, including educational measurement. It certainly is not necessary for all educators to be measurement specialists, but a basic body of concepts and procedures should be known by all teachers. This text addresses those concepts and procedures.

Some Definitions:
Measurement, Assessment, Testing, and Evaluation

The terms **assessment** and **evaluation** are commonly associated with measurement and testing, and although all of these terms are related, they are not necessarily synonymous. Consistent meanings of measurement terms, though desirable, are a characteristic not always found when terms are used in a general sense or when used with people outside the schools. The definitions below have a degree of precision about them that is important for developing an understanding of educational measurement and its procedures.

Measurement as Quantification

Measurement accompanies a host of activities in our society and involves varying degrees of precision, depending upon the measuring instrument and the use to be made of the findings. It is relatively easy to understand the measurement of something like the dimensions of the rooms of a school in terms of length and width. Having an adequate yardstick readily makes such measurement possible. It is, however, much more difficult to conceptualize and operationalize the measurement of personality.

A broad definition of measurement is often stated as the assignment of numerals to objects or events according to rules. Actually, the numerals represent some specific characteristic of the object or event. A numeral is a symbol, such as 1, 2, 3, and so on. However, the numeral itself has no relevance to measurement until it is assigned quantitative meaning. Sometimes numerals are used simply for convenience, such as the assignment of numbers to the players of a baseball team. Such assignment may or may not follow a rule but, in any event, does not comprise measurement.

Measurements involving length, weight, and volume are commonplace and readily understood by most people, since the quantification in such measurement is quite apparent. That measurement of educational attributes—such as cognitive performance, intellectual ability, and attitudes—involves the same general concepts and ideas is not as easily understood. The crucial element is, of course, the rule. For this reason, the rule and what goes into it require specific attention.

Suppose a student is measured on science achievement through the use of a twenty-item test, each item representing five points. The rule is that a correct response to an item receives five points; the points are then totaled for the achievement score. Even if the rule is applicable and produces a score representing quantification, the test cannot produce measurement relevant to the achievement unless the test items are appropriate. This is somewhat analogous to measuring the length of a room with a tape measure having inconsistent gradations for inches. It is much easier to standardize the length of an inch than the quantitative values of test items, but as long as the rule can be operationally defined, measurement is possible.

> Technically, measurement is the assignment of numerals to objects or events according to rules that give numerals quantitative meaning.

Assessment and Testing

The terms assessment and test are quite closely associated with measurement and are not always used with consistent meaning. For all practical purposes, assessment and measurement can be considered synonymous. When assessment is taking place, information or data are being collected and measurement is being conducted. Assessment does not include making judgments about the data, which is reserved for evaluation, as we will see subsequently.

Test, on the other hand, has a narrower meaning than either measurement or assessment. Test most commonly refers to a set of items or questions designed to be presented to one or more students under specified conditions. When a test is given, measurement takes place; however, all measurement is not necessarily testing. For example, suppose a teacher records information about the learning styles preferred by a student. This is an example of measurement, but we do not consider it testing. Testing is, of course, the process of administering a test, and in this sense, testing is subsumed under measurement. The test is the stimulus to which the response is made. Tests are not limited to paper-and-pencil inventories. For example, we may have oral tests for communication skills and physical performance tests for psychomotor skills.

In summarizing the relationship of the terms test, assessment, and measurement, using the definitions above, we see that all testing is subsumed under assessment, and assessment and measurement are synonymous. If a test is used for data collection, then the assessment or measurement is being conducted through testing.

Evaluation

In the meaning of terminology, evaluation is a process that includes measurement and possibly testing, but it also contains the notion of a value judgment. If a teacher administers a science test to a class and computes the percentages of correct responses, measurement and testing have taken place. The scores must be interpreted, which may mean converting them to values like A's, B's, C's, and so on, or judging them to be excellent, good, fair, or poor. This process is evaluation, because value judgments—either implicit or explicit—are being made. Evaluation sometimes is based only on objective data; however, more commonly, it involves a synthesis of information from two or more sources, such as test scores, values, and impressions. Some sources may provide quite subjective information. In any event, evaluation does include making a value judgment, and hopefully, in education, such judgments are based on objective information. Figure 1.1 shows the relationships among the terms testing, measurement, and evaluation. Note that measurement is not completely contained in evaluation. Measurement can occur without prompting a judgment or decision; thus, we would not have evaluation. Measurement may also include theory, which would not be evaluation. Figure 1.1 may be somewhat simplistic, but it illustrates the distinctions among the terms.

The Need for Measurement in Education

Sometimes the necessity of conducting measurement in the schools and classrooms seems so obvious that it hardly merits discussion. Without measurement, how could we determine student knowledge, performance levels, attitudes, aptitudes, interests, and the like? Although all of educational measurement is not conducted through testing, certainly a substantial and important portion is. The need for measurement can best be understood by considering the functions measurement serves, especially as it occurs through the testing in schools.

Functions of Measurement

Educational measurement serves several specific functions. These functions can be grouped into three general categories: instructional, guidance and counseling, and administrative. Of the three, the teacher is most extensively involved with instructional functions. We have heard the saying, "Taking a test should be a learning experience," and certainly, providing a useful learning experience for the student is an important function of testing. But testing also motivates learning by causing the student to prepare for the test, engaging in cooperative study with other students, and so forth. Therefore, if tests are well constructed and reflect course objectives, they

Figure 1.1.
Relationships among the Terms Testing, Measurement, and Evaluation

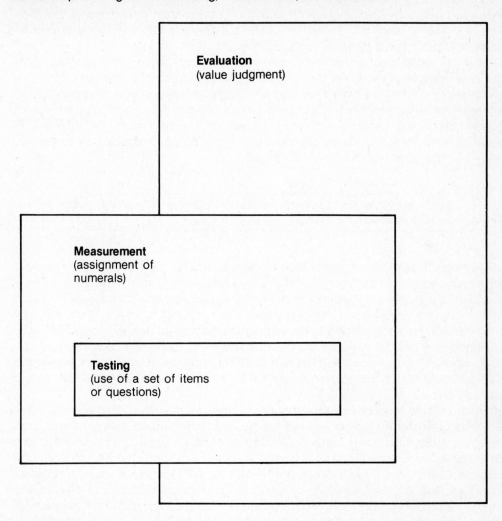

147   motivate and enhance learning. As a corollary, appropriate and fair tests enhance
148   student morale; unfair and irrelevant ones discourage students. So not only is there
149   a need for measurement from the student's perspective, measurement must be suit-
150   able whether conducted through tests, work samples, or other means.
151   From the standpoint of the teacher, measurement serves a very important func-
152   tion by providing feedback about the students. Measurement results may be used
153   for diagnosis of possible student weaknesses, as well as for evaluation of student

performance. But measurement results, especially test results, also provide feedback about instruction, such as: Has instruction been effective? Is there certain content that was poorly covered? Do the students indicate consistent misconceptions, possibly because of confused instruction? This type of important feedback about students and instruction is provided through measurement.

A more subtle function of measurement directly applicable to the teacher is that the preparation for measurement (for example, constructing a test) stimulates the teacher to clarify course objectives and enhances the preparation for teaching. This is true whether the teacher works individually or as part of a teaching team. Participation in planning measurement and preparing tests makes teachers focus directly on objectives, content, and processes, resulting not only in improved measurement and evaluation, but also in improved instruction.

> **Tests and other measurement instruments provide the teacher with information about the students, as well as the instruction.**

Tests and inventories that measure student aptitude, interest, and achievement serve guidance and counseling functions. To a large extent, tests used for guidance purposes are published tests that provide specific information about how and with whom they are to be used. Numerous tests are available, and it is important that each test be used as intended to avoid misinterpretation of results. Information from any one test is only an indicator of what is measured; counseling decisions are usually based on multiple sources of information. For example, the decision to select a college would not be based on a single test score, such as the score on a scholastic aptitude test.

Tests also serve administrative functions, often related to program evaluation. Many school systems participate in yearly student achievement testing using a battery of standardized tests. This is basically a means of self-evaluation; curriculum deficiencies, as well as program strengths, may be identified. Test information indicates whether or not student needs are being met; for example: Is student achievement sufficient for acceptance to college? Program accreditation and certification almost invariably include decisions made on the basis of test data. In some school systems, school boards use student test results for the evaluation of teaching performance. Thus, tests serve a valuable function for administrative decisions, as well as for those made in instruction and guidance.

> **In addition to instructional functions, tests provide useful information for guidance and counseling, along with administrative and program evaluation decisions.**

Classroom Measurement and Testing

A good bit of the measurement of student performance in the classroom is done through testing. Since measurement is such an integral part of instruction, the teacher must be proficient at conducting measurement through teacher-constructed tests. Because of the uniqueness of the classroom as an instructional unit, it is extremely unlikely that all measurement needs can be met through the use of standardized or published tests.

The typical elementary or secondary student spends most of the school day in the classroom, so it follows that most of the important educational outcomes (such as learning to read or add) are generated or evidenced there. Are all important educational outcomes measurable? The answer is yes, at least in theory. An educational outcome, in order to be important, must make some observable difference. If, for example, an educational outcome is the acquisition of reading skill, then there must be some discernible difference between students who have attained different "amounts" or levels of reading skill. In order for a difference to be detected or identified, the outcome must be measurable.

Although this argument may seem straightforward enough, the educational process is complex and our understanding of learning is incomplete. Consequently, some educational outcomes are not measurable by the procedures and tests presently available. Also, there are qualitative as well as quantitative differences in outcomes. But overall, the cognitive outcomes of most concern to teachers—those most affected by instruction—can be measured in some manner.

Important educational outcomes change students in ways that can be measured.

Knowledge, Performance, Objectives, and Measurement

Ebel (1982) has developed an excellent description of the meanings of knowledge, thought, and performance, especially as these terms are used in the context of education. Often we have a tendency to distinguish between knowing and thinking as if they were completely independent. Sometimes we mistake knowledge for memorized information, which, at best, is the lowest form of knowledge. Aaron (1971, 103) has described thinking as a *process* and knowledge as a *product,* but the two are closely related. A knowledgable person must possess information and must also be able to use that information to think; the information is thus a basis for solving problems and forming beliefs. Knowledge is not an end in itself. In summary:

Acquiring knowledge and learning how to think thus would seem to be identical goals. One simply cannot assimilate knowledge without knowing how to think, and assimilated knowledge is the kind most worth having. A mind stuffed with memorized facts possesses very little useful knowledge. (Ebel 1982, 269)

The reasoning above indicates we cannot teach students how to think without teaching them knowledge. Of course, we can construct tasks that vary in the extent of thinking required or the demand made on the student's knowledge. Items on intelligence tests often are intended to reflect *using* knowledge rather than *having* knowledge. So although thinking and knowing are not the same, little can be gained by attempting to separate them to the point of being independent.

Where does performance fit in all this? We all know people who seem to have a great store of knowledge but have difficulty using that knowledge for related tasks. Examples include a mechanical engineer who cannot repair an automobile motor or an economist who cannot solve financial problems. It thus appears that knowledge and thinking are not enough to ensure adequate performance. But if an individual cannot perform adequately, maybe that person lacks some essential knowledge, because the application of knowledge is itself a form of knowledge. This broader concept of knowledge emphasizes the importance of knowledge as a requisite for adequate performance. Of course, there may be factors such as personality or psychomotor characteristics that prohibit adequate performance, regardless of the extent of knowledge.

Objectives and Educational Outcomes

What does measurement have to do with knowledge and performance? Within recent years, there has been much emphasis on conducting instruction through the use of *instructional objectives* that reflect the intended outcome of the instruction. A number of taxonomies for objectives have been developed; one that is used extensively has been developed by Bloom et al. (1956). This taxonomy contains six major categories in the cognitive domain; these categories are basically hierarchical with respect to the *complexity of knowledge* required to attain the objective. However, it is questionable whether or not Bloom's taxonomy is a true hierarchy for all categories. For example, evaluation is the highest-level category (see below), but synthesis may not be required for evaluation. Research data are inconclusive on this point. Note that the focus is on the cognitive domain, not the psychomotor or affective domains.

The first or lowest category of Bloom's taxonomy is called *knowledge,* and this may be somewhat unfortunate. According to our concept of knowledge (as developed above), a better term for this first category would be *recall* or *recall and recognition.* Knowledge, then, would run through all the categories, since having knowledge also includes the ability to use it. Nonetheless, Bloom's six categories, with descriptive definitions, are as follows:

1. *Knowledge:* The recall of a wide range of previously learned content, processes, procedures, patterns, structures, and the like. Knowledge includes recall of specifics and generalities. However, all that is required is the remembering of information.
2. *Comprehension:* The lowest level of understanding. The individual knows what is being communicated and can explain the concept of whatever is being communicated. However, use is only direct and does not involve applying or relating to other concepts, materials, or situations.
3. *Application:* The use of learned concepts in particular and concrete situations. Rules, theories, concepts, and methods are the types of things that are applied.
4. *Analysis:* The breakdown of what is communicated (concepts, methods, and so on) into its component parts so that the structure is understood.
5. *Synthesis:* The ability to construct parts or elements together to form a whole. Synthesis may require developing a new pattern or structure or a plan for proceeding.
6. *Evaluation:* The ability to judge the value of concepts, materials, procedures, and so forth for a specified purpose.

If instruction is conducted with the use of objectives, then measurement should be, too. Although it is not the purpose of this text to provide a detailed discussion of the preparation of instructional objectives, it is important to identify the components and how they relate to measurement.

Criteria for Instructional Objectives. Instructional objectives may be written in various forms and in varying degrees of completeness, but whatever the form, objectives should describe the desired behavior of the learner. To satisfy this condition, Mager (1962, 12) recommends that objectives meet the following three criteria:

1. *First identify the terminal behavior by name; we specify the kind of behavior which will be accepted as evidence that the learner has achieved the objective.*
2. *Second, further define the desired behavior by describing the important conditions under which the behavior is expected to occur.*
3. *Third, specify the criteria of acceptable performance by describing how well the learner must perform to be considered acceptable.*

Objectives meeting these three criteria are useful for instruction. However, avoid elaborate statements of objectives, and sometimes the descriptions for (2) and (3) should be minimal, or the nature of the objective implicitly contains descriptions of (2) and (3). Objectives should be stated so that student behavior can be observed;

...es called *behavioral objectives*. This characteristic
...asurement.
...ssified along two independent dimensions or character-
...gnitive task and the content. Bloom's taxonomy and our dis-
...ocused on the level of a cognitive task. But objectives must also
... a content or skills area, such as mathematics or reading. In the
objectives that follow, the content areas will be apparent.

...ples of Instructional Objectives. Instructional objectives are quite specific, and it is usually helpful to organize them under more general objectives, sometimes called *educational objectives* or simply *general instructional goals*. Below are listed five educational objectives, each with two instructional objectives, taken from Nussel, Inglis, and Wiersma (1976). These objectives are from intermediate level mathematics.

1. *Students will show mastery of addition of two numbers up to five digits.*
   a) *The student will solve correctly a minimum of 40 of 50 problems on the addition of five-digit numbers.*
   b) *The student will describe correctly the positions of units, tens, hundreds, thousands, and ten thousands in the sum of two five-digit numbers.*
2. *Students will show mastery of subtraction of two numbers with up to five digits.*
   a) *The student will correctly identify 80 percent of the subtraction problems, presented in story problem form.*
   b) *The student will correctly solve 80 percent of the subtraction problems, presented in a set of 10 story problems.*
3. *Parallelogram identification will be 100 percent correct by age 11.*
   a) *Given a poster with numerous two-dimensional geometric figures, the student will correctly identify all the parallelograms on the poster.*
   b) *The student will correctly define a parallelogram when contrasting the definitions of triangle, rectangle, parallelogram, and square.*
4. *Students will master the basic division operation with problems that involve quotients with remainders.*
   a) *The student will compute the remainders on a set of 50 division problems with 80 percent accuracy.*
   b) *The student will correctly demonstrate the division of a number less than 1,000, by a one-digit number, using the method of successive subtractions.*
5. *Students will master the identification of basic, three-dimensional figures. Identification will be 100 percent correct, with 80 percent of the students attaining the 100 percent criterion by age 11, 90 percent by age 12, and 100*

percent by age 13.
  a) When presented with a collection of figures on a poster, the student will correctly identify for each figure whether it involves length, area, or volume. Identification with 90 percent or greater accuracy will comprise satisfactory performance for a student.
  b) Presented with a collection of 12 three-dimensional figures, the student will correctly name each of them. (1976, 75)

Consider the characteristics of these instructional objectives. Each objective identifies a student behavior that is observable and measurable, evidence that the student is attempting to meet the objective. That is, the objective identifies the learning outcome. The criterion of acceptable student performance has been indicated, and in some cases (such as 3[a] and 3[b]), the criterion requires 100 percent accuracy. The verbs used in the objectives are not vague, and in each case, the verb calls for only one behavior.

The ten instructional objectives call for learning outcomes that fall within the lower levels of Bloom's taxonomy. Verbs such as "describes" and "identifies" usually refer to knowledge level outcomes. Objectives 2(b) and 4(b) call for outcomes that would most likely fit into the application category of the cognitive domain.

The objectives are all written as *power objectives.* This means that none of the criteria has time requirements. The implicit assumption is that students will be given adequate time to perform what the objective requires and that their performance will improve little, if any, given additional time. Time criteria can be built into objectives, although such criteria would not be used extensively with instructional objectives.

Instructional objectives provide the context for measuring student performance and they indicate the behavior expected, whether this will be demonstrated through testing or by some other means. The criteria of the objectives can be translated into performance standards for the test.

Assuming that teachers use the objectives and that the objectives accurately reflect what is being taught, objectives and the content of tests (or other means used to measure student performance) should closely correspond. In the context of competency testing (discussed in chapter 14), court decisions have emphasized that students should be tested only on what they have been taught. Such decisions imply legal responsibility, as well as an educational one, for accomplishing this close correspondence in the classroom.

> Instructional objectives provide direction for measurement, such as testing. Objectives indicate behaviors expected of students and specify criteria for student performance.

Norm-Referenced
and Criterion-Referenced Measurement

When we contrast **norm-referenced** measurement (or testing) with **criterion-referenced** measurement, we are basically referring to two different ways of interpreting information. Although certain characteristics tend to go with each specific type of measurement or test, an item or a test is neither norm-referenced or criterion-referenced until an interpretation is made of its score. This concept is analogous to a pitch in baseball: It is neither a ball nor a strike until the umpire makes a call.

Whether a test is norm-referenced or criterion-referenced depends upon the interpretation made of its score.

Norm-referenced interpretation historically has been used in education; norm-referenced tests continue to comprise a substantial portion of the measurement in today's schools. The terminology of criterion-referenced measurement has been around for a little over two decades, having been formally introduced with Glaser's (1963) classic article. Over the years, there has been occasional confusion with its terminology and how its measurement applies in the classroom. Do not infer that just because a test is published, it will necessarily be norm-referenced, or if teacher-constructed, criterion-referenced. Again, we emphasize that the type of measurement or testing depends upon how the scores are interpreted. Both types can be used effectively by the teacher.

Norm-Referenced Interpretation

Norm-referenced interpretation stems from the desire to differentiate among individuals or to discriminate among the individuals of some defined group on whatever is being measured. In norm-referenced measurement, an individual's score is interpreted by comparing it to the scores of a defined group, often called the *normative group*. Norms represent the scores earned by one or more groups of students who have taken the test. (Norms are provided in various forms, consisting of descriptive statistics, which are discussed in the next chapter.)

Norm-referenced interpretation is a relative interpretation based on an individual's position with respect to some group, often called the normative group. Norms consist of the scores, usually in some form of descriptive statistics, of the normative group.

In norm-referenced interpretation, the individual's position in the normative group is of concern; thus, this kind of positioning does not specify the performance in absolute terms. Depending on the norms being used, the same score may be high or low. It is the norm as the basis of comparison that influences the score designation.

An Example Using an Achievement Test.   Most standardized achievement tests, especially those covering several skills and academic areas, are primarily designed for norm-referenced interpretations. However, the form of results and the interpretations of these tests are somewhat complex and require concepts not yet introduced in this text; an example using norm-referenced interpretation of scores on a standardized test is presented in a later chapter. Scores on teacher-constructed tests are often given norm-referenced interpretations. "Grading on the curve," for example, is a norm-referenced interpretation of test scores on some type of performance measure. Specified percentages of scores are assigned the different grades, and an individual's score is positioned in the distribution of scores. (We mention this only as an example; we do not endorse this procedure.)

Suppose an algebra teacher has a total of 150 students in five classes, and the classes have a common final examination. The teacher decides that the distribution of letter grades assigned to the final examination performance will be 10 percent A's, 20 percent B's, 40 percent C's, 20 percent D's, and 10 percent F's. (Note that the final examination grade is not necessarily the course grade.) Thus, across the five classes, fifteen students will receive A's on the examination, thirty B's, and so on. Since the grading is based on all 150 scores, do not assume three students in each class would receive A's on the final exam.

James receives a score on the final exam such that 21 students have higher scores and 128 students have lower scores. What will James' letter grade be on the exam? The top fifteen scores will receive A's, and the next thirty scores (20 percent of 150) will receive B's. Counting from the top score down, James' score is positioned 22d, so he will receive a B on the final exam. Note that in this interpretation example, we did not specify James' actual numerical score on the exam. That would have been necessary in order to determine that his score positioned 22d in the group of 150 scores. But in terms of the interpretation of the score, it was based strictly on its position in the total group of scores.

Criterion-Referenced Interpretation

As Popham (1981, 26–27) indicates, the concepts of criterion-referenced testing have developed with a dual meaning for *criterion-referenced*. On one hand, it means referencing an individual's performance to some criterion that is a defined performance level. The individual's score is interpreted in absolute rather than relative terms. The *criterion,* in this context, means some level of specified performance that has been determined independently of how others might perform.

A second meaning for criterion-referenced involves the idea of a defined behavioral domain—that is, a defined body of learner behaviors. The learner's performance on a test is referenced to a specifically defined group of behaviors. The criterion in this context is the desired behaviors.

> Criterion-referenced interpretation is an absolute rather than relative interpretation, referenced to a defined body of learner behaviors, or, as is commonly done, to some specified level of performance.

Criterion-referenced tests require the specification of learner behaviors prior to constructing the test. The behaviors should be readily identifiable from instructional objectives. Criterion-referenced tests tend to focus on specific learner behaviors, and only a limited number are covered on any one test.

An Example Involving Reading Objectives. Consider the following three objectives that deal with the skill of structural analysis in reading (Otto and Chester 1976).

O_1: The child uses simple contractions (for instance, I'm, it's, can't) correctly in sentences.
O_2: The child identifies the root word in familiar inflected words (such as jumping, catches, runs).
O_3: The child identifies the possessive forms of nouns used in context.

These objectives clearly specify the learner behaviors. The teacher would prepare test items to measure the attainment of these three objectives. A teacher-constructed item or exercise relative to O_2 might be to give the students a list of inflected words; then have each student read each word and identify its root. The exercise might be put into the form of a written or oral test.

The above example deals with a limited domain of learner behaviors. There are no specific criteria for performance given in the objectives, but such criteria can be specified. Suppose before the test is administered to any student, an 80 percent correct criterion is established as the minimum performance required for mastery of each objective. A student who does not attain the criterion has not mastered the skill sufficiently to move ahead in the instructional sequence. (This type of testing may also be referred to as *mastery testing.*) The criterion is, to a large extent, based on teacher judgment. No magical, universal criterion for mastery exists, although some curriculum materials that contain criterion-referenced tests do suggest criteria for mastery. Also, unless objectives are appropriate and the criteria for achievement relevant, there is little meaning in the attainment of a criterion, regardless of what it is.

Some Distinctions between Norm-Referenced and Criterion-Referenced Tests

Although interpretations, not characteristics, provide the distinction between norm-referenced and criterion-referenced tests, the two types do tend to have some differing features. Norm-referenced tests are usually more general and comprehensive. This follows, since criterion-referenced tests focus on a specific group of learner behaviors. For example, arithmetic skills represent a general and broad category of student outcomes and would likely be measured by a norm-referenced test. On the other hand, behaviors such as solving addition problems with two five-digit numbers or determining the multiplication products of three- and four-digit numbers are much more specific and may be measured by criterion-referenced tests. A criterion-referenced test tends to focus more on subskills than on broad skills. Thus, criterion-referenced tests tend to be shorter.

Norm-referenced test scores are transformed to positions within the normative group. Criterion-referenced test scores are usually given in the percentage of correct answers or another indicator of mastery or the lack thereof. Criterion-referenced tests tend to lend themselves more to individualizing instruction than do norm-referenced tests. In individualizing instruction, a student's performance is interpreted more appropriately by comparison to the desired behaviors for that particular student, rather than by comparison with the performance of a group.

One final comment on using standardized norm-referenced tests: When measuring attitudes, interests, and aptitudes, it is practically impossible to interpret the results without comparing them to a reference group. The reference groups in such cases are usually typical students or students with high interests in certain areas. Teachers have no basis for anticipating these kinds of scores; therefore, in order to ascribe meaning to such a score, a referent group must be used. For instance, a score of 80 on an interest inventory has no meaning in itself. On the other hand, if a score of 80 is the typical response by a group interested in mechanical areas, the score takes on meaning.

Comments about Test Terminology

Almost any professional area has a body of unique terminology; testing is no exception. Early in this chapter, we introduced basic measurement terminology. Several terms have developed around testing that are used to describe tests or their intended uses. Criterion-referenced and norm-referenced—certainly two very basic descriptors—have already been discussed. Other terms (again, descriptive in nature) appear in educational literature, and, in most instances, these terms describe exactly what they mean.

Diagnostic tests are used to measure a student's strengths and weaknesses, usually to identify deficiencies in skills or performance. Such tests may also be used to identify learning problems. Most often, diagnostic tests are designed to provide in-depth measurement to help locate the source of a particular problem. These tests are related to **prescriptive tests,** which extend to prescribing learning activities intended to overcome student deficiencies.

> Diagnostic tests are intended to identify student deficiencies, weaknesses, or problems and to locate the source of the difficulty. If related learning activities are prescribed, the term prescriptive tests may be used.

Formative and **summative** are terms often used with evaluation, but they also may be used with testing. Formative testing is done to monitor student progress over a period of time. The test results indicate how well students attain the instructional objectives. Weekly quizzes in a course are an example of formative testing. Formative test results may be used for evaluating instruction and for indicating adjustments. Decisions about day-to-day instruction in the classroom, as applied to the entire class or to individual students, are then based on such results. Formative testing may be considered a form of diagnostic testing; however, it does not deal with persistent individual problems, nor does it provide the in-depth information usually associated with diagnostic testing.

Comprehensive tests given at the completion of a course are summative tests. These tests are of broad scope, as the name implies, and their results are used primarily for decisions about grades. Even though they are summative, which suggests a concluding evaluation, such tests can provide information about the effectiveness of instruction. To some extent, the results may also be used for individual diagnosis. But summative testing is end-of-instruction testing done primarily to measure the extent to which intended student outcomes have been attained.

> Formative testing occurs over a period of time, intending to monitor student progress. Summative testing is done at the conclusion of instruction to measure the extent to which students have attained the desired outcomes.

SUMMARY

This chapter has introduced the basic terminology associated with measurement and testing. Measurement is such a routine activity associated with instruction that often it is taken for granted and not given the attention it merits. Classroom teachers—and all educators, for that matter—must have a clear understanding of the nature and purpose of measurement and testing.

We have seen that testing serves a number of educational functions. It provides information about students, student performance, and instruction. Testing is also an important component of school operation. Instruction could not proceed efficiently in an informational vacuum.

Numerous controversies and issues are associated with testing in the schools (see chapter 14). Are tests used properly? Do tests tend to be biased against minorities? Is there too much testing? Are test results given too much weight in important educational decisions? Should we require minimum competency testing? These current issues are probably not as concerned with the concept of testing as with the procedures for implementation.

Certainly, important questions and issues are associated with educational measurement and testing. Some of these are discussed in the final chapter of this book. There has been possibly too much testing of students over recent decades, and there have certainly been misuses of testing. But hardly anyone would advocate a halt to all testing. Would medicine discontinue all surgery because there have been cases of needless treatment or because some doctors seem to recommend surgery too quickly? Hardly. The more logical approach would be to improve the practice of medicine so that surgery is done only when necessary and most effective. So, too, with educational testing: It should be used when it can aid instruction effectively and provide useful information about students and instruction.

KEY TERMS AND CONCEPTS

Measurement   Criterion-referenced
Test   Diagnostic test
Assessment   Prescriptive test
Evaluation   Formative testing
Norm-referenced   Summative testing

REVIEW ITEMS

1. The characteristic that distinguishes evaluation from measurement is:
   a. evaluation requires quantification.
   b. measurement includes testing, evaluation does not.
   c. evaluation involves a value judgment.
   d. evaluation includes assessment, measurement does not.

2. If test data are being used to advise a student about applying for admission to certain colleges, the function being served is:
   a. instructional.
   b. administrative.
   c. program evaluation.
   d. guidance and counseling.

3. The Bloom taxonomy for educational objectives in the cognitive domain is a hierarchy based on:
   a. extent of recall required to attain the objective.
   b. complexity of knowledge required to attain the objective.
   c. reading level required to attain the objective.
   d. aptitude required to attain the objective.

4. Most instructional objectives are "power" objectives, which means that:
   a. students are to complete them within specified time periods.
   b. their completion requires cognitive skills more complex than the recall of knowledge.
   c. there are no time requirements for completion of the objectives.
   d. testing is used to determine whether or not they have been attained.

5. Traditionally, the use of tests in the schools has been:
   a. predominately norm-referenced.
   b. predominately criterion-referenced.
   c. about evenly split, norm-referenced and criterion-referenced.
   d. neither norm-referenced nor criterion-referenced.

6. Norm-referenced interpretations of test results are directed primarily to the purpose of:

a. discriminating among individuals.
b. discriminating among groups.
c. discriminating among programs.
d. discriminating between a program and a standard.

7. Norms for published standardized tests are commonly based on the performance of:
   a. individual students at specified grade levels.
   b. one or more groups of students.
   c. students in a typical school system.
   d. a random sample of students from one state.

8. Criterion-referenced interpretations of test results are directed to:
   a. relative interpretations of individual scores.
   b. absolute interpretations of individual scores.
   c. relative interpretations of group scores.
   d. absolute interpretations of group scores.

9. If criterion-referenced testing is used, it is most likely used for measuring:
   a. attitudes.
   b. interests.
   c. aptitudes.
   d. achievement.

10. Grading on the curve is a criterion-referenced interpretation of test scores.

    T   F

11. Whether a test is norm-referenced or criterion-referenced depends upon the format of the items included in the test.

    T   F

12. Most standardized achievement tests are designed for norm-referenced interpretations.

    T   F

13. Items on intelligence tests often are intended to emphasize *having* knowledge rather than *using* knowledge.

    T   F

14. If an educational outcome makes a difference, then, in some sense, it must be measurable.

           T   F

15. Criterion-referenced tests tend to be more general and comprehensive than norm-referenced tests.

           T   F

16. In measuring student interests, it is desirable to have local norms for interpreting scores on an interest inventory.

    X   T   F

17. Tests designed to identify student weaknesses or deficiencies are called _diagnostic_ tests.

18. For each of the following situations, identify whether the type of testing would most likely be formative testing or summative testing:

   _S_   a. semester exam in an English literature course.

   _F_   b. weekly test in spelling.

   _F_   c. pretest given at the beginning of an Algebra II course.

   _S_   d. standardized achievement test given to all students in a school during the final week of May.

   _F_   e. test covering four science objectives given midway through a curriculum unit.

EXERCISES

1.1 Although the terms *measurement* and *testing* are related in education, they are not synonymous. Describe the meaning of each term.

1.2 For each of the following measurement situations, indicate whether or not evaluation is involved.

    a. All students, grades 1–6, of a school are tested using a standardized achievement test.

    b. A college professor administers a final exam and assigns course grades on the basis of performance on the exam.

    c. A teacher scores fifteen essays of approximately ten pages each and ranks them in order from one to fifteen.

d. The curriculum committee of a high school administers a standardized science test and, on the basis of the results, makes decisions about revising the science curriculum.

e. An English teacher scores a three-paragraph response to an essay question on the basis of number of punctuation errors.

1.3 Describe the difference between formative testing and sumative testing. Provide an example of each in a classroom situation.

1.4 Select an academic or skills area found in a typical elementary or secondary school and write three instructional objectives for that area. Check your objectives to determine whether or not they meet the three criteria suggested by Mager.

1.5 For each of the following uses of tests and test results, indicate whether (primarily) an/a (1) instructional, (2) administration, or (3) guidance and counseling function is being served:

a. Students are tested in an algebra class to provide part of the information for assigning midterm grades.

b. Scholastic Aptitude Test (SAT) scores are used to help a student decide which college to attend.

c. A standardized mathematics test is administered to all students in a middle school in order to determine if the math program is developing the desired skills.

d. Pretest scores are used in sixth-grade mathematics for grouping students.

e. Scores on an interest inventory are used to help students make vocational choices.

1.6 Describe the difference in meaning between norm-referenced and criterion-referenced measurement.

1.7 For each of the following, indicate whether norm-referenced or criterion-referenced measurement is being used.

a. Total points obtained on tests and homework are used for assigning grades in a class, such that specified percentages of students receive the possible grades.

b. Standardized test scores are used to determine the relative performances in reading of students in a fourth-grade class.

c. A teacher assigns grades to fifth-grade students on the basis of number and level of reading objectives attained.

    d. Test results on advanced placement tests are used by college counselors for placing students in foreign language classes.

    e. A college has 1,210 applicants for a freshman class of 500, and the admissions officers use scores on the American College Testing Program (ACT) as part of the admission standards.

1.8 Select an article from a professional publication, such as *Educational Measurement; Issues and Practice* (the article by Joan Bollenbacher, "Testing in the public schools—a view from the middle," in the Spring 1982 issue of the above publication is an example), that deals with a measurement and/or testing issue; review the article, identify the issue, and analyze the position taken by the author. Is there an adequate argument for the position? Do you agree with the position? If not, develop a counterposition or explain why you are in disagreement.

REFERENCES

Aaron, R. I. 1971. *Knowing and the function of reason.* Oxford: Oxford University Press.

Bloom, B. et al. 1956. *Taxonomy of educational objectives: The classification of educational goals. Handbook I, Cognitive Domain.* New York: McKay.

Ebel, R. L. 1982. Proposed solutions to two problems of test construction. *Journal of Educational Measurement* 19 (4): 267–78.

Glaser, R. 1963. Instructional technology and the measurement of learning outcomes: some questions. *American Psychologist* 18:519–21.

Mager, R. 1962. *Preparing instructional objectives.* Palo Alto, Calif.: Fearon.

Nussel, E., J. Inglis, and W. Wiersma. 1976. *The teacher and individually guided education.* Reading, Mass.: Addison-Wesley.

Otto, W. R., and R. D. Chester. 1976. *Objective-based reading.* Reading, Mass.: Addison-Wesley.

Popham, W. J. 1981. *Modern educational measurement.* Englewood Cliffs, N.J.: Prentice-Hall.

2
Statistical Concepts Used in Measurement and Testing

Since measurement was defined in the last chapter as quantification—that is, giving numbers meaning in terms of the quantity of an attribute that a person has or demonstrates—a language must exist for expressing those numbers. This language is **statistics.**

Statistics is a term used in everyday conversation when talking about sports, the weather, or economic trends. However, we also use statistics in a technical sense, with precise mathematical meaning. The statistics introduced in this chapter have this mathematical precision and are also the statistics that help us to understand and use test scores. Measurement concepts introduced in later chapters, concepts such as *reliability* and *validity,* will depend heavily on these statistics.

The act of quantification—measurement—can take a wide range of forms, from counting noses in a line of third-graders on the playground to timing speeds of particles within atoms. Measurements can be precise or rough estimates, as the degree of necessary accuracy varies with different purposes. Thus, the quality of measurements, including test scores, can vary. Such differences affect the meaning we give to the numbers generated, and they affect the statistics that should be used. Common distinctions among scales of measurement are given below.

Scales of Measurement

Measurement scales vary in their *sophistication,* which is the amount of information contained in a score. Measures of student instructional outcomes are rarely as precise as those of physical characteristics such as height and weight. Student outcomes are more difficult to define, and the units of measurement are usually not physical units. Thus, measures of students can vary widely in their quality. Terms that describe the levels of quality inherent in these scales are: **nominal, ordinal, interval,** and **ratio.**

> Measurements may differ in the amount of information the numbers contain. These differences are distinguished by the terms nominal, ordinal, interval, and ratio scales of measurement.

The terms nominal, ordinal, interval, and ratio actually form a hierarchy. Nominal scales of measurement are the least sophisticated and contain the least information. Ordinal, interval, and ratio scales increase respectively in sophistication. The arrangement is a hierarchy because the information contained in the lower levels is also contained in the higher levels, along with additional data. For example, numbers from an interval scale of measurement contain all of the information that nominal and ordinal scales would provide, plus some supplementary input. A ratio scale of the same attribute would, however, contain even more information than the interval scale. This idea will become more clear as each scale of measurement is described.

Nominal Measurement

The least sophisticated scales are those that merely classify objects or events by assigning numbers to them. These numbers are arbitrary and imply no quantification, but the categories must be mutually exclusive and exhaustive. For example, one could nominally designate baseball positions by assigning pitchers the numeral 1, catchers, 2, first basemen, 3, second basemen, 4, and so on. These assignments are arbitrary; no arithmetic of these numbers is meaningful. For example, one plus two does not equal three, because a pitcher plus a catcher does not equal a first baseman.

Ordinal Measurement

Ordinal scales classify, but they also assign rank order. An example of ordinal measurement is ranking individuals in a class according to their test scores. Student scores could be ordered from first, second, third, and so forth to the lowest score. Such a scale gives more information than nominal measurement, but it still has limitations. The units of ordinal measurement are most likely unequal. The number of points separating the first and second students probably does not equal the number separating the fifth and sixth students. These unequal units of measurement are analogous to a ruler in which some inches are longer than others. Addition and subtraction of such units yield meaningless numbers.

Interval Measurement

In order to be able to add and subtract scores, we use interval measurement, sometimes called *equal interval* or *equal unit measurement.* This measurement scale contains the nominal and ordinal properties and is also characterized by equal units between score points. Examples include thermometers and calendar years. For instance, the difference in temperature between 10° and 20° is the same as that between 47° and 57°. Likewise, the difference in length of time between 1946 and 1948 equals that between 1973 and 1975. These measures are defined in terms of physical properties such that these intervals are equal. For example, a year is the time it takes for the earth to orbit the sun. The advantage of equal units of measurement is straightforward: Sums and differences now make sense, both numerically and logically. Note, however, the zero point in interval measurement is really an arbitrary decision; for example, 0° does not mean that there is no temperature.

Ratio Measurement

The most sophisticated type of measurement includes all the preceding properties, but in this scale, the zero point is not arbitrary; a score of zero indicates the absence of the quality being measured. For example, if a man's wealth equalled zero, he would have no wealth at all. This is unlike a social studies test, where missing every item (that is, receiving a score of zero) may not indicate the complete absence of social studies knowledge. Ratio measurement is rarely achieved in educational assessment, either in cognitive or affective areas. The desirability of ratio measurement scales is that they allow ratio comparisons, such as Ann is 1½ times as tall as her little sister, Mary. We can seldom say that one's intelligence or achievement is 1½ times as great as that of another person. An IQ of 120 may be 1½ times as great numerically as an IQ of 80, but a person with an IQ of 120 is not 1½ times as intelligent as a person with an IQ of 80.

Note that carefully designed tests over a specified domain of possible items can approach ratio measurement. For example, consider an objective concerning multiplication facts for pairs of numbers less than ten. In all, there are fifty such combinations. However, the teacher might randomly select five or ten test problems to give to a particular student. Then, the proportion of items that the student gets correct could be used to estimate how many of the fifty possible items the student has mastered. If the student answers four of five items correctly, it is legitimate to estimate that the student would get forty of the fifty items correct if all fifty items were administered. This is possible because the set of possible items was specifically defined in the objective, and the test items were a random, representative sample from that set.

Most educational measurements are better than strictly nominal or ordinal measures, but few can meet the rigorous requirements of interval measurement. Educational testing falls usually somewhere between ordinal and interval scales in sophistication. Fortunately, empirical studies have shown that arithmetic operations on these scales are appropriate, and the scores do provide adequate information for most decisions about students and instruction. Therefore, the following development of statistical concepts assumes that the measurement scales are adequate for use with addition and multiplication.

The four levels of measurement can be summarized as follows:

- *Nominal* scales categorize but do not order.
- *Ordinal* scales categorize and order.
- *Interval* scales categorize, order, and establish an equal unit in the scale.
- *Ratio* scales categorize, order, establish an equal unit, and contain a true zero point.

Descriptive Statistics

As we said earlier, statistics is the means by which we are able to communicate about the numbers that measurement procedures produce. Whole books are written about statistical procedures, and many of the topics are very elaborate and esoteric. These very theoretical and sophisticated aspects may have given statistics the common reputation of being a field of mathematical mystique, beyond the understanding of most mortals. However, the kind of statistics needed to understand test scores and basic measurement concepts is quite simple, requiring only a few arithmetic operations and the use of several basic formulas.

The purpose of the statistics we will use is to *describe* individual test scores, distributions or sets of test scores, and the relationship between sets of test scores. Although descriptive statistics is only a small portion of the total field, it is probably the most useful portion.

Statistics are merely numbers that synthesize and represent sets of scores. It is often more efficient to report a single value, a summary statistic, than to report the score of every individual. The statistical techniques that follow allow us to describe sets of scores in a number of ways.

Frequency Distributions

A simple, almost common sense technique for describing a set of test scores is through the use of a **frequency distribution.** A frequency distribution is merely a listing of the possible score values and the number of persons who achieved each score. Such an arrangement presents the scores in a more simple and understandable manner than merely listing all of the separate scores. Consider a specific set of scores to clarify these ideas.

A set of scores for a group of twenty-five students who took a fifty-item test is listed in Table 2.1. It is easier to analyze the scores if they are arranged in a simple frequency distribution. (The frequency distribution for the same set of scores is given in Table 2.2.) The steps that are involved in creating the frequency distribution are first, to list the possible score values in rank order, from highest to lowest. Then, a second column indicates the frequency or number of persons who received each score. For example, three students received a score of 47, two received 40, and so

Table 2.1.
Scores of 25 Students on a Fifty-Item Test

Student	Score	Student	Score
A	48	N	43
B	50	O	47
C	46	P	48
D	41	Q	42
E	37	R	44
F	48	S	38
G	38	T	49
H	47	U	34
I	49	V	35
J	44	W	47
K	48	X	40
L	49	Y	48
M	40		

Table 2.2.
Frequency Distribution of the 25 Scores of Table 2.1

Score	Frequency	Score	Frequency
50	1	41	1
49	3	40	2
48	5	39	0
47	3	38	2
46	1	37	1
45	0	36	0
44	2	35	1
43	1	34	1
42	1		

forth. There is no need to list score values below the lowest score that anyone received.

When there is a wide range of scores in a frequency distribution, the distribution can be quite long, with a lot of zeros in the column of frequencies. Such a frequency distribution can make interpretation of the scores difficult and confusing. A *grouped* frequency distribution would be more appropriate in this kind of situation. Groups of score values are listed, rather than each separate possible score value.

If we were to change the frequency distribution in Table 2.2 into a grouped frequency distribution, we might choose intervals such as 48–50, 45–47, and so forth. The frequency corresponding to interval 48–50 would be 9 (1 + 3 + 5). The choice of the width of the interval is arbitrary, but it must be the same for all intervals. In addition, it is a good idea to have an odd-numbered interval width (we used 3 above), so that the midpoint of the interval is a whole number. This strategy will simplify subsequent graphs and description of the data. The grouped frequency distribution is presented in Table 2.3.

Table 2.3.
Grouped Frequency Distribution

Score Interval	Frequency
48–50	9
45–47	4
42–44	4
39–41	3
36–38	3
33–35	2

> Frequency distributions summarize sets of test scores by listing the number of people who received each test score. All of the test scores can be listed separately, or the scores can be grouped in a frequency distribution.

Measures of Central Tendency

One often wishes to represent a set of test scores with one representative measure of how the scores tend to average. Since most sets of scores have more persons in the middle of the distribution than at the extremes, such statistics are called measures of **central tendency.** There are three commonly used measures of central tendency: the **mean,** the **median,** and the **mode.** Each is described below.

The Mean

The mean of a set of scores is the arithmetic average. It is found by summing all the scores and dividing by the number of scores. The mean is the most commonly used measure of central tendency, because it is easily understood and is based on all of the scores in the set; hence, it summarizes a lot of information. The formula for the mean is as follows:

$$\bar{X} = \frac{\Sigma X}{N}, \tag{2.1}$$

where $\bar{X}$ is the mean,
    X is the symbol for a score,
    Σ is the summation operator (it tells us to add all the X's), and
    N is the number of scores.

For the set of scores in Table 2.1,

$$\Sigma X = 1100$$

and

$$N = 25,$$

so then

$$\bar{X} = \frac{1100}{25} = 44.$$

The mean of the set of scores in Table 2.1 is 44. The mean does not have to equal an observed score; it is usually not even a whole number.

When the scores are arranged in a grouped frequency distribution, the formula is:

$$\bar{X} = \frac{\Sigma f x_{mdpt}}{N},$$

where fx_{mdpt} means that the midpoint of the interval is multiplied by the frequency for that interval.

The Median

Another measure of central tendency is the median. The median is the point that divides the distribution in half; that is, half of the scores fall above the median, and half of the scores fall below the median.

When there are only a few scores, the median can often be found by inspection. If there is an odd number of scores, the middle score is the median. When there is an even number of scores, the median is halfway between the two middle scores. However, when there are tied scores in the middle of the distribution or when the scores are in a frequency distribution, the median may not be so obvious.

Consider again the frequency distribution in Table 2.2. There were twenty-five scores in the distribution, so the middle score should be the median. A straightforward way to find this median is to augment the frequency distribution with a column of cumulative frequencies. Cumulative frequencies indicate the number of persons at or below each score. Table 2.4 indicates the cumulative frequencies for the data in Table 2.2. For example, seven persons are at or below a score of 40, and twenty-one persons are at or below a score of 48.

To find the median, we need to locate the middle person in the cumulative frequency column, because his score is the median. Since there are twenty-five persons in the distribution, the middle one is the thirteenth person; his score is 46. Thus, 46 is the median of this distribution; half of the people scored above 46, and half scored below.

When there are ties in the middle of the distribution, there may be a need to interpolate between scores to get the exact median. However, such precision is not needed for most classroom tests. The whole number closest to the median is usually sufficient.

The Mode

The measure of central tendency that is the easiest to find is the mode. The mode is the most frequently occurring score in the distribution. The mode of the set of scores

Table 2.4.
Frequency Distribution and Cumulative Frequencies for the Scores of Table 2.2

Score	Frequency	Cumulative Frequency
50	1	25
49	3	24
48	5	21
47	3	16
46	1	13
45	0	12
44	2	12
43	1	10
42	1	9
41	1	8
40	2	7
39	0	5
38	2	5
37	1	3
36	0	2
35	1	2
34	1	1

in Table 2.1 is 48. Five persons had scores of 48, and no other score occurred as often.

Each of these three measures of central tendency—the mean, the median, and the mode—is a legitimate definition of "average" performance on this test. However, each does provide different information. The arithmetic average was 44, half the people scored at or below 46, and more people received 48 than any other score.

The mean, the median, and the mode all describe central tendency:

- The mean is the arithmetic average.
- The median divides the distribution in half.
- The mode is the most frequent score.

There are some distributions in which all three measures of central tendency are equal, but more often than not they will be different. The choice of which measure of central tendency is best will differ from situation to situation. The mean is used most often, perhaps because it includes information from all of the scores. When a distribution has a small number of very extreme scores, though, the median may be a better definition of *central* tendency. The mode is the type of average that is used least often.

Measures of Dispersion

The measures of central tendency are very useful for summarizing average perform-ance, but they tell us nothing about how the scores are distributed around the av-erages. Two sets of test scores may have equal measures of central tendency, but they might differ in other ways. One of the distributions may have the scores tightly clustered around the average, and the other distribution may have scores that are widely separated. As you may have anticipated, there are descriptive statistics that measure **dispersion,** which is how spread out the scores tend to be.

The Range

The **range** indicates the difference between the highest and lowest scores in the overall distribution. It is simple to calculate, but it provides limited information.

A problem with using the range is that only the two most extreme scores are used in the computation. There is no indication of the spread of scores between the highest and lowest. Measures of dispersion that take into consideration every score in the distribution are the **variance** and the **standard deviation.** The standard deviation is used a great deal in interpreting scores from standardized achievement or aptitude tests.

The Variance

The variance measures how widely the scores in the distribution are spread about the mean. In other words, the variance is the average squared difference between the scores and the mean. As a formula, it looks like this:

$$s^2 = \frac{\Sigma\,(X - \bar{X})^2}{N}.$$

(2.2)

An equivalent formula that is sometimes easier to compute is:

$$s^2 = \frac{\Sigma X^2}{N} - \bar{X}^2.$$

(2.3)

Table 2.5.
Computation of the Variance for the Scores of Table 2.1

Student	Score X	Score − Mean $X - \bar{X}$	(Score − Mean)² $(X - \bar{X})^2$
A	48	4	16
B	50	6	36
C	46	2	4
D	41	−3	9
E	37	−7	49
F	48	4	16
G	38	−6	36
H	47	3	9
I	49	5	25
J	44	0	0
.	.	.	.
.	.	.	.
.	.	.	.
W	47	3	9
X	40	−4	16
Y	48	4	16
Totals	1100	0	570

To determine the mean:

$$\bar{X} = \frac{1100}{25} = 44$$

Then, to determine the variance:

$$s^2 = \frac{\Sigma(X - \bar{X})^2}{N} = \frac{570}{25} = 22.8$$

The computation of the variance for the data in Table 2.1 is illustrated in Table 2.5. The data for students K through V are omitted to save space, but these values are included in the column totals.

The Standard Deviation

The standard deviation also indicates how spread out the scores are, but it is expressed in the same units as the original scores. The standard deviation is computed by finding the square root of the variance:

$$s = \sqrt{s^2}.$$

For the data in Table 2.1, the variance is 22.8. The standard deviation is $\sqrt{22.8}$, or 4.77.

Most of the scores in distributions are within two standard deviations of the mean. In this case, the mean minus two standard deviations is 34.46, and the mean plus two standard deviations is 53.54. Therefore, only one score is outside of this interval; the lowest score, 34, is slightly more than two standard deviations from the mean.

The usefulness of the standard deviation becomes apparent when scores from different tests are compared. Suppose that two tests are given to the same class: one on fractions and the other on reading comprehension. The fractions test has a mean of 30 and a standard deviation of 8; the reading comprehension test has a mean of 60 and a standard deviation of 10. If John scored 38 on the fractions test and 55 on the reading comprehension test, it appears from the raw scores that he did better in reading than in fractions, because 55 is greater than 38. But, relative to the performance of the others in the class, the opposite is true. A score of 38 on the fractions test is one standard deviation above the mean, a score that is much better than average. A score of 55 on the reading comprehension test is one-half of a standard deviation below the mean, a score that is lower than average. Clearly, when comparison is made relative to the class mean, John's performance on the fractions test is better than his performance on the reading comprehension test.

Descriptive statistics that indicate dispersion are the range, the variance, and the standard deviation. The range is the difference between the highest and lowest scores in the distribution. The standard deviation is a unit of measurement that shows by how much the separate scores tend to differ from the mean. The variance is the square of the standard deviation. Most scores are within two standard deviations from the mean.

Graphing Distributions

A graph of a distribution of test scores is often better understood than is the frequency distribution or a mere table of numbers. The general pattern of scores, as well as any unique characteristics of the distribution, can be seen easily in simple graphs. There are several kinds of graphs that can be used, but a simple bar graph, or **histogram,** is as useful as any.

The bar graph for the scores in Table 2.1 is presented in Figure 2.1. Note how the height of the bar corresponds to the frequency for each interval. The width of each bar corresponds to the width of the interval, and the vertical lines in the graph meet the axis at the limits.

Figure 2.1.
Bar Graph of the Grouped Frequency Distribution

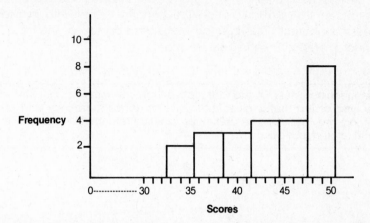

The general shape of the distribution is clear from the graph. Most of the scores in this distribution are high, at the upper end of the graph. Such a shape is typical for classroom tests.

Many distributions have graphs that are symmetric and bell-shaped, with most of the scores in the middle of the distribution and progressively fewer scores toward the extremes. Such distributions are called **normal** and are often used as a point of reference. Distributions that are not symmetric have **skewness.** The graph in Figure 2.1 is negatively skewed, because most of the scores are high. When most of the scores fall at the lower end of the distribution, the shape is said to be positively skewed.

Descriptive Statistics for Norm-Referenced and Criterion-Referenced Tests

The descriptive statistics that have been presented can be applied to any set of scores. However, as the purpose for which the test is given varies, so does the meaningfulness of the statistics. Norm-referenced measures are used to quantify differences between persons. Spreading out the scores results in a large standard deviation. The adequacy of a norm-referenced test may, in part, be judged by the size of the standard deviation. Scores from norm-referenced tests are often interpreted by comparing an individual's score to the average performance of some relevant reference group. Thus, the measures of central tendency are important here, too.

In criterion-referenced testing, the measures of central tendency and dispersion are useful but not of primary concern. Criterion-referenced scores are interpreted relative to the scale of measurement or to an established standard of performance, rather than relative to the mean. It is more useful to speak of the percentage of the class that scores above a criterion than it is to speak of average performance on a criterion-referenced test. Similarly, since the concern is not with individual differences, there is no inherent virtue in a large standard deviation. The range of scores and the standard deviation are largely irrelevant.

> The meaningfulness of the descriptive statistics will vary in terms of the type of test that is given. Measures of central tendency and dispersion may not be as useful for criterion-referenced tests as for norm-referenced tests.

Correlation

One other statistic commonly used in measurement is the **correlation** coefficient, which quantifies the direction and degree of the relationship between two variables. There is sometimes confusion about the term *correlation,* because it may have an associated meaning in common usage. However, correlation has a very specific meaning. The correlation between two variables is a value that quantifies the association between them. Correlation is expressed as a numerical coefficient.

The correlation coefficient is a number that can range between -1 and $+1$. A graph, or **scatterplot,** of the pairs of scores for two variables (which may be tests) can be plotted to give a visual illustration of the relationship between the two variables.

For example, suppose that eight students each take two tests, one in reading and one in science. Each test has ten items. The pairs of scores and the scatterplot appear in Figure 2.2. Notice that persons with low scores in reading also tend to have low scores in science. Similarly, persons with high scores in reading tend to have high scores in science. Such a direct relationship has a *positive* direction. Inverse relations are said to have *negative* direction, *inverse* meaning that high scores on one variable go with low scores on the other variable. Suppose X and Y represent the two tests scores to be correlated. The formula for calculating the Pearson product-moment correlation is:

$$r = \frac{N \, \Sigma XY - \Sigma X \, \Sigma Y}{\sqrt{(N \, \Sigma X^2 - (\Sigma X)^2)\,(N \, \Sigma Y^2 - (\Sigma X)^2)}} . \tag{2.5}$$

The computation of the correlation coefficient for the data in Figure 2.2 is shown in Table 2.6.

Figure 2.2.
Scatterplot of Reading and Science Scores

Student	Reading	Science
Bill	4	7
Ann	3	2
Paul	7	6
Jim	8	8
Pete	3	5
Mary	5	8
Jane	10	7
Sue	2	4

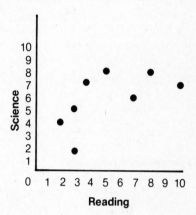

A correlation of +0.58 indicates a moderate degree of association between the two variables. The points of the scatterplot could be contained by an ellipse indicating some departure from the straight line, characteristic of perfect correlation.

Other degrees of association are illustrated by the scatterplots in Figure 2.3. As you can see, the direction of the relationship is indicated by the sign, and the strength of the relationship is indicated by the closeness to +1 or −1. Correlations close to zero indicate no relationship between the variables.

> The correlation coefficient can range from −1 to +1. The sign tells the direction of the relationship, and the numerical value indicates its strength. Scatterplots visually depict correlations.

The strength of the correlation is better described by r^2 than by r. The **coefficient of determination**, r^2, indicates the percentage of the variance in one variable that is predictable from the other variable. For example, if scores from a science test and from a reading test correlated 0.4, then 0.4^2 (or 16 percent) of the variance in the scores of the science test is predictable from the scores on the reading test. Or similarly, 16 percent of the variance in the reading scores is associated with the scores on the science test. The correlation can be interpreted in either direction.

Correlations are used in several ways in measurement applications. The correlation is based on pairs of scores from two variables. If at least one of the variables is an item or a test, it is a measurement application. Obviously, there are a great many possibilities.

Table 2.6.
Computation of the Correlation Coefficient for the Data of Figure 2.1

X	Y	X^2	Y^2	XY
4	7	16	49	28
3	2	9	4	6
7	6	49	36	42
8	8	64	64	64
3	5	9	25	15
5	8	25	64	40
10	7	100	49	70
3	5	9	25	15
Totals 43	48	281	316	280

To determine the correlation:

$$r = \frac{N \, \Sigma XY - \Sigma X \, \Sigma Y}{\sqrt{(N \, \Sigma X^2 - (\Sigma X)^2)(N \, \Sigma Y^2 - (\Sigma Y)^2)}}$$

$$r = \frac{(8 \times 280) - (43 \times 48)}{\sqrt{((8 \times 281) - 43^2)((8 \times 316) - 48^2)}} = .58$$

Scores on individual items are often correlated with total test scores to see whether performance on the item is consistent with performance on the total test. Scores on two measures of the same thing are often correlated to see whether the two measures are equivalent. Scores from tests are also correlated with performance on other variables. An example of this is correlating aptitude scores with subsequent grade point average in college. In each of these instances, the correlation coefficient is primary evidence from which decisions are made.

The measurement concepts of *reliability* and *validity* will be developed in later chapters, discussing these ideas in terms of correlation coefficients. Quite simply, reliability is defined as the correlation of two tests of the same thing, and validity is the correlation of the test with measures of other variables.

Correlations are also used to make predictions from one variable to another. If we know a person's score on X, and we know the correlation between X and Y, then we can predict the person's score on Y. For example, if we know that aptitude and achievement correlate positively, we can predict that an individual who is above average in aptitude will be above average in achievement. Similarly, if a student scores high on form A of a test, it can be predicted that this student will also score high on form B of the test, if scores on the two forms of the test are positively correlated.

Figure 2.3.
Scatterplots for Various Correlations

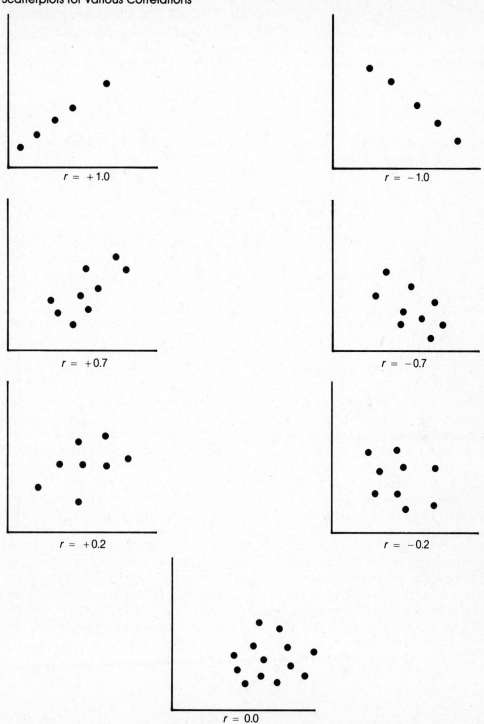

Item Statistics

All of the descriptive statistics that have been introduced to this point have been developed in terms of total test scores. There are also some very useful statistics that are used on the separate items contained in a test. Two of the most commonly used **item statistics** are the **difficulty** index and the **discrimination** index.

Difficulty

Item difficulty is an index that shows the percentage of students who answered an item correctly. Given in formula form, it is:

$$p = \frac{\text{Number of correct responses to an item}}{\text{Number of persons responding}}. \qquad (2.6)$$

For example, if an item has a difficulty level of 0.90, this means that 90 percent of the persons taking the test answered that item correctly. It clearly would be a very easy test item. The difficulty index can range from zero to 1. It is an inverse scale, since high p values correspond to easy items, and low p values correspond to difficult items.

Teachers may choose to delete or revise items, based on their difficulty levels. Criterion-referenced tests often are constructed from items with difficulty levels of 0.80 or 0.90. The difficulty index preferred for norm-referenced test items is about 0.50. A norm-referenced test is designed to measure individual differences; items of middle difficulty will help spread out the scores.

An inspection of difficulty can be very revealing to teachers. Often there are concepts that everyone assumes are well understood, but corresponding test items have surprising difficulty levels. The teachers must then determine whether the problem lies with the test item or the instruction and take what action seems necessary.

Suppose, for example, that a teacher has a test item over some concept that was stressed in class; she would thus expect a high p value for that item. The test, which includes that item as a multiple-choice question with four options, is administered to her class of 30 students. The number of persons that chose each option is listed in Table 2.7, along with the calculation of the p value.

The calculated value of p was 0.20, a value much lower than the teacher expected. In fact, more students picked option b than the preferred response. This result should cause the teacher to try to find out why the students did so poorly on the item. Maybe the scoring key was wrong, and (b) was really the correct response. Perhaps the item was ambiguous, or maybe the learning that the teacher assumed took place did not occur. In any case, the teacher now has information that can lead to improved instruction.

Table 2.7.
Calculation of the Difficulty Index

Option	Number Selecting Each Option
a	4
b	18
c*	6
d	2

*Denotes the keyed response

To determine the difficulty index, p:

$$p = \frac{\text{Number correct}}{\text{Number of responses}} = \frac{6}{30} = .20$$

The difficulty index p is an inverse index—the lower the value, the more difficult the item. An inspection of item difficulty levels can reveal problems with the test and even the instruction.

Discrimination

Item discrimination for *norm-referenced* tests means that the test item is effective in separating those with high scores on the total test from those with low total test scores. One way to calculate this measure is to correlate success on the item (0 = incorrect, 1 = correct) with the scores from the whole test. The **item-total correlation** indicates how well an individual test item predicts scores on the total test. The correlation can range from −1.0 to +1.0. This is sometimes called a *point-biserial correlation.*

Positive correlations show that the item is measuring something in common with the total test; getting the item correct predicts a higher total test score. This is what we would hope to find for each of the items.

A zero correlation shows that performance on that item is not related to performance on the total test. Such an item is not a useful contributor to the total test and may need to be eliminated or possibly replaced by another item before the test is used again.

If the item-total correlation is negative, there is a problem. This means that getting that item correct is predictive of a *low* total test score. This could only occur if the item were misleading to the better students (better in terms of total test scores). Items that have negative item-total correlations should be eliminated from the test. Class discussions about the item might disclose the item's weaknesses.

A discrimination index that provides virtually the same information as the item-total correlation coefficient can be found as follows:

1. Separate the test scores into three groups: the highest 27 percent, the middle 46 percent, and the lowest 27 percent. (Twenty-seven percent is used because it has been shown that this value will maximize differences in normal distributions while providing enough cases for analysis. This is a guideline figure, not a strict rule.)
2. Find the difficulty index for an item for the highest group; call this *PH*.
3. Find the difficulty index for the same item for the lowest group; call this *PL*.
4. Discrimination (*D*) can then be calculated:

$$D = PH - PL.$$ (2.7)

> The discrimination index, *D*, can range from -1 to $+1$. It indicates how well an item separates the high and low scores on the total test. Negative discrimination indexes alert the teacher to problems in the item or in the instruction.

The discrimination index would not be appropriate for criterion-referenced tests without some modification. In a criterion-referenced test, it is important for an item to discriminate between persons who are above and below the criterion on the total test. A similar index could be developed, dividing students into groups depending on whether they were above or below the criterion on the total test. Then the tallies of correct responses to each item would indicate how well each item separated students, with respect to the criterion. When proportionally more persons who were below criterion than above criterion answered an item correctly, it would correspond to a negative *D* value.

SUMMARY

This chapter introduced the descriptive statistics that are used with sets of test scores, as well as individual items. The amount of information contained in test scores can vary widely; the terms nominal, ordinal, interval, and ratio describe these differences.

Statistics were introduced that describe both the central tendency and the dispersion of distributions of test scores. The mean (arithmetic average), the median (middle point of the distribution), and the mode (most frequently occurring score) were the measures of central tendency developed. The range, variance, and standard deviation were introduced as useful measures of dispersion, or how spread out the test scores were.

It was shown that the correlation coefficient can be used to quantify the direction and strength of the relationship between two variables. In testing applications, the variables are often scores on individual items, scores on tests or other measuring instruments, and scores on external criteria that we try to predict, such as future grade point average. The correlation coefficient will also be used in future chapters to develop the concepts of validity and reliability.

Two item statistics—difficulty and discrimination—were introduced and shown to be useful in evaluating the performance of individual items. The difficulty index indicated the percentage of persons who answered an item correctly, while the discrimination index showed how well the item separated those who had high and low scores on the total test.

The statistics introduced in this chapter comprise a very small part of the field of statistics, but they are sufficient for understanding the basic theoretical concepts of measurement that are developed in the remaining chapters of this book. A little practice with using the formulas on different sets of scores will enhance your understanding of these statistics. The exercises below should provide you with an opportunity to apply the concepts of this chapter.

KEY TERMS AND CONCEPTS

Statistics	Variance
Measurement scales	Standard deviation
Nominal	Histogram
Ordinal	Normal distribution
Interval	Skewness
Ratio	Correlation
Frequency distribution	Scatterplot
Central tendency	Coefficient of
Mean	determination
Median	Item statistics
Mode	Difficulty
Dispersion	Discrimination
Range	Item-total correlation

REVIEW ITEMS

1. Except in trivial cases, the range is larger than the standard deviation.

    T   F

2. If the mode and median of a distribution of scores are equal, the mean will also have to be equal to the median.

        T   (F)

3. Which of the following provides a measure of dispersion in the same units as the original scores?

    a. variance.

    b. median.

    (c.) standard deviation.

    d. correlation.

4. Which of the following indicates the greatest degree of correlation?

    a. −0.52.

    (b.) −0.61.

    (c.) +0.23.

    d. +0.42.

5. The standard deviation is as important for norm-referenced tests as for criterion-referenced tests.

        T   (F)

6. The scores from a typical classroom test are probably better than _____ measurement, but not quite _____ .

    a. ordinal, nominal.

    b. interval, ratio.

    c. nominal, ordinal.

    (d.) ordinal, interval.

7. To compute a correlation between attitude and achievement, one must have:

    a. achievement scores from one group of people and attitude scores from another group.

    b. achievement and attitude scores on the same group of people.

    c. achievement scores from two points in time and attitude scores from two points in time.

    d. the same tests given twice to the same group of people.

8. Generally, the larger the numerical value of the median, the larger the value of the standard deviation.

        T   F

EXERCISES

2.1 An eight-item test (items 1 through 7) was given to ten children. Each item was scored right (1) or wrong (0). The data are given below.

Person	Item 1	2	3	4	5	6	7	8
Al	1	1	1	1	0	0	0	0
Bob	1	1	1	1	1	1	0	0
Cheryl	1	0	1	0	1	1	0	0
Diane	1	1	1	1	1	1	1	1
Fred	1	1	0	0	0	0	0	0
George	1	1	0	0	1	1	0	0
Helen	1	0	0	1	0	0	1	0
Ilsa	1	1	1	0	0	1	1	0
John	1	1	1	1	1	1	1	1
Karen	1	1	1	1	1	1	0	0

a. Find the total score for each person.

b. Find the mean, median, and mode for this distribution of scores.

c. Find the range for these scores.

d. Find the variance and standard deviation.

e. What person(s) had tests scores that were more than one standard deviation above the mean?

f. What is the difficulty index for item 1? What is the difficulty index for item 3?

g. What is the discrimination index for item 2? What is the discrimination index for item 4?

h. What is the correlation between the scores on item 3 and the total test scores?

2.2 The following frequency distribution is given for eight scores, scores indicated by X, frequency by f.

X	f
20	1
19	2
18	0
17	3
16	1
15	1

a. What is the median of the distribution?

b. What is the mode of the distribution?

c. What is the mean of the distribution?

d. What is the range of the distribution?

2.3 Create a distribution of ten scores in which the mean, median, and mode are equal.

2.4 Consider the following pairs of scores, X and Y.

X	Y
10	15
8	12
7	8
4	6
2	2

a. Draw a scatterplot for these scores.

b. Estimate the size and sign of the correlation in the scatterplot.

c. Compute the actual value of the correlation for the scores in problem a.

SUGGESTED READING

Gay, L. R. 1980. *Educational evaluation and measurement.* Columbus: Merrill.

Hinkle, D. E., W. Wiersma, and S. G. Jurs. 1982. *Basic behavioral statistics.* Boston: Houghton Mifflin.

Isaac, S., and W. B. Michael. 1981. *Handbook in research and evaluation.* 2d ed. San Diego: Edits.

3

Interpreting Test Scores

It isn't enough to select, create, and administer valid and reliable tests. The real significance of a testing program is in how the test scores are used. Our purpose in this chapter is to explain how to present test scores in a number of different ways. To do this, we examine several commonly used score-reporting methods. We also provide some practical suggestions about aggregating several test scores into a single score, and then we discuss how that score might be used in assigning grades.

The discussion is in terms of using the scores provided by test publishers, rather than computing the scores directly. Most of the development is concerned with norm-referenced scores, rather than criterion-referenced scores.

Norms and Norm Groups

We have already explained that there are two major ways to interpret scores from tests. The first, the criterion-referenced way, requires that a student's test performance be compared to some previously established standard of performance or to the levels on the scale of measurement itself. A student could, for example, correctly answer 20 percent of the items on some well-defined area of content before instruction and 70 percent after instruction. This performance is interpreted in an *absolute* sense, not relative to the performance of other people.

The second way to interpret test scores is norm-referenced, wherein the score of an individual is compared to the performance of others. Usually, the basis of comparison is the average performance of some well-defined group of people who took the test under similar testing conditions. The **norm,** then, is the average performance of the relevant comparison group.

It is obviously very important that the appropriate **norm group** be used. It would not be very useful to compare a second-grader's test performance to the norms for fifth-graders or a law school applicant's performance to the average score of graduate students in astronomy. The need for relevant norm groups has been met by the use of **national** and **local norms,** as well as norms for various sexes or majors.

> It is essential that the norm group for standardized tests is well described and relevant for the interpretations that are to be made.

National Norms

Most standardized achievement and aptitude tests require national norms, because the tests are intended for use across the country. The tests would be quite limited if the basis for the interpretation of the test scores was 150 students from Nebraska. The norms should be based on a large, representative sample from across the country. The key word here is *representative*. The norm group should represent the population of students in the country, especially with regard to factors such as age, geographic region, ethnic background, socioeconomic factors, and the like.

Test manuals should contain a complete description of the norm groups used for their norm-referenced scores. *Standards for Educational and Psychological Tests* states:

> *Norms presented in the test manual should refer to defined and clearly described populations. These populations should be the groups with whom users of the test will ordinarily wish to compare the persons tested. (1974, 20)*

Most of the commonly used standardized tests have done a careful and thorough sampling of the population when constructing their national norms. Information about specific tests can be found in the reviews in Buros' *Mental Measurements Yearbook* (1978).

An example of the steps taken in securing national norms is that of the STEP tests (The Sequential Tests of Educational Progress) (STEP Test Development and Content Description 1979, 5–6). The standardization of the STEP III, done in 1977–78, was based on over 200,000 students from 200 school districts across the country. The sample was stratified by geographical region, socioeconomic status, minority status, and rural, suburban, or urban setting. The actual variables were:

A. Region of the country
  1. Western states
  2. Central states
  3. Northeastern states
  4. Southern states
B. Type of community
  1. Cities of 250,000 or more
  2. Districts where more than 90 percent of the population is urban (as reported by the Census Bureau)
  3. Districts where between 10 and 90 percent of the population is urban
  4. Districts where less than 10 percent of the population is urban

C. Percentage of black and Hispanic heritage population
   1. Less than 10 percent
   2. 10 to 40 percent
   3. Greater than 40 percent
D. Socioeconomic status
   1. Low
      a) Less than 60 percent of the parent-age population graduated from high school, and more than 20 percent of the children under 18 came from homes below the poverty level (as reported by the Census Bureau)
      b) Less than 50 percent of the parent-age population graduated from high school, and more than 10 percent of the children under 18 came from homes below the poverty level
   2. Medium
      a) 60 to 70 percent of the parent-age population graduated from high school, and 5 to 10 percent of the children under 18 came from homes below the poverty level
      b) 50 to 60 percent of the parent-age population graduated from high school, and 5 to 20 percent of the children under 18 came from homes below the poverty level
   3. High
      a) More than 70 percent of the parent-age population graduated from high school, and less than 10 percent of the children came from poverty-level homes
      b) More than 60 percent of the parent-age population graduated from high school, and less than 5 percent of the children came from poverty-level homes (*STEP Test Development and Content Description* 1979, 5)

Local Norms

There are many communities where the local norms are much more useful than the national norms. For instance, cities such as Palo Alto, California, Boulder, Colorado, and New Haven, Connecticut, have citizens who are above national averages in educational and socioeconomic levels. It is not surprising, then, that the children in these communities tend, on the average, to be above the national norms. In these situations, local norms are probably more relevant than national norms.

Consider the plight of the student whose test performance is above the national norm but below the local norm. An apparent contradiction occurs when he is told that his tested achievement level is above average (on the national norm), but he knows that he is in the bottom third of his class (the local norm). Which norm group is most relevant for him? The local norm is probably the most useful, because it shows how he is doing compared to those students with whom he must compete on a regular, day-to-day basis. The national norm might be useful to him only for decisions about the likelihood of success in college or how realistic some career goal might be, decisions that require a broader context than local norms.

Some test publishers provide local norms as one of several scoring services that a school district can purchase. There are other tests, though, for which local norms must be developed. This is usually done by the school district offices responsible for evaluation, testing, and research.

Norms for Subgroups

When the average test performances of subgroups of the population differ significantly, it may be important to have separate normative data for the subgroups. The Graduate Record Examination (GRE) is used to predict the likelihood of success in graduate school. The same score that might predict success in one major may predict less success in another major. A person with a Quantitative Aptitude score of 600 would be well above the norm for English or education majors but below the average for physics majors. Thus, it is important that separate norms be available for each possible major field. In addition, when there are sex differences in performance, separate norms must also be presented for males and females.

The overall point is clear: The norm group used must be appropriate for the purpose for which the test is used. Additionally, a norm-referenced interpretation of a score is meaningless unless the norm group is well understood. Being "below average" is useless information when we do not know on whom that average is based.

National, local, and subgroup norms provide different perspectives for interpreting the results of tests.

Norms Are Not Standards

One cautionary note that must be mentioned is that norms are *not* standards. Norms are measures of the actual performance on a test by some well-described group of test takers. The norms depict the *average* performance; they do not connote adequate or inadequate performance. Essentially, the norms describe "what is"; they do not necessarily imply what "should be."

People sometimes mistakenly present norms as standards. Therefore, they set goals, such as getting all students to read at or above grade level—that is, to have all students at or above average. Achieving such a goal is impossible, because, by definition, some students will be below the average.

Deciding what level of achievement to strive for should be based on information beyond that which the achievement test provides. For example, what level of achievement is necessary to perform in a variety of occupations? What level of achievement is needed in one content area in order to be successful in another? The answers to these questions require further analysis of the relationship between the test scores and these criteria. The information contained in the norm-referenced test scores is not sufficient in itself.

Norms are measures of the actual performance of a group on a test. They are not meant to be standards of what performance levels should be.

Norm-Referenced Scores

Norm-referenced scores can be expressed in several ways. We will describe some of the commonly used methods and then provide an example from a standardized test.

Percentiles

The **percentile** rank of a score is a whole number between one (1) and ninety-nine (99) that indicates the percentage of persons in the norm group who scored at or below that particular score. For example, suppose that Bob received a score of 65 on a one hundred–item test and is told that his percentile rank is 80. This means that 80 percent of the people in the norm group had scores of 65 or less.

The middle score in a distribution of scores is the one that equals or exceeds 50 percent of the scores. This score, at the fiftieth percentile, is also called the *median*. The median describes the average performance in the percentile distribution.

Percentiles are simple, useful numbers that describe how an individual score compares to the scores obtained by the norm group. Most audiences can easily understand percentiles because they require no sophisticated statistics; they are expressed in terms of percentages.

A disadvantage of percentiles is that they form an ordinal rather than an equal interval scale. Most distributions of test scores are roughly bell-shaped, with most of the scores in the middle of the distribution and fewer scores at either extreme. Therefore, a given amount of achievement—say, five more correct items—could result in a large change in percentile rank if it occurred in the middle of the distribution, but it might mean a small increase in the percentile rank if it occurred near the high end of the distribution. The consequence of the percentiles being unequal in width is that we are limited in the arithmetic that can be meaningfully done with them. We should not average percentiles, for example.

> Percentiles indicate the percentage of students in the norm group who are at or below a particular score.

Standard Scores

One way to achieve an equal-unit norm-referenced score is by using the standard deviation as the unit of measurement. The **standard score,** or z-score, does just that. A standard score expresses the position of an individual score in terms of how many standard deviations the score is above or below the mean of the distribution.

$$z = \frac{X - \bar{X}}{S}. \tag{3.1}$$

Suppose, for example, that John has a score of 55; the average score for the norm group is 60 and the standard deviation is 15. John's standard score would be:

$$z = \frac{55 - 60}{15} = -.33 .$$

This would mean that John is one-third of a standard deviation away from the mean. The negative sign shows that he is one-third of a standard deviation *below* the mean.

Standard scores are useful because they have equal units—they can be meaningfully averaged. The mean of the z-scores is zero, and almost all of the z-scores are between the values of -3.0 and $+3.0$.

A problem with standard scores is that they contain decimal points and minus signs. Both of these properties can confuse nonmathematical audiences. To eliminate these problems, **transformed standard scores** are often used.

The formula for transforming a standard score is as follows:

$$X' = \bar{X}' + S'z, \tag{3.2}$$

where X' is the transformed standard score,
$\bar{X}'$ is the transformed mean, and
S' is the transformed standard deviation.

A frequently used transformed score is the T-score, which has $\bar{X}' = 50$ and $S' = 10$. Thus, most T-scores are between 20 and 80. The Wechsler Intelligence Scale for Children-Revised (WISC-R), for example, uses $\bar{X}' = 100$ and $S' = 15$ so that the distribution of IQ scores has a mean of 100 and a standard deviation of 15. An IQ of 115 on the WISC-R would be 1 standard deviation above the average for the norm group.

Any values of $\bar{X}'$ and S' can be used. The College Entrance Examination Board tests use a mean of 500 and a standard deviation of 100, while the Miller Analogies Test uses a mean of 50 and standard deviation of 10. In either case, the transformed standard scores indicate how many standard deviation units an individual is above or below the mean.

> Standard scores and transformed standard scores express the relative position of a score in a distribution in terms of standard deviation units from the mean.

Stanines

The **stanines,** or standard nine-point scale, divide the distribution into nine parts, each half a standard deviation wide. A normal distribution is assumed so that the percentage of cases in each of the stanines is as follows:

Stanine	Percentage
1	4
2	7
3	12
4	17
5	20
6	17
7	12
8	7
9	4

Therefore, if Mary has a stanine score of 1, we know that she is somewhere in the bottom 4 percent of the scores. If Sue has a stanine of 5, she is somewhere among the middle 20 percent of the scores. Similarly, if Pat is in the 7th stanine, her score is somewhere between the 77th percentile and the 89th percentile (since 77 percent of the scores are below the 7th stanine, and 11 percent of the scores are above the 7th stanine).

Stanines can be meaningfully averaged, and because they represent a band of scores rather than a particular score, they tend to limit overinterpretation of small differences in test scores. This is especially good when tests have modest reliability coefficients. A disadvantage of stanines is that the nine points may not be enough differentiation on some tests. The stanine distribution has a mean of 5 and a standard deviation of 2.

> Stanines provide equal units of measurement. Each stanine contains a band of scores.

Comparison of Percentiles, Standard Scores, and Stanines

Figure 3.1 shows how percentiles, standard scores, and stanines can be used to show the standing of an individual's score, compared to the distribution of scores for the norm group.

It is clear from Figure 3.1 that the choice of whether to present the norm-referenced scores as percentiles, standard scores, or stanines can be a very arbitrary decision. The score-reporting system that is best for a given situation may depend most on the statistical sophistication of the audience and whether the scores are to be used in further calculations. A single score could be reported in several ways, including $z = 1.0$, a percentile rank of 84, or at the 7th stanine.

Grade Equivalent Scores

Another type of norm-referenced score is the **grade equivalent score**. This score uses the within-grade average performance to define "at grade level" and then interpolates between grade levels or provides measures at other points in the year so that a continuous, monthly definition of grade-level performance can be obtained.

The grade equivalent score is expressed as the grade and month. Thus, a score of 3.6 denotes the average performance of third-graders in the sixth month of school (February). A grade equivalent score of 4.2 means that the score is equal to the average performance of fourth-graders in the second month of school (October). This system is based on a September-to-June school calendar, which may not be used in all schools.

The advantage of grade equivalent scores is that "performing at grade level" is a concept that most people can easily understand. The disadvantages of grade equivalents are:

1. They are often ordinal rather than equal interval scales.
2. The performance at grade level is often seen as a standard rather than a norm.
3. Extrapolated scores are a problem: What does it mean for a fourth-grader to get a grade equivalent score of 7.5 in reading?

> Grade equivalent scores are intended to indicate the average level of performance for students in each month of each grade. Unfortunately, grade equivalents do not form an equal interval scale.

Figure 3.1.
Comparison of Various Norm-Referenced Scores

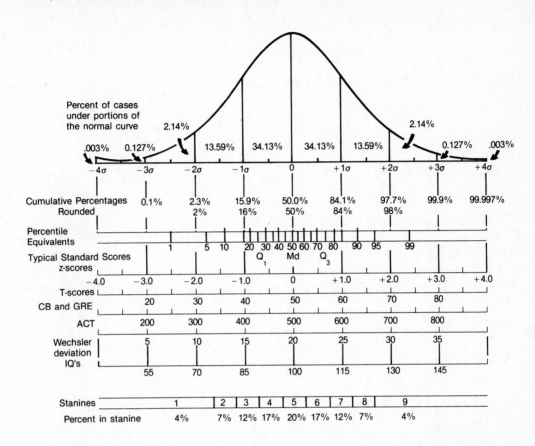

Source: Reproduced from Test Service Notebook No. 148. Courtesy of the Psychological Corporation, Cleveland, Ohio.

An Example from a Standardized Test

Table 3.1 presents part of a table of norms from the STEP Mathematics Basic Concepts Test (STEP Individual Norms Tables 1979). This table packs a lot of information into a small space. Note that there are two levels of the test (I and J) and two forms of the test (X and Y). A raw score of 25 on Level I corresponds to a standard score of 280. A ninth-grader who has a raw score of 25 in the spring testing has a percentile rank of 24; this is in the 3rd stanine. The grade level of this performance is 7.3.

Table 3.1.
STEP Individual Norms: Mathematics Basic Concepts

Standard Score	Raw Scores — Level I Form X	Level I Form Y	Level J Form X	Level J Form Y	Percentile Ranks — Spring Grade 9	Fall Grade 10	Spring Grade 10	Fall Grade 11	Spring Grade 11	Fall Grade 12	Spring Grade 12	Stanine	Grade Level Indicator — Level I	Level J
286	29	29	21	20	36	34	27	27	26	26	23	4	8.3	8.3
285	28	28		19	33	31	26	26	25	25	22		8.2	8.2
284			20		32	30	24	24	23	23	20		8.1	8.1
283	27	27	19	18	30	28	23	23	22	23	19		7.9	7.9
282	26	26			27	25	21	21	20	22	17	3	7.5	7.9–
281				17	26	24	19	19	18	20	16		7.4	7.9–
280	25	25	18		24	22	17	17	16	18	15		7.3	7.9–
279	24	24			22	19	16	16	15	16	14		7.2	7.9–
278			17	16	21	18	14	14	13	15	13		7.0	7.9–
277	23	23			19	17	13	13	12	13	13		6.9–	7.9–
276	22	22			17	15	12	12	11	12	12		6.9–	7.9–
275			16	15	16	14	11	11	11	11	11	2	6.9–	7.9–
274	21	21			15	13	10	10	10	10	10		6.9–	7.9–
273					15	13	9	9	9	9	9		6.9–	7.9–
272	20	20	15	14	14	12	8	8	8	8	8		6.9–	7.9–
271	19	19			12	11	8	8	8	7	7		6.9–	7.9–
270			14	13	11	10	7	7	7	6	6		6.9–	7.9–
269	18	18			10	9	6	6	6	5	5		6.9–	7.9–
268	17	17			8	8	6	6	6	5	5		6.9–	7.9–
267			13		7	7	5	5	5	4	4		6.9–	7.9–
266	16	16			7	7	5	5	5	4	4		6.9–	7.9–
265				12	6	6	4	4	4	3	3		6.9–	7.9–

Score				Grade Equivalents						6.9	7.9
264	15	15	12	11	5	5	4	4	4	3	3	—	6.9	7.9
263	15	15			5	5	4	3	3	3	3		6.9	7.9
262	14	14	11	10	4	4	3	3	3	2	2		6.9	7.9
261	13	13			4	4	3	3	2	2	2		6.9	7.9
260	12	12	10	9	3	3	3	2	2	1	1		6.9	7.9
259					3	3	2	2	1	1	1		6.9	7.9
258	12	12	10		2	2	2	1	1	1	1		6.9	7.9
257					2	2	2	1	1	1	1		6.9	7.9
256					2	2	1	1	1	1	1		6.9	7.9
255	11	11	9	8	2	2	1	1	1	1	1		6.9	7.9
254					1	1	1	1	1—	1—	1—		6.9	7.9
253					1—	1—	1—	1—	1—	1—	1—		6.9	7.9
252	10	10	8	7	1—	1—	1—	1—	1—	1—	1—		6.9	7.9
251					1—	1—	1—	1—	1—	1—	1—		6.9	7.9
250					1—	1—	1—	1—	1—	1—	1—		6.9	7.9
249	9	9	7	0–6	1—	1—	1—	1—	1—	1—	1—		6.9	7.9
248			0–6		1—	1—	1—	1—	1—	1—	1—		6.9	7.9
247					1—	1—	1—	1—	1—	1—	1—		6.9	7.9
246	8	8			1—	1—	1—	1—	1—	1—	1—		6.9	7.9
245		0–6			1—	1—	1—	1—	1—	1—	1—		6.9	7.9
244	8				1—	1—	1—	1—	1—	1—	1—		6.9	7.9
243	7				1—	1—	1—	1—	1—	1—	1—		6.9	7.9
242					1—	1—	1—	1—	1—	1—	1—		6.9	7.9
241					1—	1—	1—	1—	1—	1—	1—		6.9	7.9
240	7	0–6			1—	1—	1—	1—	1—	1—	1—		6.9	7.9
239					1—	1—	1—	1—	1—	1—	1—		6.9	7.9
238					1—	1—	1—	1—	1—	1—	1—		6.9	7.9
237	0–6				1—	1—	1—	1—	1—	1—	1—		6.9	7.9

Source: From Sequential Tests of Educational Progress. Reprinted with permission of the publisher, CTB/McGraw-Hill, 2500 Garden Road, Monterey, CA 93940. Copyright © 1979 by Educational Testing Service. All rights reserved. Printed in the United States of America.

Similarly, an eleventh-grader who takes level J, form X in the fall and has a raw score of 15 has a standard score of 272, a percentile rank of 8, a 2nd stanine level, and a grade-level score of 7.9.

This is just part of the complete table; only the bottom third of the norm group is represented. However, it does illustrate how a table of norms can be used to express raw scores as various norm-referenced scores.

Relating Scores to Grades

One of the most difficult tasks for any teacher is grading: taking a set of test scores from a ten-week period or an entire semester and using them to determine a grade. At some time in this procedure, there must be a subjective, professional judgment about what constitutes quality performance. The judgment is outside of the realm of measurement, but there are some things that can be done to ensure that the measures that provide the basis for that judgment are as sound as possible.

1. *Consider the reliability of the information.*

    The various tests, quizzes, and other measures are likely to vary in their reliability. Other things being equal, the more reliable measures should be given greater influence in the decisions about grades.

2. *Weight the scores properly.*

    Many teachers take the simple average across a set of tests to arrive at a single score. Other teachers prefer to **weight** some tests more heavily than others. Both of these approaches are incorrect, unless standard scores (*z*-scores) are used. If *z*-scores are not used, the actual greatest weight will accrue to that test that had the largest standard deviation. Sometimes this is not the test that the teacher wanted to weight the most heavily.

    The formula that would allow for the intended weighting is:

$$z' = \frac{\Sigma W_i z_i}{\Sigma W_i} \qquad (3.3)$$

where z' is the weighted standard score,
  w_i is the weight for a particular test, and
  z_i is the standard score on a particular test.

Suppose, for example, that a teacher gives two four-week tests, plus a final exam. He wishes to weight the final exam as being twice the value of each four-week test. Suppose, too, that test 1 has a mean of 20 and standard deviation 5, test 2 has a mean of 30 and standard deviation of 8, and the final has a mean of 60 and standard deviation of 10.

	Test 1	Test 2	Final Exam
Mean	20	30	60
Standard deviation	5	8	10

What would Bill's weighted score be if he had 30 on test 1, 34 on test 2, and 70 on the final exam?

His standard scores, using the formula $z = (X - \bar{X}) / S$, would be $+2.0$, $+0.5$, and $+1.0$. Thus, his weighted score would be:

$$z' = \frac{(1)(2.0) + (1)(0.5) + (2)(1.0)}{1 + 1 + 2} = 1.125 .$$

Bill's weighted z-score would be 1.125, or 1⅛ standard deviations above the mean.

3. *Understand the problems of grading on the curve.*

A neat, statistical procedure is to "grade on the curve," which is to use the areas under the normal curve to assign grades. Suppose that a teacher wishes to assign 10 percent F, 20 percent D, 40 percent C, 20 percent B, and 10 percent A grades. The areas under the normal curve can be obtained from any statistics textbook to show what z-scores correspond to these cut-off points (see Hinkle et al. 1982, for example).

Figure 3.2 indicates that the scores for these cut-off points are -1.28, -0.525, $+0.525$, and $+1.28$. Thus, any student with a final z-score of 1.28 or better would receive an A. Those with z-scores between 0.525 and 1.28 would receive a B, and so forth. In our example above, Bill would receive a grade of B.

The danger of grading on this or any other curve is that it prejudges the results. Ten percent of the students are destined to receive F's, regardless of how well the class does as a whole. Old testing legends speak of days shortly after the Korean War, when students on the GI bill had their wives sit in the class, merely to fill in the lower half of the "curve." Thus, it clearly is better to apply a subjective, professional judgment to the set of scores after they are in and thoroughly perused, instead of deciding the students' fate before the scores are even collected and analyzed.

> Translating test scores into grades is likely to require some arithmetic manipulation, such as averaging or weighting. But, at some point, it also requires a subjective, professional judgment that is beyond the realm of measurement.

Figure 3.2.
Cut-off Points for Grading "On the Curve"

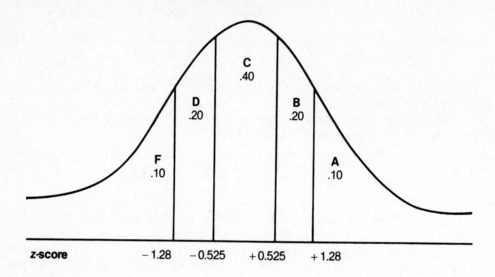

SUMMARY

The scores from tests can be interpreted in a variety of ways, including percentiles, stanines, standard scores, and grade equivalent scores for norm-referenced tests. The choice of which of these scores is most appropriate for a particular situation depends primarily on the statistical sophistication of the audience and whether further computations will be done on the scores. The development of these scores in this chapter was intended to help in accurately interpreting the scores, rather than doing the actual computations to arrive at these scores.

The nature of norm-referenced scores makes it clear just how important it is that the norm group is well described and well understood. Just being at the 99th percentile on a test is meaningless, unless you know what norm group you are being compared to. The importance of national, local, and subgroup norms was emphasized.

The idea of converting test scores to grades was also addressed. Although no specific procedures for assigning grades were given, some guidelines for averaging and weighting test scores were provided.

KEY TERMS AND CONCEPTS

Norms
Norm groups
National norms
Local norms
Percentiles
Standard scores

Transformed standard
  scores
Stanines
Grade equivalent
  scores
Weighted scores

REVIEW ITEMS

1. It is most important that the norm group for a nationally used achievement test:
   a. is large.
   b. is representative.
   c. is from at least three grade levels.
   d. has persons from each state.

2. Local achievement and aptitude norms might be more important than national norms in decisions about:
   a. future occupations.
   b. the likelihood of success in certain colleges.
   c. selection into special high school programs.
   d. allocations among different school districts.

3. A student that scores at the 45th percentile on a test:
   a. answered 45 percent of the items correctly.
   b. is above average in performance.
   c. equalled or surpassed 45 percent of the other examinees.
   d. had at least 45 percent of the right answers.

4. Percentiles are more of an ordinal scale than an equal interval scale.

               T   F

5. Standard scores express an individual's position in the distribution of scores in terms of:

   a. standards of performance.

   (b.) standard deviations from the mean.

   c. standard deviations from the maximum possible score.

   d. deviations from a standard of performance.

6. A test score that is at the 42d percentile could also be said to be at which stanine?

   a. 3d.

   b. 4th.

   (c.) 5th.

   d. 6th.

7. A z-score of 1.5 would have what value if it were converted to a T-score?

   a. 120.

   b. 50.

   c. 35.

   (d.) 65.

$$T = 1.5 \frac{0}{10}$$
$$1 \frac{5.0}{50}$$

8. Which of these cannot be meaningfully averaged because the scores are ordinal rather than interval?

   (a. percentiles.

   b. stanines.

   c. standard scores.

   d. none of the above.

9. Converting test scores to grades requires a great deal of subjective judgment.

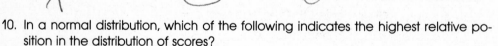

   X   (T)   (F)

10. In a normal distribution, which of the following indicates the highest relative position in the distribution of scores?

   a. $z = 1.5$.

   b. percentile rank $= 80$.

   c. $T = 65$.

   (d.) stanine $= 8$.

EXERCISES

3.1 Select at least two manuals from standardized aptitude or achievement tests and compare the procedures that were used to establish the norm groups.

3.2 Read at least two reviews of standardized achievement tests in Buros' *Mental Measurements Yearbook*. Pay special attention to the reviewer's comments about the adequacy of the norm groups.

3.3 Identify an aptitude test that presents separate norms for males and females. Inspect the tables to see which group has the higher average performance on that test.

3.4 Using Figure 3.1, express a z-score of -1.0 as: (1) a stanine, (2) a percentile rank, and (3) a transformed standard score from a distribution with a mean of 100 and a standard deviation of 15.

3.5 The fifth stanine contains which percentile ranks? The ninth stanine contains which percentile ranks?

3.6 Explain why stanines might be preferred to percentiles for a teacher that wants to base grades on ten fairly short quizzes.

3.7 John had z-scores on five quizzes of -0.40, -0.15, $+0.84$, $+1.21$, and $+1.30$. What would be his weighted composite score if each test is weighted twice the value of the preceding test?

3.8 Compare stanines, percentiles, and transformed standard scores in terms of which would be the easiest to explain to a group of parents of third-grade children.

3.9 Explain the relevance of norm groups for criterion-referenced tests.

3.10 Explain what factors besides test scores might enter into decisions about grades.

REFERENCES

Buros, O. K., ed. 1978. *Mental measurements yearbook.* Highland Park: Gryphon Press.

Hinkle, D. E., W. Wiersma, and S. G. Jurs. 1982. *Basic behavioral statistics.* Boston: Houghton Mifflin.

1974. *Standards for educational and psychological tests.* Washington, D.C.: American Psychological Association.

1979. *STEP individual norms tables.* Menlo Park, Calif.: Addison-Wesley Testing Service.

1979. *STEP test development and content description.* Menlo Park, Calif.: Addison-Wesley Testing Service.

4

Reliability

It is desirable, indeed necessary, for tests to possess certain characteristics, two of which are **reliability** and **validity.** Intuitively, most educators have an understanding of these terms. But, as used in the context of educational measurement, reliability and validity are somewhat complex concepts, in terms of both practical application and theoretical background. In this chapter, we provide a conceptual description of reliability and discuss its application in educational measurement; we also discuss the theory connecting reliability and variance. In a preceding chapter, statistical concepts applicable to educational measurement were developed; these concepts will now be used throughout the discussion of reliability and validity.

In a word, reliability of measurement is *consistency.* If a test is reliable, it will consistently measure whatever it measures. Reliability deals with the question, Do we get the same score (or close to it) every time we measure this person with this instrument (test)? It may be that the test is not measuring what was intended, but it is measuring in a consistent manner. For example, a bathroom scale may measure 10 pounds light. This measurement is reliable, although it is not the true measure.

> Reliability of measurement is consistency—consistency in measuring whatever the instrument is measuring.

Stability and Equivalence Reliability

As indicated above, reliability is consistency of measurement. But in what sense are test scores consistent? Ebel provides the following operational definition of a **reliability coefficient:**

The reliability coefficient for a set of scores from a group of examinees is the coefficient of correlation between that set of scores and another set of scores on an equivalent test obtained independently from the members of the same group. (1979, 275)

Since a reliability coefficient is a correlation, its maximum value is +1.0. Correlation coefficients can take on negative values (to −1.0), but reliability coefficients, at least theoretically, cannot be less than zero; a reliability coefficient of zero would indicate a complete lack of reliability. We will use the symbol r_{11} with a double subscript for reliability to distinguish it from a correlation coefficient.

Equivalent tests or equivalent forms of a test are tests of the same type covering the same content. Difficulty levels of items would have the same distributions across the tests, and, if a group of students was administered both tests, the two distributions of scores would have the same mean and variability.

The definition above indicates that reliability is situation specific. That is, a test may vary in reliability as it is used with two or more groups of students or under varying conditions. Also, the reliability coefficient involves correlation, a statistical measure of agreement or relationship between two sets of scores. Finally, the definition requires at least two independent measures of whatever the test measures from the group being tested. The way in which these independent measures are obtained brings us to **equivalence** and **stability reliability.**

Suppose we administer a test to a group of students and then, at some later time, again administer the same test—a test-retest situation. The correlation between the two sets of scores, one from each test administration, gives us a measure of reliability. But what type of reliability is being measured? The same test is being used, so the reliability coefficient is an indicator of the stability of the trait, skill, or whatever is being measured, over time. A reliability coefficient based on two measures taken over time (using the same test would certainly make the measures equivalent) is an indicator of stability. A reliability coefficient so computed is called a coefficient of stability.

When considering stability reliability, any lack of reliability is due to measurement errors, such as mistakes in scoring, and any changes in what is being measured. For example, students may learn from the original testing, which will have an effect upon the second test score, if this learning is not consistent across students. In some situations, we are deliberately attempting to change a trait, and under those conditions, we would not expect scores to be stable across time.

Stability reliability is consistency of measurement across time.

Another approach to reliability, one more commonly used in educational measurement, is to base reliability on scores taken at a single point in time. The scores on two measures, which are **parallel forms** of a test, are correlated. The parallel forms are often two halves of a single test, called a **split-half,** which is a special case of parallel forms. Parallel forms of tests are tests that are very much alike but not exactly equivalent. Therefore, the reliability coefficient based on parallel forms of a test administered at the same time is a measure of the equivalence of the two tests; thus, it is called a coefficient of *equivalence*. Reliability is reduced by measurement errors and any lack of equivalence between the two parallel forms of the test. Differences due to item sampling or content sampling may introduce some lack of equivalence. In contrast to stability reliability, for which time varies, equivalence reliability involves different items.

> Equivalence reliability is consistency of measurement across two parallel forms of a test.

The differences between stability and equivalence reliability are summarized in Figure 4.1. In this figure, X_1 represents the score on the first administration of a test, X_2 the score on a parallel form of the test, and X_R the score on a retest given at a later time. The upper part of the figure represents stability reliability, and the lower part represents equivalence reliability.

A possibility that is not indicated in the figure is the situation in which a parallel test is used at a later time. This happens on occasion in education. Under this condition, both time and items vary, and reliability involves both equivalence and stability.

Many of the reliability coefficients computed for educational tests are based on a single test administration. The items and their scores are then divided in some manner, such as splitting the test into two halves, and a measure of **internal consistency reliability** is computed. Measures of internal consistency are measures of equivalence reliability—the extent to which the parts of the test are equivalent. In the section on estimating reliability, we will consider several procedures that are based on splitting a single test and determining an estimate of internal consistency reliability.

Procedures for Estimating Reliability

There are a number of ways in which the reliability of a test can be estimated. Some involve only one administration of a test, while others involve two. However, before discussing specific procedures, we must consider factors that affect test reliability.

Factors That Affect Reliability— Errors of Measurement

There are any number of factors that can cause scores to fluctuate. Before discussing specific procedures for estimating reliability, we will consider these factors, some of which are beyond the control of the test administrator or teacher.

Figure 4.1.
Summary of the Difference between Stability and Equivalence Reliability

Stability Reliability

Correlate a test with a retest using the same test

$$X_1 \text{-----------------------} X_R$$
Time Varies

Any lack of reliability is due to instability in the trait (or whatever is being measured) and measurement errors.

$$\text{Stability reliability} = r_{1R}$$

Equivalence Reliability

Correlate parallel forms of a test administered simultaneously

$$X_1 \text{-----------------------} X_2$$
Items Vary

Any lack of reliability is due to lack of equivalence between the two forms and measurement errors.

$$\text{Equivalence reliability} = r_{12}$$

If the same test is administered twice or if parallel forms are used, there may be changes in the individual student from one administration to the next. An individual may change in his rate of work, for example. In addition, there may be other personal factors, such as fatigue, that cause instability in an individual's performance. Factors of this sort are usually beyond the control of the teacher.

Variations may develop in the measurement procedure itself. Inconsistency in directions is an example of such a factor. Another example is confusion with the use of a separate answer sheet by one or more students. Lack of consistency in scoring also certainly reduces reliability. The effects of these factors can be reduced and possibly even eliminated by making the measurement procedure or test administration as clear and consistent as possible. The procedures must be clearly defined, appropriate for the students being tested, and then adhered to during the testing.

The kinds of factors discussed above are errors of measurement. Some of these factors, such as scoring errors, can be controlled by the teacher; but others, such as individual fatigue, cannot. Overall, measurement conditions should be so structured so as to minimize errors of measurement as much as possible.

Factors That Affect Reliability—
Characteristics of the Test
and Those Being Tested

There are characteristics of the test and of the individuals being tested that affect test reliability. Test length has an effect upon reliability; if all other factors remain constant, the longer the test, the greater the reliability. However, this relationship between test length and reliability is not a straight line relationship—that is, a test twice as long will not be twice as reliable. This formula, called the **Spearman-Brown formula,** expresses this relationship:

$$r'_{11} = \frac{Kr_{11}}{1 + (K - 1)r_{11}}$$
(4.1)

where r'_{11} = reliability of the new test, usuallly the longer test;
r_{11} = reliability of the original test; and
K = factor by which test length has been increased—that is, the ratio of new test length to original test length.

Note that K is a *ratio of length,* not the number of additional items. For example, if the test length was increased from 20 to 30 items, $K = 1.5$, not 10.

> Test length affects reliability in such a way that, the longer the test, the greater the reliability, assuming other factors remain constant.

The Spearman-Brown formula is used for estimating reliability when test length is increased. Suppose an original test of 30 items, with $r_{11} = 0.60$, is increased to 40 items. What would be the estimated reliability of the 40-item test?

In this case, $K = 40 \div 30 = 1.33$, and $r_{11} = 0.60$. Applying the Spearman-Brown formula, we have:

$$r'_{11} = \frac{1.33(.60)}{1 + (1.33 - 1)(.60)} = \frac{.80}{1.20} = .67 .$$

The reliability of the test would thus be increased from 0.60 to 0.67, an increase of 0.07.

Suppose the original test had been increased from 30 to 50 items. In that case, $K = 50 \div 30 = 1.67$, and the reliability of the new test would be:

$$r'_{11} = \frac{1.67(.60)}{1 + (1.67 - 1)(.60)} = \frac{1.00}{1.40} = .71 .$$

Now, the increase in reliability is 0.11, from 0.60 to 0.71, over that of the original test. But the added 10 items over the 40-item test increased reliability by only 0.04, whereas the 10-item increase from 30 to 40 items increased reliability by 0.07. Generally, as tests become longer, it requires increasing numbers of items to have a substantial impact upon reliability by lengthening the test.

Generally, the greater the similarity of item content, the greater the reliability of the test. Similar items tend to produce scores that are moderately to highly correlated. As the intercorrelations of items decrease (which means that they are measuring different concepts or content), the observed test score variance decreases. If the observed test score variance is restricted, reliability will be reduced.

Another factor that affects the observed test score variance is the range of performance of the students taking the test. If this range is restricted, test scores will be homogeneous, and observed test score variance will be small. For example, if a group of fifth-graders, all about equally proficient in mathematics, takes a mathematics exam, the scores will tend to be similar and show little variance. If students with a wide range of mathematics proficiency take the exam, their scores will have a good deal of variance. Increased range of performance tends to increase test reliability.

> Item similarity and increased range of performance of the students being tested tend to enhance reliability.

Finally, item difficulty affects reliability. A common definition of item difficulty is the proportion of students taking the test that respond correctly to the item. The smaller this proportion, the more difficult the item. Items that are either very easy or very difficult—such that practically all students get them either correct or incorrect—contribute little to the variance of the observed test scores. Items for which about 50 percent of the students respond correctly contribute the most to this variance. Thus, reliability is decreased as items tend to be very easy or very difficult.

> Item difficulty affects reliability such that items of moderate difficulty, around 50 percent correct response per item, enhance reliability.

# of those who got it correct over the # of those taking it.

There are a number of ways in which reliability of a test can be estimated, the specific procedure used depending upon the type of reliability that is of interest. Some procedures involve two or more test administrations; others involve only one test administration. If two or more administrations are conducted at different times, stability reliability is involved. Single test administrations are concerned with internal consistency or equivalence reliability.

Procedures for Estimating
Stability Reliability

Test-retest or parallel forms administered at different times are procedures for estimating stability reliability, or, in the case of parallel forms, a combination of stability and equivalence reliability. For test-retest, the same test is administered twice with an intervening time period. The reliability coefficient is the correlation coefficient between the scores on the two test administrations; for parallel forms, it is the correlation coefficient between the scores on the two forms of the test.

> Test-retest and parallel forms administered at different times, provide estimates of stability reliability. The reliability coefficient is the correlation coefficient between the scores of the two test administrations.

Procedures for Estimating
Internal Consistency Reliability

It is often not practical to have two test administrations. Therefore, reliability estimates based on a single test administration are commonly used. These reliability estimates are internal consistency estimates, which essentially involve equivalence reliability. Conceptually, internal consistency deals with the question, Do the items of the test, taken in some combination, measure the same thing? If, for example, a test of 20 items was split into two tests of 10 items each, and the two 10-item tests measured the same thing, the original 20-item test would be internally consistent in what it measured. The term "internally" is used because all items involved were internal or part of the original tests. No items of some other test were involved. With other factors being equal, the more similar the test content, the greater the internal consistency reliability.

Split-Half Procedure. The split-half procedure essentially performs a parallel forms reliability, given that the parallel forms were administered at the same time. The items of the test are separated into two parallel parts—two half-tests, so to speak.

One commonly used method of splitting the test is to divide it into odd-numbered and even-numbered items; the scores on the two halves of the test are then correlated. This correlation is the reliability estimate for a test one-half as long as the original test. The Spearman-Brown formula is then used to estimate the reliability of the entire test. Reliability based on the split-half procedure rests on the equivalency of the two halves of the test: The greater the extent to which the two halves of the test measure the same things, the greater the equivalency.

Consider an example. An 80-item test is administered to 35 students, and the test is divided into two 40-item, parallel parts. The correlation between the scores on the two parts is 0.70. Let this correlation be symbolized by r_{11}. What is the reliability of the total test?

In applying the Spearman-Brown formula (Formula 4.1), $K = 2$, since the total test is twice as long as the two parallel halves. If r_t equals the total test reliability, then:

$$r_t = \frac{2r_{11}}{1 + r_{11}}.$$

Substituting the information into the formula, we get:

$$r_t = \frac{2(.70)}{1.70} = \frac{1.40}{1.70} = .82.$$

Thus, the reliability estimate for the total test is 0.82.

> The split-half procedure divides the test into two parallel halves; the scores on the two halves are then correlated. The reliability of the total test is then estimated using the Spearman-Brown formula.

Kuder-Richardson Formula-20 Procedure. The split-half procedure bases the reliability estimate on one specific division of the test, when actually, for most tests, there is a large number of possible splits. One approach to avoiding the single-split problem is to compute r_t for all possible splits and then take the mean of the r_t's. However, for most tests, this is an overwhelming task and certainly not a practical approach. Several people (Kuder and Richardson 1937; Hoyt 1941; Cronbach 1951) have developed shortcut procedures that, in essence, provide the mean for all split-half reliability estimates. In computation, these methods do not require the correlation coefficient between two test halves. Instead, they involve the proportions of correct responses to individual test items and/or the variances of the scores on individual items.

Kuder and Richardson (1937) developed two formulas—designated as *KR-20* and *KR-21*—that estimate internal consistency reliability. KR-20 provides the mean of all possible split-half reliability coefficients. The coefficient, which we will designate as r_{20}, is given by:

$$r_{20} = \frac{n}{n-1}\left(1 - \frac{\Sigma pq}{s^2}\right)$$ (4.2)

where n = number of items,
p = proportion passing an item,
q = proportion failing an item, and
s^2 = variance of the total scores.

Note that as we consider scores on individual items, a student will have one of two scores, either correct or incorrect, hence the p and q that indicate proportions. Σpq tells us to add or sum the products of p times q for the n items.

> The KR-20 formula gives an estimate of internal consistency relia-
> bility (r_{20}), which, in essence, is the mean of all possible split-half
> coefficients.

Consider an example that, in order to limit the computation, will be based on a test with only 5 items. The proportions of correct responses to the items are 0.8, 0.6, 0.8, 0.6, and 0.4, respectively, with a variance of 1.68 for the total test scores. The p, q, and pq by item are:

Item	p	q	pq
1	.8	.2	.16
2	.6	.4	.24
3	.8	.2	.16
4	.6	.4	.24
5	.4	.6	.24

$$\Sigma pq = 1.04$$

In addition, $n = 5$, so, substituting into the KR-20 formula, we get:

$$r_{20} = \frac{5}{4}\left(1 - \frac{1.04}{1.68}\right) = \frac{5}{4}(.38) = .48\,.$$

Kuder-Richardson Formula-21 Procedure. There is another Kuder-Richardson formula, KR-21, that is computationally easier to use than KR-20. Its use requires the assumption that item difficulty levels are similar for the items of the test. If this assumption holds, the KR-21 formula gives a reasonably good approximation of the reliability, although it always gives an underestimation of the reliability coefficient if the items vary in difficulty. The KR-21 formula is given by:

$$r_{21} = \frac{n}{n-1}\left(1 - \frac{\bar{X}(n - \bar{X})}{ns^2}\right) \tag{4.3}$$

where n = number of items on the test,
$\bar{X}$ = mean score on the test, and
s^2 = variance of the total scores.

KR-21 avoids computing the proportion of correct responses to each item of the test, which can become tedious, especially for a long test. The mean and variance are readily obtained and may be substituted directly into the KR-21 formula.

Consider an example. A 40-item test is administered to a group of students; the test scores have a mean of 25 and a variance of 26. It is known that difficulty levels of the items are about the same, so KR-21 applies. Substituting the given values into the KR-21 formula, we get:

$$r_{21} = \frac{40}{39}\left(1 - \frac{25(40 - 25)}{40(26)}\right) = 1.03\ (1 - .36) = .66 .$$

The r_{21} may be substituted for r_{20} if item difficulty levels are similar; r_{21} is computationally easier, but it underestimates reliability if the items vary in difficulty.

Cronbach Alpha Procedure. Cronbach (1951) developed a more generalized reliability coefficient called Cronbach alpha or just alpha, designated by r_α, which is based on parts of a test. If the parts of the test are individual items and the items are dichotomously scored, the alpha coefficient equals r_{20}, determined by KR-20. The formula for r_α, involves variances of the parts of the test and is given by:

$$r_\alpha = \frac{J}{J-1}\left(1 - \frac{\Sigma s_j^2}{s^2}\right) \tag{4.4}$$

where J = number of parts into which the test is divided,
s_j^2 = variance of the *j*th part, and
s^2 = variance of the total scores.

The alpha coefficient does not require the right-wrong scoring of individual items if subtests or subscales are scored.

Suppose a test consists of three subtests, each containing several items. The variances of the three subtests are $s_1^2 = 6$, $s_2^2 = 4$, and $s_3^2 = 7$. Therefore, $\Sigma s_j^2 = 6 + 4 + 7$, or 17. The variance of the total test scores is 32. The reliability estimate for the test, using the alpha coefficient, is:

$$r_\alpha = \frac{3}{2}\left(1 - \frac{17}{32}\right) = \frac{3}{2}\,(.53) = .80\,.$$

The alpha coefficient provides an estimate of internal consistency reliability, based on two or more parts of a test. If each item is considered a part, the r_α is equivalent to r_{20}.

Internal consistency reliability estimates are widely used for educational tests, especially the KR-20 formula. However, it should be noted that internal consistency estimates and the split-half procedure are *not* appropriate for **speeded tests,** only for **power tests.** Power tests are tests on which students would not perform better even if given additional time. These procedures will give spuriously high reliability estimates if used with speeded tests. For speeded tests, only the parallel forms method is appropriate for reliability estimation.

Reliability of Criterion-Referenced Tests

Classical reliability theory and procedures for estimating reliability are closely related to the concept of variance, that is, differences among individuals being measured. Criterion-referenced measurement—which often takes on the characteristic of a dichotomy in scoring, such as pass-fail, adequate-inadequate, with the majority of examinees falling in one category—would not seem to lend itself to the usual procedures of estimating reliability. With dichotomous scoring, the variance of the observed test scores would be very small. So, how is reliability estimated for criterion-referenced tests?

Ebel (1979, 281–82) makes the case for using traditional procedures of reliability estimation (the internal consistency procedures discussed earlier) with criterion-referenced tests. The difference with applying the procedures to criterion-referenced tests versus norm-referenced tests is that for norm-referenced tests, reliability estimates are based on the total test score; for criterion-referenced tests, reliability estimates apply to clusters of items, each cluster associated with an objective. Thus, two or more reliability coefficients might be generated for a single test. It would seem that because of the relatively small numbers of items per objective, reliability estimates would be low. But, in fact, the similarity of item content of the items in a cluster increases reliability to acceptable levels.

> Reliability of criterion-reference tests can be determined by the usual reliability estimation procedures, applying them to clusters of items as the clusters are associated with different objectives.

There are other procedures for estimating the reliability of criterion-referenced tests. One of these will be discussed later in this chapter, after the necessary concepts have been introduced.

The Size of the Reliability Coefficient

Of course, it is desirable to have reliability coefficients as close to 1.00 as possible. However, we have seen that various factors affect the size of the reliability coefficient, such as test length and homogeneity of content. Another factor that affects reliability is the variable being measured. For instance, height can be measured very reliably, much more so than attitude toward school. The expected magnitudes of reliability coefficients will thus differ with the variables being measured.

As far as educational tests or inventories are concerned, reliability coefficients on achievement and intelligence tests tend to be higher than those on interest and attitude inventories. However, among the tests within any one area, such as achievement in academic subjects and skills, there may be a considerable range of reliability coefficients. Table 4.1 contains examples of typical reliability coefficients for selected tests and inventories. When a range is provided for the reliability coefficient (r_{11}), the reliability coefficients are from multiple test administrations.

What, then, is a high reliability coefficient? The answer is relative, as the magnitude depends on the variables measured. Standardized tests, especially those in achievement areas, tend to have higher reliability coefficients than teacher-constructed tests. For one thing, standardized tests tend to be longer, and second, since more effort is put into their development, they tend to be better constructed, technically. But standardized tests need to be reliable because of the decision-making purposes for which their results are used. Often a decision is based heavily on the results of one or two tests, such as test results used for college admission decisions. Results of classroom tests are used more commonly with other performance results in arriving at a decision.

It has been noted that, theoretically, reliability coefficients can take on values from zero to +1.00, inclusive. In practice, however, negative reliability coefficients may appear. For example, the correlation between the scores on parallel forms of a test could be negative. In that case, there is no consistency in the measurement,

Table 4.1.
Examples of Reliability Coefficients Reported for Selected Tests

Test	r_{11}
Stanford Early School Achievement Tests	.61–.94
Chemistry Achievement Examination	.65
Differential Aptitude Test	.88
Screening Test of Academic Readiness	
total	.89–.90
subtests	.42–.80
Wechsler Intelligence Scale for Children—Revised	.73–.83
Slossen Intelligence Test	.83
Comprehensive Ability Battery	
females	.79
males	.78
Strong Vocational Interest Blank	.70–.90
Survey of School Attitudes	.60–.80
Attitudes Towards Mathematics Scales	.51–.78
Screening Inventory for Assessing Psychological Impairment	.76
Piers-Harris Children's Self-Concept Scale	.62

Source: These coefficients were obtained from a number of sources in the *Journal of Counseling and Clinical Psychology* 44 (1976), and *Educational and Psychological Measurement* 37 (1977). Reproduced with permission from W. Wiersma, *Research Methods In Education*, 3rd ed. (Table 9.1, p. 215), Itasca, Ill.: F. E. Peacock Publishers, Inc., 1980.

and reliability would be completely lacking. In this case, the reliability coefficient is usually reported to be zero.

Quantitative Concepts of Test Scores

Thus far, we have discussed the practical aspects of *test reliability:* what it means and procedures for estimating reliability. At this point, we provide theoretical background underlying the concept of reliability. This section may be considered optional, depending on the extent of theoretical background desired.

Suppose a test is administered and scored, and we have a distribution of scores, each representing the performance of one student. What does any one score, such as 75, represent quantitatively with respect to the student? We can partition this score, at least conceptually, into meaningful components.

It is generally recognized that few, if any, tests are perfect; therefore, scores obtained on a test contain some error. We will call this error, which is part of the observed score, an **error component.** The error component may be due to several factors, as discussed earlier, associated with a specific administration of the test to the students. *Error variance* is random or unsystematic variance; an example of a factor contributing to error variance would be mistakes in scoring. The nonerror part of the observed score is called the **true component**. *True variance* is systematic variance or variance due to systematic sources, such as the ability or competence of the students being tested.

> An observed test score may be considered as consisting of two parts, the true component and the error component.

Conceptually, what is the true component of a test score? It may be considered as the student's score if we had a perfect test. Suppose the test had been independently administered a large number of times to a single student and we assume that the error components are randomly distributed around zero. That is, both positive and negative error scores would appear and tend to cancel each other over a large number of scores. Under these circumstances, the true component can be defined as the mean of this large number of scores. This is a theoretical concept of the true component, since a large number of independent administrations to the same student is generally impossible.

Suppose we let X_o represent the observed score, X_t the true component, and X_e the error component. We can then express the observed score as the sum of two components. In equation form, this expression would consist of $X_o = X_t + X_e$. This represents a partitioning of the observed score of a single student into the two independent parts. The error and true components are independent, which means that they are uncorrelated, or the correlation coefficient between the two parts is zero.

Consider an example. Suppose a woman's true weight is 105 pounds. She is weighed on a scale at the local health club and her weight is registered at 106 pounds. The reading is in error by one pound. In her case, the observed score (106) is the sum of her true score (105) and the error component (+1 pound).

We need to consider the entire distribution of scores, not just the score of a single student. If we think of the observed scores in terms of their two components, we have three distributions, two of which are theoretical. The error and true components are uncorrelated, and the error components can be both positive and negative. This means that some of the observed scores may be larger than the true scores, some may be less, and, in some cases, the observed score may equal the true score, in which case the error score would be zero. However, over a large distribution of scores, the positive and negative error scores tend to "balance out"; thus, the mean of the error scores would be zero. Also, it is assumed that the distribution of error scores is a normal distribution.

If, in any one of the three distributions, we summed all scores and then divided this sum by the number of scores, we would have the mean of the distribution. (This is operationally possible only for the observed distribution, however.) Since the true and error components are independent, the relationship between the means may be expressed as $\bar{X}_o = \bar{X}_t + \bar{X}_e$. However, we have assumed that for a large number of scores the mean of the distribution of error components ($\bar{X}_e$) is zero. Therefore, the observed mean is equal to the mean of the true components.

Consider the variances of the three distributions. (Recall that the variance is a measure of the dispersion or spread of the scores in a distribution.) The variance of the observed distribution can be represented by s_o^2. The theoretical components would also have their respective variances, if the distributions were known. Since the true and error components are uncorrelated, the variance of the observed scores may be expressed as the sum of the variances of the component distributions. In keeping with our notation, the s_o^2 may be expressed as $s_o^2 = s_t^2 + s_e^2$. This expression is helpful in developing the connection between reliability and variance, which is discussed in the following section.

> In considering the distributions of the observed, true, and error scores:
>
> $$\bar{X}_o = \bar{X}_t + \bar{X}_e \text{ and } s_o^2 = s_t^2 + s_e^2.$$

Reliability and Variance

Reliability can be thought of as the theoretical partitioning of a test score into the true and error components, which were introduced in the preceding section. We have seen that a score can be partitioned into these two parts; correspondingly, if we have a distribution of observed scores, the variance can also be partitioned into the true components and the error components.

One definition of reliability is the ratio of the *true score* variance to that of the *observed* scores; that is, reliability is the proportion of the variance in the observed scores that is nonerror. If we let r_{11} represent the reliability, the expression $r_{11} = s_t^2/s_o^2$ defines the reliability. We know that $s_o^2 = s_t^2 + s_e^2$. Therefore, an equivalent expression for reliability is $r_{11} = 1 - s_e^2 / s_o^2$.

> Reliability is the proportion of the variance in the observed scores that is true or nonerror variance.

The symbol r_{11} is the reliability coefficient. The formulas for r_{11} above show that r can take on values from zero to $+1.0$, inclusive. A reliability coefficient of zero indicates that all the observed variance is error variance, certainly an undesirable situation. If that were the case, all dispersion—that is, differences among scores—in the observed distribution would be due to measurement error. None of the differences would be due to differences in student performance.

A reliability coefficient of 0.85 indicates that 85 percent of the observed variance is true variance. Of course, it is desirable to have the reliability coefficients of tests as great as possible: The greater the coefficient, the greater the proportion of the observed variance that is true variance.

The Standard Error of Measurement *is a standard deviation*

In chapter 2, we introduced the standard deviation, which is a measure of dispersion in a distribution of scores. In fact, the standard deviation is the square root of the variance. The standard deviation of the distribution of error scores is called the **standard error of measurement**. Since $s_o^2 = s_t^2 + s_e^2$, the smaller the standard error of measurement, the larger the reliability. Conversely, the greater the reliability, the smaller the standard error of measurement. The formula for the standard error of measurement is:

$$s_e = s_o \sqrt{1 - r_{11}}. \qquad (4.5)$$

We can see that if reliability is 1.0, s_e will be zero; on the other hand, if reliability is zero, $s_e = s_o$ and all observed variance will be error variance, as was indicated earlier. Formula 4.5 shows the inverse relationship between reliability and the standard error of measurement.

> The standard error of measurement is the standard deviation of the distribution of error scores. As reliability increases, the standard error of measurement decreases.

A characteristic of the standard error of measurement is that, as test length increases, the standard error of measurement also increases, but only in its absolute size, not in its size relative to the variation in the observed scores. The reason it increases in absolute size is that the variance of the observed test scores tends to increase with additional items. However, the relative size of the standard error of measurement decreases as test length is increased, thus increasing reliability.

The standard error of measurement also has a direct application in one procedure for estimating the reliability of criterion-referenced tests. Hopkins and Stanley (1981, 134–35) suggest that the standard error of measurement (s_e) be used as an indicator of measurement consistency. Of course, the smaller the standard error, the greater the consistency of measurement. If close to all students tested attain the criterion, Hopkins and Stanley consider s_e / number of items. If this ratio is less than 5 percent, the test will have high consistency, regardless of what the reliability coefficient might be using other procedures.

Reliability and an Individual Score

Thus far, we have discussed reliability in the context of an entire distribution of test scores. But does reliability have any application to an individual test score? The answer is yes, and, of course, the standard error of measurement is involved.

Earlier in the chapter, we said that the standard error of measurement is the standard deviation of the distribution of error scores. The error scores are the differences between true and observed scores across all individuals taking the test. Now, instead of having an error for each individual, suppose one individual is tested a large number of times using the same test. (Generally, this is practically not possible.) The individual receives a score each time the test is taken; these scores will be similar, but they will not likely be identical. The mean of this distribution of scores is the best estimate of the individual's true score, and the standard deviation of this distribution is the standard error of measurement. With a large number, these scores will be normally distributed. In administering the test once to an individual, we have conceptually selected one score from this distribution. If we know the standard error of measurement for the test, we can draw some conclusions about how an individual's score might fluctuate.

> We can use the concepts of reliability and standard error of measurement in making inferences about how an individual's score would fluctuate on repeated use of the same test. The distribution of scores would have a mean approaching the individual's true score and a standard deviation equal to the standard error of measurement.

Consider an example illustrating the above concepts. An achievement test in mathematics is administered to a group of 93 eighth-grade students. The distribution of observed scores has a standard deviation of 12, and the reliability of the test is 0.87. Sally received a score of 78. The question we will pose is: What is the probability that Sally would have obtained a score of 78 or less, if her true score is 80?

In order to answer this question, we must compute the standard error of measurement. Using formula 4.5, which involves the reliability coefficient, we get:

$$s_e = s_o \sqrt{1 - r_{11}} = 12\sqrt{1 - .87} = 12(.36) = 4.32 .$$

We assume Sally's true score is 80, and the theoretical distribution of all Sally's observed scores on repeated testing has a mean of 80 and a standard deviation of 4.32, the standard error of measurement. We locate the observed score of 78 in this normal distribution and determine the area to the left of 78. The relative positioning of scores and the distribution are given in Figure 4.2.

In order to use the standard normal distribution, we convert the observed score of 78 to a z-score:

$$z_{78} = \frac{78 - 80}{4.32} = -.46 \, .$$

A z-score of -0.46 has 0.1772, or 0.18, of the area between it and the mean; 0.32 of the area in the distribution thus lies at or below the score of 78. So, the probability is 0.32 that Sally would have received a score of 78 or less if her true score is 80.

Since reliability influences the standard error of measurement, it also influences conclusions about an individual's score. The higher the reliability, the less an individual's observed scores will fluctuate around the true score, if the individual was tested repeatedly. We can provide probability estimates of obtaining an observed score, given a true score. The standard error of measurement is clearly informative about individual scores, as well as an entire distribution of scores.

SUMMARY

In this chapter, the concept of reliability has been developed, presenting the various procedures for estimating reliability. Reliability is consistency of measurement; the reliability coefficient is the indicator of reliability. Reliability coefficients take on values from zero to 1.0, inclusive; the greater the coefficient, the more reliable the measurement.

Educational tests and measures are less than perfect, and any lack of reliability is due to measurement error caused by unsystematic factors, such as scoring errors. Conceptually, the variance of a distribution of observed scores may be partitioned into the variance of the true scores and the variance of the error scores. Reliability is the ratio of the variance of the true scores to the variance of the observed scores.

There are different types of reliability and different procedures for estimating it. A summary of reliability coefficients is presented in Table 4.2. Internal consistency reliability, a form of equivalence reliability, is the most commonly used with educational tests. Estimates of internal consistency reliability require only one test administration, which is certainly an advantage over reliability estimates that require two test administrations. The Kuder-Richardson formulas and the Cronbach alpha formula are commonly used procedures for estimating internal consistency reliability.

Reliability is affected by a number of factors. Longer tests tend to be more reliable than shorter tests. Homogenous items—that is, items of similar content—enhance reliability. If the students being tested have a wide range of ability, reliability

Figure 4.2.
Theoretical Distribution of Observed Scores if an individual's true score is 80 and the standard error of measurement is 4.32

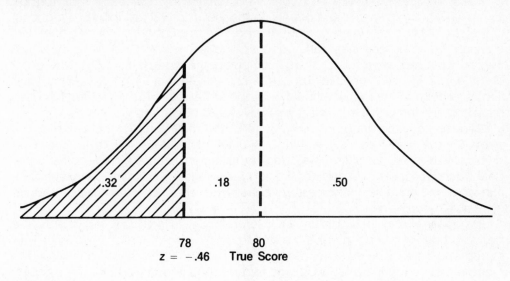

78   80
z = −.46   True Score

Table 4.2.
Summary of Reliability Coefficients and the Type of Reliability Involved

Coefficient	Symbol	Type of Reliability
Test-retest	r_{1R}	Stability
Parallel forms administered at the same time	r_{12}	Equivalence (If parallel forms are administered at different times, both equivalence and stability.)
Split-half	r_t	Internal consistency (equivalence)
Kuder-Richardson 20	r_{20}	Internal consistency (equivalence)
Kuder-Richardson 21	r_{21}	Internal consistency (equivalence)
Cronbach alpha	r_{α}	Internal consistency (equivalence)

will be greater than if the students have a restricted range of ability. Items of moderate difficulty level increase reliability over items that are either very easy or very difficult. The factors that affect reliability can, at least to some extent, be controlled by the test constructor and the test user.

Why are we concerned about reliability? Of what use are reliability coefficients? Concern is primarily a matter of confidence. Unless tests are consistent in their measurement, we cannot be confident of what they measure. Thus, reliability is a necessary but not sufficient condition for test validity, a concept discussed in the next chapter. Also, without reliability, we would have little confidence in interpreting test scores.

Reliability coefficients are important in educational measurement. It is probably safe to say that they merit more attention than they receive. Reliability is of concern in the selection of tests, such as standardized tests of academic achievement. Test manuals should provide information about reliability, including the group for which the test was used when reliability was computed, the type of reliability considered, and the magnitude of the reliability coefficients. Any test for which there is no mention of reliability in the manual should be suspect. If all other factors for test selection are equal, the test with the greatest reliability should be chosen.

Teachers commonly do not compute reliability coefficients for the tests they develop for use with their classes, which is unfortunate. Reliability of teacher-constructed tests should be determined. Possibly, with computer assistance in the future, determining reliability of locally constructed tests will become more prevalent. Confidence in the educational process will certainly be enhanced if there is assurance of reliable measurement.

Reliability is also important in the interpretation of individual test scores. The standard error of measurement is the standard deviation of the distribution of error scores, and it also is an indicator of how much individual scores would vary (due to measurement error) if the test was used repeatedly. Since the greater the reliability coefficient, the smaller the standard error of measurement, the coefficient provides an indication of the confidence to be placed in an individual score.

Finally, in summary, reliability is an essential concept in understanding educational measurement. Tests lacking in reliability are basically of no use and may lead to erroneous conclusions. Reliability should thus be considered in any test selection; reliability coefficients provide valuable information about the extent of measurement error associated with the test.

KEY TERMS AND CONCEPTS

Reliability
Validity
Reliability coefficient
Equivalence reliability
Stability reliability
Parallel forms
Split-half
Internal consistency
    reliability

Spearman-Brown
    formula
Test-retest
Kuder-Richardson
    formulas
Speeded tests
Power tests
Error component
True component
Standard error of
    measurement

REVIEW ITEMS

1. The variance of a distribution is a measure of:
   a. dispersion.
   b. central tendency.
   c. relationship.
   d. location.

2. The reliability coefficient can take on values:
   a. from zero to +1.00, inclusive.
   b. from −1.00 to +1.00, inclusive.
   c. of any positive number.
   d. from −1.00 to zero, inclusive.

3. If the reliability of a test is 1.0, the standard error of measurement is:
   a. 1.0 also.
   b. greater than 1.0.
   c. undeterminable.
   d. zero.

4. Two or more equivalent forms of a test are tests:
   a. whose distributions of scores have the same mean.
   b. whose distributions of scores have the same variance.
   c. whose items have difficulty levels with the same distributions.
   d. all of the above.

5. If a group of students was measured in September using a mathematics achievement test and then tested again in May using the same test, the correlation coefficient between the scores of the two test administrations would be a measure of:
   a. stability reliability.
   b. equivalence reliability.
   c. internal consistency reliability.
   d. both stability and equivalence reliability.

6. In estimating stability reliability, error variance can be due to:
   a. measurement errors.
   b. changes in what is being measured.
   c. both a and b.
   d. neither a nor b.

7. Reliability estimates of a test:
   a. may be based on content or logical analysis of the test.
   b. require some correlation coefficient.
   c. increase with repeated test usage.
   d. are the same for all applications of the test.

8. If a reliability estimate is based on a single administration of a test, the reliability of interest is *not:*
   a. stability reliability.
   b. split-half reliability.
   c. equivalence reliability.
   d. parallel forms reliability.

9. On a given test, the observed standard deviation of the scores is 20, and the reliability of the test is 0.84. The standard error of measurement is:
   a. 8.00.
   b. 18.33.
   c. 3.20.
   d. 16.80.

10. A test of 40 items has a reliability of 0.70. If the test is increased to 80 items, the reliability will be:
    a. 0.99.
    b. 0.54.
    c. 0.82.
    d. 0.90.

11. A test of 100 items is increased to 120 items by the addition of similar items. The original test had a reliability of 0.80. The additional items will:
    a. increase the reliability very little.
    b. increase the reliability to over 0.90.

c. decrease the reliability slightly.

d. have no effect on the reliability.

12. A reading test is given to two groups of sixth-grade students: Group A consists of high ability (IQ 120 or greater) students; Group B consists of students of hetero-geneous ability (IQ range 90 to 150). The most likely reliability situation is:

   a. test reliability will be the same for both groups.

   b. test reliability will be greater for Group A than Group B.

   c. test reliability will be greater for Group B than Group A.

   d. no inference can be made about test reliability.

13. Mr. Jones teaches two classes of algebra; the students in the classes are of sim-ilar heterogeneous ability. To one class, Mr. Jones administers Test A, which has items of similar content; to the other class, he administers Test B, which has items of heterogeneous content. The two tests are the same length. The most likely reliability situation is:

   a. Test A has greater reliability than Test B.

   b. Test B has greater reliability than Test A.

   c. the tests have equal reliability.

   d. no inference can be made about which test will have the greater reliability.

14. Two chemistry classes, with students of very similar background and ability, are administered tests. The tests are of equal length and cover the same content, but Test A has very difficult items, while Test B has items of moderate difficulty. The most likely reliability situation is:

   a. Test A has greater reliability than Test B.

   b. Test B has greater reliability than Test A.

   c. the tests have equal reliability.

   d. no inference can be made about which test will have the greater reliability.

15. Identify the reliability estimation procedure appropriate for determining stability reliability of a test:

   a. split-half.

   b. Kuder-Richardson Formula-20.

   c. parallel forms administered at the same time.

   d. parallel forms administered at different times.

16. In applying the split-half procedure for estimating reliability, the reliability coefficient for one-half the test is computed. To estimate the reliability of the entire test, we use the:

   a. Kuder-Richardson Formula-20.

   b. Kuder-Richardson Formula-21.

   c. Spearman-Brown formula.

   d. Cronbach alpha procedure.

17. A 70-item test has a reliability of 0.75. If the test is divided into two shorter tests of 35 items each, the reliabilities of the shorter tests likely will be:

   a. 0.75.

   b. less than 0.75.

   c. greater than 0.75.

   d. no inference can be made about the reliabilities of the shorter tests.

18. The Kuder-Richardson 20 procedure (KR-20) is a procedure for estimating reliability that provides:

   a. an internal consistency coefficient.

   b. the mean of all possible split-half coefficients.

   c. both a and b.

   d. neither a nor b.

19. The Kuder-Richardson Formula-21 for estimating reliability is an adequate substitute for Kuder-Richardson Formula-20 if the:

   a. test covers homogeneous content.

   b. item difficulty levels are similar.

   c. test is a power test.

   d. reliability of the test is high, greater than 0.80.

20. A test of 100 items is divided into five subtests of 20 items each. If we are interested in internal consistency reliability, the most appropriate procedure for estimating reliability is:

   a. Kuder-Richardson Formula-20.

   b. Kuder-Richardson Formula-21.

   c. Cronbach alpha.

   d. parallel forms.

21. The internal consistency reliability of a speeded test is being estimated. The appropriate procedure is:

    a. Kuder-Richardson Formula-20.

    b. Kuder-Richardson Formula-21.

    c. Cronbach alpha.

    d. parallel forms.

22. With criterion-referenced tests, the usual reliability estimation procedures tend to give low reliability coefficients because:

    a. error variance is small.

    b. error variance is large.

    c. observed variance is small.

    d. observed variance is large.

23. We would expect reliability coefficients for aptitude and intelligence tests to be in the range of:

    a. 0.30–0.50.

    b. 0.55–0.65.

    c. 0.70–0.90.

    d. 0.90–0.95.

24. A mathematics test is given to a class of gifted students and also to a regular ungrouped class. The reliability of the test would likely be:

    a. greater for the gifted class.

    b. greater for the ungrouped class.

    c. about the same for both classes.

    d. unable to infer anything until the reliability coefficient is computed.

25. A reliability coefficient of 0.75 for a test indicates that:

    a. most of the observed variance is true variance.

    b. most of the observed variance is error variance.

    c. 75 percent of the observed variance is error variance.

    d. 75 percent of the true variance is observed variance.

26. A reliability coefficient for a test is computed to be zero. This means that:

    a. error variance and true variance are equal.

    b. observed variance and error variance are equal.

c. true variance and observed variance are equal.

d. all of the above are true.

27. Conceptually, if a test has been administered a large number of times to a single student, we expect error scores to be:

a. randomly distributed around the observed mean.

b. randomly distributed around zero.

c. positively biased, if the student tends to do well on the test.

d. negatively biased, if the student tends to do poorly on the test.

28. In the variance of a distribution of test scores, variance due to the competence of the students being tested is a part of:

a. true variance.

b. error variance.

c. both true and error variance.

d. neither true nor error variance.

29. Conceptually, the true component and the error component of a test score are such that:

a. the greater the true component, the greater the error component.

b. the greater the true component, the smaller the error component.

c. the components are equal.

d. the components are correlated.

30. Conceptually, if we consider a distribution of scores and the true components of the scores:

a. all observed scores are greater than true scores.

b. all observed scores are less than true scores.

c. some observed scores are greater than true scores, and some are less than true scores.

d. the observed scores and true scores are equal.

31. In conceptualizing the distributions of observed, true, and error scores, the following is true for the means:

a. the observed mean equals the true mean.

b. the error mean equals zero.

c. the observed mean equals the true mean plus the error mean.

d. all of the above.

32. Conceptually, the variances of the distributions of the observed, true, and error scores are such that:
    a. the variance of the error scores is zero.
    b. the error variance plus the true variance equal the observed variance.
    c. the observed variance is less than the true variance.
    d. the observed variance and the true variance are equal.

33. Theoretically, with respect to variance, reliability can be considered the ratio of:
    a. observed variance to true variance.
    b. error variance to observed variance.
    c. true variance to error variance.
    d. true variance to observed variance.

34. The standard error of measurement is a measure of:
    a. location.
    b. central tendency.
    c. variability.
    d. association.

35. As the standard error of measurement increases, the reliability of a test:
    a. also increases.
    b. decreases.
    c. remains unchanged.
    d. may increase or decrease.

36. Theoretically, if an individual is tested repeatedly using the same test, as reliability increases, the:
    a. variance in the distribution of the individual's scores will also increase.
    b. individual's scores will vary less around the true score.
    c. variance of the error scores will increase.
    d. variance of the individual's scores will be zero.

37. Conceptually, if a test is administered a large number of times to one individual, a distribution of test scores for the same individual will be obtained. This distribution will have:
    a. a mean equal to the individual's true score.
    b. a standard deviation equal to the standard error of measurement.

c. both a and b.

d. neither a nor b.

38. Reliability estimates for achievement tests tend to be higher than those for attitude inventories.

T   F

39. Increasing the heterogeneity of item content but retaining the same number of items tends to decrease reliability.

T   F

40. Error variance is unsystematic variance.

T   F

41. Increasing the difference between true variance and observed variance increases test reliability.

T   F

EXERCISES

4.1 Discuss the difference between *stability reliability* and *equivalence reliability*. Specifically, what will be the different sources of measurement error between situations in which stability reliability and equivalence reliability are being considered?

4.2 A test consisting of 45 items is extended to 65 items, the new items consisting of content similar to the original items. The reliability of the original test was 0.62.

a. Find the estimated reliability of the 65-item test.

b. Assuming all other factors to be constant, how many items need to be added to the original test in order to increase reliability to 0.75?

4.3 The reliability of a 50-item test is estimated by splitting the test into two 25-item halves. The correlation between the two halves is 0.65. Find the reliability coefficient for the total test.

4.4 A 10-item test is administered to a group of students with the following pass-fail results by item:

Item Number	Proportion Pass	Proportion Fail
1	.7	.3
2	.6	.4
3	.8	.2
4	.4	.6
5	.5	.5
6	.7	.3
7	.5	.5
8	.6	.4
9	.3	.7
10	.6	.4

The variance of the total test scores is 5.32. Find the reliability coefficient using KR-20.

4.5 A test consists of three subtests. On a single test administration, the variances of the scores on the three subtests are 3.9, 4.8, and 5.1, respectively. The variance of the total scores is 25.2. Estimate the reliability of the test using the Cronbach alpha coefficient.

4.6 A 75-item test is administered and the results show a mean of 57.2 and a variance of 39.1 It is known that difficulty levels are about the same for the items. Compute a reliability estimate for the test.

4.7 A 50-item test is to be administered and the reliability of the test estimated. There is no information about the similarity of item difficulty levels, and the items do not group into specific clusters. Identify an appropriate procedure for estimating reliability, and describe the computations required to obtain a reliability coefficient.

4.8 A criterion-referenced test is administered to 40 students; 38 receive passing scores and two students fail. Explain why, in this situation, the traditional approaches to estimating reliability will result in a very low reliability coefficient. Why will such a coefficient not be a good indicator of measurement consistency?

4.9 Describe the concept of test reliability in terms of the variance of the observed scores, error variance, and true variance.

    a. Suppose the variance of a distribution of test scores is 270, and the error variance is 40. What is the true variance? What is the reliability of the test in this situation?

    b. The scores on Test A have a variance of 300, and the scores on Test B a variance of 145. The error variance for Test A is 32, and the error variance for Test B is 24. Which test has the higher reliability? Explain.

    c. The reliability of a test is 0.75, and the true variance is 201. What is the variance of the observed scores? What is the standard error of measurement?

4.10 If, for a given test, the error variance equals the observed variance, what does this indicate about the measurement using this test?

4.11 If the error variance and the true variance for a distribution of test scores are equal, find the reliability of the test.

4.12 Conceptually, reliability coefficients cannot take on negative values or values greater than +1.0. Explain.

4.13 If the variance of a distribution of observed test scores is 256, and the reliability of the test is 0.8, find the standard error of measurement.

4.14 A 60-item criterion-referenced test is administered, and the standard error of measurement is found to be 2.63. If we use the ratio of s_e to number of items, as suggested by Hopkins and Stanley, what can be concluded about the consistency of the test? Explain.

4.15 A test is used to measure a cognitive skill. The same test is administered a second time, after a three-month interval, to the same group of 10 students that were initially tested. The correlation coefficient between the scores of the two administrations is negative. What type of reliability is being considered? What can be concluded about the reliability of the test in this situation and the nature of the cognitive skill being measured?

4.16 A test has a reliability of 0.75. The test is administered to a group of 150 students, and the standard deviation of the observed scores is 15. Find the standard error of measurement. Jack had a score of 90 on the test. What is the probability that he would have obtained this score or less if his true score is 100? If his true score is 95? What is the probability of Jack obtaining a score of 90 or less if his true score is 90?

REFERENCES

Cronbach, L. 1951. Coefficient alpha and the internal structure of tests. *Psychometrika* 16:297–334.

Ebel, R. L. 1979. *Essentials of educational measurement.* Englewood Cliffs, N.J.: Prentice-Hall.

Hopkins, K. D., and J. C. Stanley. 1981. *Educational and psychological measurement and evaluation.* 6th ed. Englewood Cliffs, N.J.: Prentice-Hall.

Hoyt, C. 1941. Test reliability estimated by analysis of variance. *Psychometrika* 6:153–60.

Kuder, G. F., and M. Richardson. 1937. The theory of the estimation of test reliability. *Psychometrika* 2:151–60.

Lemke, E., and W. Wiersma. 1976. *Principles of psychological measurement.* Boston: Houghton-Mifflin.

stance, the criterion measure may be another test. The correlation coefficient can be computed between the scores on the test being validated and the scores on the criterion. A correlation coefficient so used is called a **validity coefficient.** In contrast to content validity, which is based on "logical" correspondence between the test and the content to be covered, criterion validity has a statistical indicator through the correlation coefficient.

> Criterion validity is based on the correlation between scores on the test and scores on a criterion. The correlation coefficient is the criterion validity coefficient.

There are two slightly different types of criterion validity: **concurrent validity** and **predictive validity.** Concurrent validity applies if data on the two measures—test and criterion—are collected at or about the same time. Predictive validity applies if there is an intervening period—for example, three months or six months—between the time of testing and the collection of data on the criterion. Operationally, this time of criterion data collection is the distinction between the two types of criterion validity. Specifically, the question of concurrent validity is whether or not the test scores estimate a specified present performance: that of predictive validity, whether or not the test scores predict a specified future performance.

> Concurrent validity is involved if the scores on the criterion are obtained at the same time as the test scores. Predictive validity is involved if the scores on the criterion are obtained after an intervening period from those of the tests.

Concurrent Validity

In educational measurement, concurrent validity finds its most frequent application in the substitution of one measure for another, such as a more convenient measure for one that is somewhat inconvenient to administer, or a shorter test substituted for a longer one. For the latter situation, the shorter test would be the test whose validity is under consideration.

The process of establishing concurrent validity is one of administering the two measures—the criterion measure and the measure being validated—at about the same time. Consider an example. Suppose that a school system establishes a minimum-competency testing program that includes minimum performance in reading and mathematics for promotion to ninth grade. A comprehensive examination has been developed, with subtests in reading and mathematics. The examination is judged to have good content validity; however, its primary disadvantage is that it requires six hours testing time. So a shorter test, requiring only one hour for administration, is developed, covering both reading and mathematics.

The validity issue here concerns the shorter test: Does the test have adequate concurrent validity, making it a suitable substitution for the longer examination? The original examination and the shorter test would both be administered to a sample of eighth-grade students near the close of the school year. A sample of fifty students would be adequate; preferably, this would be a random sample. The students would take both tests with a short intervening time period, say a week or so. Then the scores on the two tests would be correlated.

The situation actually involves three scores: a total score and one for each of the reading and mathematics subscores. Correlation coefficients would be found for the total score, reading score, and mathematics score, and these three coefficients would be the validity coefficients for the shorter test. Of course, validity is specific to situations, groups, and conditions, and, like reliability coefficients, validity coefficients can vary considerably. In the example described above, substantial correlations, say 0.70 or greater, would be considered necessary to have adequate concurrent validity, allowing the shorter test to be substituted for the longer test. It is possible that not all three coefficients would be adequate. If so, the shorter test would require revision or another test could be tried as a potential substitute.

> Concurrent validity applies if it is desirable to substitute a shorter test for a longer one. In that case, the score on the longer test is the criterion, and validity is that of the shorter test.

Predictive Validity

Predictive validity is involved if we are concerned about a test score's relationship with some criterion measured in the future. In fact, the correlation coefficient between the predictor scores and the criterion scores is called the *predictive validity coefficient.* When test scores are used for selection purposes, such as choosing individuals for jobs or acceptance for admission to college, predictive validity of the test is of concern. In the former, scores on the test must be related to some measure of job performance, which is the criterion, in order for the test to have predictive validity. For the latter, scores on tests such as the Scholastic Aptitude Test (SAT) or the American College Testing (ACT) Assessment Tests are considered valid predictors of college success, if they are related to a measure such as the freshman-year grade point average (GPA). The GPA is often the criterion measure when predicting college success.

Since scores on the ACT Assessment Tests are widely used as at least one criterion for college admission, it stands to reason that the predictive validity of the tests is important and quite good as far as success in college is concerned. We will therefore use the ACT as an example for predictive validity.

There are four tests in the ACT:

- English Usage Test
- Mathematics Usage Test
- Social Studies Reading Test
- Natural Sciences Reading Test

Scores on individual tests are available, and a composite score across the four tests is determined. Other information, such as out-of-class accomplishments in high school, may also be included in a student profile, but for the purposes of this example, we will concern ourselves only with ACT scores and high school GPA.

It is generally accepted that college admission should not be based on a single criterion, such as a test score. Furthermore, it seems reasonable that students that do well in high school will most likely do well in college. So, high school GPA, as well as scores on the ACT, should be valid predictors of college success. The college GPA is undoubtedly the most widely accepted criterion of success in college, and for predictive validity studies of the ACT, first-semester college GPA is usually used as the criterion measure.

A very comprehensive study, involving almost 300,000 college students, produced the predictive validity results summarized in Table 5.2. In this study, high school GPA and ACT scores were used in combination as predictors of college GPA. For that reason, the multiple correlation coefficient is used. This correlation coefficient means that the high school GPA and ACT scores were used in combination and correlated with the college GPA. In the table, the correlation interval midpoint is given at the far left. High school GPA and ACT scores are reported singly, and then they are given in combination. The frequencies indicate the numbers of colleges for which the corresponding validity coefficients (correlation coefficients) were obtained. The PR stands for the percentile rank based on the 419 colleges reporting data for the study.

As indicated near the bottom of Table 5.2, the two predictors, high school GPA and ACT scores, had a median correlation of 0.576 in the 419 colleges, which was somewhat higher than the correlation for either predictor singly. This is considered a relatively high predictive validity coefficient. Of course, the coefficients vary for individual colleges, and, as would certainly be expected, the ACT score is a better predictor of success in some colleges than in others. In the ACT Assessment Student Profile Report, which is provided for high school seniors having taken the ACT tests,

Table 5.2.
Distributions of Multiple Correlations of High School Grades and ACT Test Scores with College GPA[a]

Mult. Cor. Interval Midpoint	High School Grades		ACT Test Scores		HS Grades and ACT Scores[b]	
	Freq.	PR	Freq.	PR	Freq.	PR
Above						
0.83	—	—	—	—	1	99
0.80	—	—	—	—	2	99
0.77	2	99	—	—	4	99
0.74	3	99	1	99	12	97
0.71	6	98	2	99	21	93
0.68	16	95	3	99	24	88
0.65	20	91	5	98	43	80
0.62	21	86	17	95	50	68
0.59	33	80	20	91	55	56
0.56	55	69	32	85	43	44
0.53	49	57	43	76	43	34
0.50	48	45	52	64	29	25
0.47	35	35	51	52	12	21
0.44	28	28	44	41	24	16
0.41	19	22	39	31	24	11
0.38	21	18	25	23	7	7
0.35	21	13	26	17	12	5
0.32	17	8	20	12	4	3
0.29	8	5	15	8	5	2
Below	17	2	24	3	4	1
Median	.512		.465		.576	

[a]Based on data from 419 colleges and 297,980 students.
[b]The correlations given are the correlations of a simple average of the best weighted combination of ACT scores and the best weighted combination of high school grades with overall college grade point average (GPA).
Source: Reproduced with permission from *Highlights of the ACT Technical Report,* Iowa City, Iowa, The American College Testing Program, 1973.

predictions of GPA are provided according to groups, such as liberal arts and engineering. Predictions are also given for specific courses. Thus, predictive validity may vary for courses and majors.

In order for a test or measure such as GPA or ACT score to be a useful predictor, it is necessary for the prediction equations to remain stable from one year to the next, since prediction equations typically are used for several years. Using the results from one sample of students to determine if the validity coefficients hold is called **cross-validation.** In a cross-validation experiment (ACT 1973b), the validity coefficients for students in 1970 were compared with the correlations of *predicted* GPA and *actual* GPA of students in 1971 for fifty colleges. That is, the 1970 prediction equation was used for 1971 students. When the number of students in a college was 250 or greater, there was no average decrease in the validity coefficient; for small samples, the average decrease was only 0.04. Thus, the prediction equations appear to be sufficiently stable for use across years.

Predictive validity can be used in a host of situations: predicting job success, predicting performance in vocational programs, predicting success in selected military occupations, and so on. In some situations—those for which training is very expensive, for example—predictive validity is very important. High predictive validity is obtained by selecting predictors that are related to the criterion measure. The stronger this relationship, the greater will be the validity coefficient.

Construct Validity

Construct validity is concerned with the psychological **constructs** that are reflected in the scores of a measure or test. A construct is a psychological trait, attribute, or quality, something that cannot be observed directly but is inferred from psychological theory. Intelligence, anxiety, honesty, spatial relations ability, and mathematical aptitude are examples of constructs. Gronlund defines construct validity as "the extent to which test performance can be interpreted in terms of certain psychological constructs" (1981, 82). This definition implies that construct validation relies, to a large extent, on psychological theory that indicates the constructs underlying a set of tests or measures.

If a test measures one or more specific constructs, then scores on the test should be correlated with scores on other tests or measures designed to measure these same constructs. Establishing construct validity is a somewhat complex process; it involves both logical analysis and empirical data.

> The construct validity of a measure or test is the extent to which scores can be interpreted in terms of specified traits or constructs.

Correlational Analysis and Construct Validity

Technically, tests do not measure constructs directly; rather, they measure performance or behaviors that *reflect* constructs. A logical analysis of test content can usually give some indication of the number and nature of the constructs reflected by the test. For example, if a mathematics test has among its constructs "conceptualization of abstract relationships," then items that logically reflect this construct can be identified and grouped. Items that do not reflect this construct presumably reflect some other construct. Usually, we would not have as many constructs as there are items. The most interpretable test scores are those based on only one construct.

As indicated above, if tests (or items) measure the same constructs, scores on the tests should be correlated; conversely, scores on tests that measure different constructs should have low correlations. Suppose we have a test that is hypothesized to measure verbal ability, say Test VA. Scores on this test are correlated with scores on seven other measures, six tests (including another known verbal ability test) and individual weight. The pattern of correlations with these measures is as follows:

Test	r
Verbal Ability Test K	.85
Creativity Test	.65
Self-Concept Test	.30
Vocabulary Test	.89
Mathematics Aptitude Test	.71
Reading Achievement Test	.57
Individual weight	.03

Does Test VA measure verbal ability? The pattern of correlation coefficients certainly provides evidence of its construct validity. It has very high correlations with scores on the known verbal ability test and the vocabulary test. Correlations with the scores on the creativity test and the mathematics aptitude test are lower but still substantial. We would expect some correlation with reading achievement tests scores, but not too high a correlation if reading performance is a different construct or contains different constructs than verbal ability. We would not expect a self-concept measure and individual weight to have constructs in common with verbal ability.

Factor Analysis.   When there is a large number of variables (scores on tests or items), visual inspection of correlation coefficients becomes too cumbersome. In such cases, we use a more complex statistical procedure—**factor analysis**—for establishing construct validity. Factor analysis is an analytical procedure by which the number and nature of constructs, factors, underlying a set of measures (for example, tests or items) are determined. The procedures of factor analysis are complex and beyond the scope of this book. However, a descriptive, nontechnical explanation is provided below, along with an example, to enhance the reader's understanding of construct validity.

Factor analysis examines the correlation coefficients among a group of measures, say test scores. As factors are generated by the analysis, one of the statistics computed is a **factor loading,** which is a correlation coefficient between a factor and the scores on a test. Tests that reflect one or more of the factors (constructs) will have relatively large correlations with these factors. If a test does not reflect a factor, its correlation with that factor will be low or near zero. Depending on patterns of these correlations, which are called *loadings,* we have different types of factors. A **general factor** has substantial loadings on all the measures or tests; a **group factor** has high loadings on two or more but not all of the tests; and a **specific factor** has a substantial loading with only one of the tests. In a particular factor analysis, more than one type of factor may appear.

Factor analysis is a procedure for analyzing a set of correlation coefficients between measures; the procedure analytically identifies the number and nature of the constructs underlying the measures. Different types of factors are general, group, and specific factors.

Factor analysis is a statistical procedure; it does not provide names for the factors or constructs. Factors may be considered *artificial* variables: They are not variables that are originally measured but variables generated from the data. So, factors must be described in terms of the variables measured. For example, suppose scores on ten mathematics tests are factor analyzed and the scores on four of the tests whose items appear to be measuring numerical relations are highly correlated with a single factor. This factor would be the *numerical relations factor,* which is an example of a group factor.

Scores on several tests can be factor analyzed, or the item scores on a single test can be analyzed. In the former, we would be interested in the number and nature of the constructs underlying the tests. In the latter, we would be interested in the number and nature of the constructs underlying the items of a single test. If a test consists of a number of subtests, the scores on the subtests can be factor analyzed to determine if they follow some hypothesized pattern. If they do, this would be evidence of the construct validity of the test with respect to the hypothesized pattern.

An Example.   Shepard (1979) did a construct validity study of the Entry Level Test (ELT), a reading examination given to all first-grade students in California as part of the state assessment program. The test has five subtests; the first four subtests have six items each, and the fifth subtest has twelve items. The subtest with twelve items is the *Language Development* subtest; the others are *Immediate Recall, Letter Recognition, Auditory Discrimination,* and *Visual Discrimination.*

Concerning the primary purpose of the ELT, Shepard stated:

The test is not used as a measure of individual pupil readiness. ELT scores are employed with demographic variables to predict differences among schools and districts, and subsequent reading achievement tests. (1979, 868)

The content of the test was determined by an advisory committee of reading specialists, and prereading skills included were those expected to predict reading performance. The intent of the test was to reflect a wide range of relevant skills within the constraints of a short test with little change in the response mode. The items were placed into the five subtests defined above, and the construct validity focused on whether or not the five traits (most of which are skills, as indicated by the subtest names) intended to be measured by the subtests were reflected in the ELT.

Data on slightly over three thousand students were analyzed by factor analysis. The subtest scores were included, along with some student characteristic variables, such as socioeconomic status and ethnic background. The results showed a distinctive factor pattern, with each subtest tending to load on one factor. These loadings ranged in magnitude from 0.70 to 0.87 for the five subtests. Actually, more than five factors emerged, if additional factors are associated with student ethnic membership. On the basis of these results, the constructs followed distinctly the pattern of the subtests. The factors essentially were named for the subtests on which they had the high loadings.

The Shepard study also investigated the predictive validity of the ELT, with respect to subsequent reading performance. The correlation coefficients between scores on the ELT and the scores on the *Reading Test: Second and Third Grades* (California State Department of Education 1976), were around 0.89, indicating high predictive validity.

Validity, Reliability, and Variance

In the preceding chapter on reliability, we saw that, *conceptually*, reliability may be expressed as the proportion of the variance in the observed scores that is true variance. For validity that involves the correlation of test scores with the scores on some other measure or test (a criterion measure), we consider the variance of the two distributions of scores, those of the test and those on the criterion. Then, to relate the two, we consider the variance that the two measures have in common. Suppose we quantify the variances in terms of Euler diagrams, as in Figure 5.2. Let s_o^2 be the variance of the observed tests scores, s_c^2 the variance of the criterion measure, and s_{co}^2 the covariation or variance that the two have in common. In the figure, s_o^2 would still contain error variance (s_e^2), and any variance not error or common with the criterion measure is variance specific to the observed distribution, represented in the diagram by s_{so}^2. The validity of a test is then defined as the proportion of the observed variance that is common variance with the criterion measure. In symbol form, validity $= s_{co}^2 / s_o^2$, or validity $= 1 - (s_{so}^2 + s_e^2)/s_o^2$.

The variance relationship between reliability and validity is also relevant here. The true variance, or s_t^2 introduced with reliability, would be made up of the s_{so}^2 and

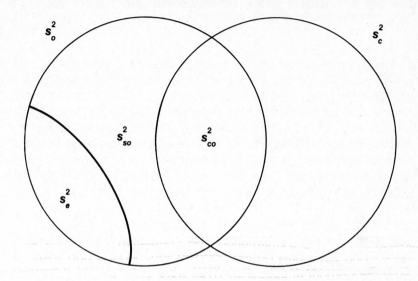

s_{co}^2 of Figure 5.2. The total variance of the observed scores is composed of three parts; that is,

$$s_o^2 = s_{so}^2 + s_{co}^2 + s_e^2.$$

If we divide this equation by s_o^2, we get:

$$\frac{s_o^2}{s_o^2} = \frac{s_{so}^2}{s_o^2} + \frac{s_{co}^2}{s_o^2} + \frac{s_e^2}{s_o^2}.$$

From this equation, we can see that the following proportion,

$$\frac{s_{so}^2}{s_o^2} + \frac{s_{co}^2}{s_o^2} = \frac{s_{so}^2 + s_{co}^2}{s_o^2} = \frac{s_t^2}{s_o^2},$$

represents the reliability, and the proportion s_{co}^2 / s_o^2 represents the validity. The validity coefficient, which is the correlation coefficient between the test and the criterion, is the square root of the ratio s_{co}^2 / s_o^2. That is, $r^2 = s_{co}^2 / s_o^2$, and the validity coefficient, r, equals s_{co} / s_o. Validity coefficients can take on values from zero to 1.0, inclusive. If the validity coefficient is zero, there is no covariation; if it is 1.0, all of the observed variance is covariation.

> For tests validated through correlation with a criterion measure, validity can be expressed as the proportion of the observed test variance that is common variance with the criterion. The validity coefficient is the square root of this proportion or ratio.

The variance equations show us that a test cannot be valid if it is not reliable. The s_{co}^2 is part of s_t^2; hence, if there were no true variance component, there could be no **covariation** component. However, the reverse is not true: The test could be reliable but not valid. The true variance component could be made up entirely of the specific variance, and hence the covariation component would be zero.

Logically, this necessity of reliability for validity can also be seen. A test that is consistently measuring the wrong thing is reliable but not valid. On the other hand, a test that is not consistent (that is, unreliable) can hardly be measuring what it is supposed to be measuring; thus, it lacks validity.

> A test cannot be valid (either conceptually or practically) if it is not reliable; however, a reliable test could lack validity. Thus, reliability is a necessary but not sufficient condition for test validity.

The Validity Coefficient

When validity coefficients associated with tests are reported, they are based on correlations between test scores and criterion measures. Validity is always specific to the particular measurement situation. When a test manual or other publication reports that a test is valid (often supported by validity coefficients), the question must be asked, Valid for what? For example, a test that is valid for measuring the scholastic aptitude of students heterogenous in scholastic ability may not be valid for measuring the aptitude of only high-ability students. Validity coefficients, therefore, must be interpreted in the context in which they were computed.

The Size of the Validity Coefficient. In preceding sections of this chapter, specific examples of validity coefficients have been given. How large must a validity coefficient be to serve as an adequate or good coefficient? Clearly, the larger the coefficient the better. However, some validity coefficients that may seem modest are, in fact, useful and informative. Again, as with reliability coefficients, the expected size of the validity coefficient depends upon the situation.

In our discussion on concurrent validity, we indicated that a validity coefficient of probably 0.70 or greater would be desirable if a shorter scholastic test were to be substituted for a longer test. But by no means will all criterion validity coefficients, concurrent or predictive, attain a value of 0.70 or greater. Actually, quite modest coefficients—some as low as in the 0.30s—can be useful. Validity deals with what can be inferred from a test score; however, the inference must be made in the context of the test use and on the basis of all available information. *Standards for Educational and Psychological Tests* summarizes this point well:

> *Validity coefficients may be presented in a manual, but validity for a particular aspect of test use is inferred from the collection of coefficients. It is, therefore, something that is judged as adequate, or marginal, or unsatisfactory.* (American Psychological Association 1974, 25)

Factors That Affect Validity

There are a number of factors, both internal and external to the test, that affect validity. Some factors may be subject to the control of the test user, while others are beyond such control. Careful selection of a test for the specific purposes of the situation does much to enhance validity. So, when published tests are used, it is important that effort and time be put into selection.

Factors Internal to the Test

A test consisting of poorly constructed items will tend to have low validity. Poorly constructed items may be ambiguous, many times confusing the better students, or they may contain clues to the correct answer. Any item characteristics that distract from what is being measured, such as inappropriate distracters in multiple-choice items, certainly lower validity. Items may be improperly arranged, so that students concentrate more on response mode than item content. Too many difficult items early in the test make it difficult for students to allot adequate time for all items of the test. Items that are not of proper difficulty level also lower test validity. Collectively, the test may be too easy or too difficult. If either situation is true, the test will not discriminate properly and validity is thus sacrificed.

Since test length affects reliability, and reliability in turn affects validity, test length also affects validity. Increasing test length with items of similar content tends to increase validity to a modest extent. If content validity is being considered, a short test may not provide a representative sample of content.

Item intercorrelations may have an effect if criterion validity is of concern. Given a complex criterion—that is, one consisting of several abilities—a test with low item intercorrelations may tend to have higher criterion validity than a test for which the items are highly correlated. This phenomenon occurs when the test with low item intercorrelations measures more of the abilities making up the criterion. A test with high item intercorrelations would measure only one or very few of the abilities.

> A well-constructed test with items of proper difficulty level will en-
> hance validity. Validity tends to increase with test length. Low item
> intercorrelation may tend to enhance criterion validity, if we have
> a complex criterion.

Factors External to the Test

Just as a poorly constructed test lowers validity, so, too, does an improperly administered test. Confusing directions or inappropriate administration, such as lack of
sufficient time, should be avoided. Of course, a test must also be scored correctly,
and any unsystematic errors, such as scoring mistakes, lower validity, as well.

The heterogeneity of the group tested on whatever is being measured affects
any validity involving correlation. Restriction of the range of either the test or the
criterion lowers criterion validity, either concurrent or predictive. The validity coefficients tend to decrease as the groups become more homogeneous. For that reason,
tests that have adequate predictive validity when used with heterogenous groups
may have little validity when applied to a homogenous subgroup. For example, a
test designed to predict first-year college grade point average will have higher predictive validity if used with the entire spectrum of college students than if used with
a homogeneous subgroup within the college population.

There may be subtle, individual factors associated with students that affect validity. Some students may simply not be motivated, while others may be emotionally
upset about the test situation; thus, performance is affected. Any of these types of
individual characteristics that may interfere with performance on the test are potential threats to validity.

> Increased heterogeneity of the group measured tends to enhance
> validity. Subtle, individual factors may also affect validity. Tests
> should be properly administered, since any procedures that
> impede performance also lower validity.

What can a test user do to enhance validity? As a very minimum, tests should
be well constructed and properly administered. If tests are being constructed, revisions are usually necessary, and it may be advisable to try out the test to obtain
information about how long it will take and the like. Students should be encouraged
to put forth their best efforts, and undue anxiety about the test should be avoided. If
a test is to be selected, the selection should be made carefully, ensuring that the
test is used for its intended purpose and audience. Relevant information should be
available in the test manual. Manuals that claim "broadside validity" but provide
little specific information should raise suspicion. It is probably best to avoid tests described by such manuals.

A Comment about Test Bias

To a large extent, the question of test bias or unfairness is a question of the validity of test use. Test publishers are quick to point out that tests, in and of themselves, are not biased: Bias results only when tests are used inappropriately. Considerations of bias or unfairness are often subtle, yet test users must be sensitive to possible biasing factors that may be present in validity studies. A test that consistently underpredicts or overpredicts for some subgroups, such as certain ethnic groups, is biased for that subgroup. Although more will be said about this in a later chapter, the point being made here is quite simple: Test bias is a concern of validity. But as validity is specific to the situation, the bias is specific to the use of the test and its results.

SUMMARY

Few educators, and especially teachers, will compute validity coefficients. Yet validity is a very important part of educational measurement, so educators should understand the concept and be able to interpret validity information when provided in test manuals. We have discussed several different types of validity and shown that validity is specific to the measurement situation.

Content validity is the validity most closely associated with teacher-constructed tests. It deals with the representativeness of the test items in covering the instructional content. Content validity is established through a correspondence between test items and content, which is done in a descriptive or tabular way through aids such as a table of specifications. There is no computation of something like a "content validity coefficient," so to speak.

When a validity coefficient is computed, it is based on the correlation of test scores with scores on a criterion measure. There are two kinds of criterion validity: concurrent and predictive. Concurrent validity is based on the correlation between test scores and scores on the criterion taken at about the same time. For predictive validity, the scores on the criterion are obtained after an intervening time period from the original testing.

Construct validity is a more abstract concept than content validity or criterion validity. It deals with the psychological traits that underlie one or more tests or measures. The establishment of construct validity is done through logical and statistical analysis. Factor analysis is a statistical procedure that indicates the nature and number of factors or constructs that underlie the set of scores being factor analyzed. Theory development and theory testing are often conducted, at least in part, through factor analysis.

These different types of validity are summarized in Table 5.3, providing the reader with a synopsis of the contrasts between these terms.

In the day-to-day operation of classrooms, content validity is undoubtedly the validity of most concern to teachers, not only for teacher-constructed tests but also

Table 5.3.
Summary Information About Types of Validity: Educational Measures

Type	Purpose	How Established
Content	To determine the extent to which test items are representative of content; often instructional content, as with teacher-constructed tests.	Through an analysis that involves the correspondence between test items and content.
Criterion		
Concurrent	To determine the extent to which one measure is an adequate substitute for another, called the criterion.	Correlational analysis; scores on the measure being validated are correlated with scores on the criterion. Scores on the two measures are obtained at about the same time.
Predictive	To establish the extent to which scores on one measure are predictive of scores on another, called the criterion.	Correlational analysis; scores on the measure being validated are correlated with scores on the criterion. Scores on the criterion are obtained sometime later than those on the measure being validated.
Construct	To determine the number and nature of the traits that underlie a set of scores, test scores or item scores.	Logical analysis and through correlational procedures, such as factor analysis.

for published tests. Of the two types of criterion validity, predictive validity is used more commonly, particularly by guidance counselors and those concerned with selection for jobs or admission to colleges or training programs. For most educators in the elementary and secondary schools, construct validity is probably of the least concern. It applies more to research and theory-testing purposes. Yet, anyone that uses tests and other measures should understand the different types of validity and the situations for which they apply.

KEY TERMS AND CONCEPTS

Validity

Content validity

Criterion validity

Construct validity

Validity coefficient

Predictive validity

Concurrent validity

Cross-validation

Construct

Factor analysis

Factor loading

General factor

Group factor

Specific factor

Covariation

REVIEW ITEMS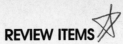

1. Which of the following types of validity does not yield a validity coefficient?
   a. predictive.
   b. concurrent.
   c. content.
   d. criterion.

2. When considering the terms *reliability* and *validity,* as applied to a test, we can say:
   a. a valid test ensures some degree of reliability.
   b. a reliable test ensures some degree of validity.
   c. both a and b.
   d. neither a nor b.

3. If a test is representative of the skills and topics covered by a specific unit of instruction, the test has:
   a. construct validity.
   b. concurrent validity.
   c. predictive validity.
   d. content validity.

4. If scores on a high school academic aptitude test are highly and positively related to freshman GPA in college, the test has:
   a. construct validity.
   b. concurrent validity.
   c. predictive validity.
   d. content validity.

5. A school system's curriculum committee is attempting to select a published achievement test to be used with all elementary students at the end of the school year. The validity of most concern is:
   a. construct.
   b. concurrent.
   c. predictive.
   d. content.

6. The index of criterion validity for a test is computed by finding the correlation between scores on:

   a. the test and those on an external variable.

   b. two forms of the test.

   c. two halves of the test, such as scores on even-numbered and odd-numbered items.

   d. two administrations of the test.

7. Which combination of test characteristics is *not* possible?

   a. low validity and low reliability.

   b. high validity and high reliability.

   c. low validity and high reliability.

   d. high validity and low reliability.

8. Which characteristic is true of criterion validity?

   a. it is based on a logical correspondence between two tests.

   b. it includes two types, concurrent and predictive validity.

   c. it is based on two administrations of the same test.

   d. all of the above.

9. A school system uses a test considered to be valid for measuring student achievement, but the test requires three hours' administration time. The principals and teachers are considering substituting a shorter test for the longer one. The validity of concern here is:

   a. concurrent.

   b. content.

   c. construct.

   d. predictive.

10. When an academic aptitude test score is used for decisions about admission to a specific college, the test validity of concern is:

    a. concurrent.

    b. content.

    c. construct.

    d. predictive.

11. The testing division of a school system is attempting to analyze the traits that are inherent in the six subscores of an academic achievement test. The validity of concern here is:

    a. concurrent.
    b. content.
    c. construct.
    d. predictive.

12. Construct validity is established through:

    a. logical analysis.
    b. statistical analysis.
    c. both logical and statistical analysis.
    d. neither logical nor statistical analysis.

13. Factor analysis is a procedure often used in establishing construct validity of a set of tests. In the analysis, the factor loadings that are computed are correlation coefficients between:

    a. scores on two or more tests of the set.
    b. factors and tests.
    c. two or more factors.
    d. none of the above.

14. A factor analysis is conducted on the scores from six different IQ tests. One of the factors has a large loading with a single IQ test and very small loadings with the other five tests. This is a:

    a. general factor.
    b. specific factor.
    c. group factor.
    d. none of the above.

15. When using criterion measures for establishing validity, a validity coefficient is computed. Theoretically, in terms of variance, the validity coefficient is the square root of the ratio of:

    a. variance common with the criterion to observed variance.
    b. observed variance to variance common with the criterion.
    c. true variance in the criterion to observed variance.
    d. true variance in the criterion to true variance in the test being validated.

16. In considering criterion validity, the validity of a test will certainly be increased if the:

    a. specific variance of the test is increased.

    b. true variance of the test is increased.

    c. error variance of the test is decreased.

    (d) the variance common with the criterion is increased.

17. A criterion is made up of several abilities, aptitudes, or traits. If a test is used to predict performance on the criterion, the intercorrelations of the test items must be:

    (a.) low.

    b. high.

    c. zero.

    d. negative.

18. If a validity coefficient is computed for a test, and the test has been used with a very homogeneous group of students, we expect that the validity coefficient will be:

    a. moderate, around 0.55.

    b. high.

    (c.) low.

    d. unable to make an inference.

19. A test is found to have high reliability but low validity. In order for this to occur, the test has:

    a. little true variance.

    b. large error variance.

    (c.) large specific variance.

    d. little observed variance.

20. Which of the following is least like the others?

    a. criterion validity.

    (b.) construct validity.

    c. concurrent validity.

    d. predictive validity.

EXERCISES

5.1 Describe what is meant by the content validity of a teacher-constructed test. How would it be established? How would the content validity of a published test be established?

5.2 Distinguish between the *reliability* and the *validity* of a test. Why do we say that a test can be reliable without being valid, but that the reverse cannot be true?

5.3 A distribution of test scores has a variance of 80; 55 of this variance is variance that the test has in common with the that of a criterion. What is the validity coefficient of the test? What sources of variance are contained in the proportion of variance not common with that of the criterion test?

5.4 A school system has three relatively large high schools. It is decided that all classes of an Introduction to American History course will have a common semester final exam. What procedures need to be followed in order to enhance the content validity of the exam, assuming this decision is made at the beginning of the semester? What will be the likely effect on content validity if this decision is not made until three weeks or so prior to the end of the semester?

5.5 The variance of a distribution of test scores consists of 75 specific variance, 15 error variance, and 105 covariance with that of a criterion variable. Determine the portion of the variance that is covariation and compute the validity coefficient.

5.6 Suppose that a group of 75 fifth-grade students was measured with a battery of six tests claiming to measure creativity. If a factor analysis were conducted on the test scores, what factor pattern would be expected if creativity is a single trait or construct? A psychologist hypothesizes that creativity consists of four constructs. If the tests, in fact, measure these four constructs, what would be an expected factor pattern?

5.7 An admissions director at a specific university is concerned about the predictive validity of an aptitude test in predicting success at the university, using freshman GPA as the measure of college success. Outline a study that could be conducted, taking a year or longer, that would check the predictive validity of the test at the university. Identify the statistics that would be computed. Suppose this is a large university containing several colleges: What would be the merits, if any, of separating results by college?

5.8 Identify five factors that influence test validity, describing the effect that each has.

5.9 Review the validity section of the manual for an achievement test, such as *The Iowa Test of Basic Skills.* Then do the same for the manual of an IQ test. For each, identify the types of validity discussed and how these types differ. Make a judgment about the adequacy of the respective validity sections.

REFERENCES

American College Testing Program. 1973a. *Assessing students on the way to college: Technical report for the ACT assessment program.* Iowa City, Iowa: American College Testing Program.

———. 1973b. *Highlights of the ACT technical report.* Iowa City, Iowa: American College Testing Program.

American Psychological Association. 1974. *Standards for educational and psychological tests.* Washington, D.C.: American Psychological Association.

California State Department of Education. 1976. *Reading test: Second and third grades.* Sacramento, Calif.: California State Department of Education.

Gronlund, N. E. 1981. *Measurement and evaluation in teaching.* 4th ed. New York: MacMillan.

Heuer, E., and W. Wiersma. 1977. A design for the content validation of standardized achievement tests. *AIGE Forum* 2 (3): 18–20.

Messick, S. A. 1975. The standard problem: Meaning and values in measurement and evaluation. *American Psychologist* 30:955–66.

Shepard L. 1979. Construct and predictive validity of the entry level test. *Educational and Psychological Measurement* 39:867–77.

Toledo Diocesan Schools. 1972. *Curriculum guide for elementary school social studies.* Toledo, Ohio: Toledo Diocesan Schools.

Yalow, E. S., and W. J. Popham. 1983. Content validity at the crossroads. *Educational Researcher* 12, no. 8 (Oct.): 10–14, 21.

6

Constructing Objective Items:
True-False and Multiple Choice

Test items can be written in a wide variety of styles and formats. Two major types are commonly called *objective* and *essay* items; of course, each of these includes several different kinds of items within it. This chapter will present two item formats under the objective label: **true-false** and **multiple choice.** (Essay items are discussed in chapter 8.)

The term *objective test item* is really a misnomer; it implies that these items are *objective*, while essay items are *subjective*. There is actually much subjectivity in every item format. Choices of what to test, how narrowly or broadly to define the domain of possible items, and how to phrase the items are all very subjective choices that the test writer must make. The only condition that sets so-called "objective" items apart is that the scoring of the items is done objectively, with a standard scoring key, which does not call for the scorer to make subjective inferences or judgments.

True-false and multiple-choice tests are the focus of this chapter; since they are used so often in testing, they deserve careful consideration. These two item formats are frequently used in commercially available tests, including standardized tests; they are also used in many teacher-constructed tests. This chapter describes these formats and provides suggestions for writing good test items. Examples of the various problems that can creep into these item formats are also provided.

> Objective items tend to be objective only with regard to scoring. The selection of content to be tested and the phrasing of items are always subjective choices.

General Characteristics of True-False and Multiple-Choice Items

There are two major positive qualities of true-false and multiple-choice questions: (1) they can be reliably scored; and (2) they allow for adequate content sampling. The one major negative quality of such tests is that they often measure trivia. Each of these qualities is explained below.

Reliable Scoring

Reliable scoring is important because anything that introduces inconsistency into the observed scores lowers the reliability of the measurement. The consistency and accuracy of the scoring surely is one such factor. Since it is also true that reliability is a necessary part of validity, reliable scoring tends to increase the validity of the measure.

The scoring of multiple-choice and true-false items is reliable because two independent scorers or one person scoring the same test twice should arrive at identical scores. Scorers are not called upon to make judgments; they only have to determine whether the answers on a test or answer sheet match the preferred responses given on the scoring key. Since no judgments are needed, the scoring can be done by clerks or machines, rather than teachers, counselors, or other highly trained staff.

Note the distinctions among **objectivity,** reliable scoring, and test reliability. Scoring is objective because it requires no judgments or inferences from the scorer; thus, it is very likely that the item scoring will be consistent. This means that the scoring is also reliable. **Scorer reliability** is one component of test reliability. There can be tests on which the scoring is reliable but the levels of performance of the individual examinees are not consistent. In this instance, the test is unreliable but the unreliability is due to something other than the scoring.

Content Sampling

The second quality of true-false and multiple-choice tests is that they do a good job of **content sampling.** In the earlier development of content validity, we said that a content-valid test provided a good match between the items actually selected for a test and the domain of possible items: all those items that could be constructed concerning the content of the course or objectives. The domain of possible items is often infinitely large, even with very specific instructional objectives. Hence, it follows that an adequate, representative sampling from the domain of possible items probably requires a reasonably large number of items. The virtue of true-false and multiple-choice items is that they require less time on the part of the examinee than do other item formats. Therefore, more items of this type can be asked in a given amount of testing time, which allows for a broader sampling of content than is provided by other item formats. Thus, there is the possibility of increased content validity for tests of true-false and multiple-choice formats.

Tendency to Measure Trivia

The attributes of true-false and multiple-choice items described above may give the impression that these item formats are so good that they have no weaknesses. To balance the description, it is necessary to describe a major weakness of these items but, at the same time, point out that the weakness can be overcome.

The weakness that we are referring to is that true-false and multiple-choice items tend to measure trivial bits of knowledge. Actually, this is the fault of the test item *writer,* not the item *format.* When used properly, these items (especially the multiple-choice items) can measure higher levels of understanding; examples of this are presented later in this chapter. However, when these item formats are used without planning the cognitive levels addressed, as is often done when a table of specifications is not used, there is a tendency to write these items at the lowest level of the cognitive taxonomy, calling for merely the *recognition* of specifics, names, dates, and facts. With a little more time and effort such items could require the student to form comparisons or draw conclusions, higher levels of outcomes in the cognitive taxonomy.

The two strengths of true-false and multiple-choice testing—reliable scoring and good content sampling—outweigh the limitation of low cognitive levels of many items, especially since a little planning and creativity can overcome this problem. Overall, these are only general strengths and weaknesses. We will continue to address additional concerns with these items throughout the chapter, providing specific examples for illustration.

True-false and multiple-choice items have three general qualities:

- They can be reliably scored.
- They can sample the domain of content extensively.
- They tend to measure memorization of unimportant facts unless care is taken in constructing the items.

True-False Items

True-false items are essentially any items that call for the examinee to select one of the two choices given as possible responses to a test item. Very often the choice is between yes-no or right-wrong, as well as true-false. And sometimes the examinee is asked to explain why a false statement is false, but usually this is not required. The following guidelines include the most commonly mentioned concerns with writing true-false items.

Make the Statement Clearly True or False

The true-false item must be clearly stated and free of ambiguity. Subtle phrasing only bothers the examinees and contributes to confusion rather than allowing one to "tease out" additional information.

Here is an example of the ambiguity that can confuse students:

1. Lengthening a test will increase its reliability.

        T   F

This item will be confusing to the better students because they know that the reliability may not increase if the additional items bear little resemblance to the original test items. A better statement of the item is:

2. Homogeneously lengthening a test will increase its reliability.

        T   F

Avoid Lifting Statements from the Textbook

It is often tempting to pick sentences directly from the textbook to serve as true-false items. When the students become aware of this, it can promote memorization of the text rather than learning of concepts and principles. In addition, textbooks are written so that sentences fit into paragraphs and paragraphs fit into sections. Sentences are not written to stand alone, out of context, as they would when serving as true-false items. It is much better to rewrite important ideas that are gleaned from whole paragraphs, rather than from single sentences.

Avoid Specific Determiners

Very often the wording of an item gives away the answer without requiring the student to know anything about the concept being tested. **Specific determiners**—such as *always, never, all,* and *none*—are often used in true-false questions, but they are frequently false. When the student knows this, there is little need to ever read the whole item. The correct answer is probably "false." Note the following item:

1. All Woodland Indians were hunters of small game.

    T   F

The answer to this item is "false." Although most Woodland Indians did hunt small game, it is possible that at least one did not, which is all that is required to make the statement false. The student does not even have to know a specific counterexample to the statement; he can merely assume the existence of one.

This is not to imply that there are no instances in which specific determiners are appropriate. In fact, consider the following item:

2. You should never use specific determiners on true-false tests.

    T   F

According to the ideas expressed above, this item implies that there are times when a specific determiner is acceptable. The following statement is an example of the appropriate use of a specific determiner:

3. All carbohydrates contain oxygen, carbon, and hydrogen atoms.

    T   F

This example demonstrates that, at times, exceptions can be made. We should thus interpret these item-writing suggestions as general guidelines, rather than strict rules.

Avoid Trick Questions

Sometimes minor adjustments are made to true statements in order to create test items that are false. These changes are often slight and have only a trivial bearing on the falseness of the statement. Consider this example:

1. FDR was succeeded in the presidency by Harry L. Truman.

    T   F

The answer is "false" because Truman's middle initial is S, not L. However, the idea that is tested for should be that Truman—rather than Harding, Eisenhower, Nixon, or anyone else—succeeded Roosevelt in the presidency.

If the test constructor in the above example wanted to know whether the students knew Truman's middle initial (an inconsequential bit of knowledge), that question should have been asked directly. Trick questions are only confusing, not clever. Nothing is gained by including them on the test.

Do Not Limit Questions to Memorized Facts

The true-false item is well suited to the measurement of knowledge of specific names, dates, and terms. However, it can also measure higher-order cognitive outcomes. Consider the following pair of items:

1. The area of an equilateral triangle with 6-inch sides is 40 square inches.

    T   F

2. Hyperbole: Exaggeration:: Tsunami: Wave

    T   F

Note that both of these questions call for understanding well beyond the knowledge level of the taxonomy. With a little creativity, a set of true-false items written at the knowledge level can be transformed into items measuring higher-level outcomes. The key is to require more than simple recall from the students; they should have to make comparisons or draw conclusions.

Make the Length and Number of True and False Statements About the Same

Students should not be given irrelevant clues about the correct answers. Some test constructors have a tendency to write more false items than true items, or the reverse. When students become aware of such a tendency, their guesses also follow that pattern.

Similarly, one often must add qualifiers to make a statement true. This sometimes causes the true statements to be longer than the false statements. This type of clue may cause the student to answer the question based on its length, rather than its content. Care should be taken to avoid such irrelevant clues in true-false questions.

True-false items can be effective when a few guidelines are followed in the construction:

- Statements must be clearly true or false.
- Statements should not be lifted directly from the text.
- Specific determiners should be avoided.
- Trick questions should not be used.
- Some statements should be written at higher cognitive levels.
- True and false items should be of the same frequency and length.

Multiple-Choice Items

Multiple choice refers to test items that require the examinee to select one or more responses from a set of three or more options. These items have two parts: (1) the **stem,** which includes all of the pertinent information needed to introduce the question; and (2) the **options,** correct answers, and **distracters,** which are the statements from which the examinee must choose. The two most frequently used multiple-choice approaches call for the examinee to select the one *correct* response or the one *best* response. Obviously, the items must be preceded by specific directions that tell the examinee how to respond.

The following sections offer some suggestions for writing multiple-choice items, along with example items for illustration.

Do Not Indicate Correct Answers by the Grammar

Sometimes the wording of the test item and options provides clues that students can capitalize on. Then, in effect, the item measures grammar skills, rather than the content area of the test. Plurals, articles, and tenses are the most common **grammatical clues.** Note their use in the following items:

1. A prehistoric birdlike animal is called an _____ .
   a. triceratops.
   b. archaeopteryx.
   c. stegasaurus.
   d. diplodocus.

2. Fruits that were once considered poisonous to humans are _____ .
   a. tomatoes.
   b. pear.

    c. apple.

    d. strawberry.

Test items are fairer to all students when they do not test for extraneous knowledge, such as grammar skills. When possible, the options should be parallel in grammar construction, such as all plurals or all singulars. Sometimes the problem can be corrected by using the terms *a(n)* or *this (these)* so the student is shown that all options are grammatically consistent.

Make All Distracters the Same Length

There is sometimes a tendency to add qualifying words and phrases to an option to make sure that it is correct. More often than not, the result is that the longest of the distracters is the correct response. Clever students recognize this pattern and select answers accordingly, rather than consider what is actually contained in the item. It is not difficult to overcome this problem; one needs only to make sure that the options are roughly the same length. Then the lengths of the options no longer provide clues to the correct answer. Note the poorly written item below and the improvement in the revised statement below it:

1. The reliability coefficient for a test:
   a. is a number between -1 and $+1$.
   b. indicates the percentage of variance in the observed scores that is due to differences in true scores.
   c. is the correlation between true and observed scores.
   d. is written in terms of raw score points.

2. The number that indicates the percentage of variance in the observed scores that is due to differences in the true scores is the:
   a. reliability coefficient.
   b. correlation coefficient.
   c. index of reliability.
   d. standard error of measurement.

Make All Distracters Plausible

It is very difficult to think of good distracters for multiple-choice items. It takes patience and creativity. However, just tacking on any old distracter is not appropriate; it invariably results in an option that students can dismiss immediately, regardless of whether or not they know the correct response. Implausible distracters are quickly rejected by examinees and therefore serve no purpose. Occasionally, a clearly implausible option may be inserted for comic relief or to keep the examinees involved and motivated, but the test constructor must be aware of the function that such a distracter serves. In the item below, two options can be quickly eliminated; thus, there is actually a 50:50 odds level for someone guessing at the item, rather than the assumed guessing level of 1:4.

1. The capital of Nebraska is:
   a. New York.
   b. Omaha.
   c. Los Angeles.
   d. Lincoln.

Another problem with implausible distracters is that they can disrupt the student's test-taking state of mind. When the student encounters an option that is tangential or unrelated to the other options, he may have a tendency to pause and imagine how the option can be made to fit the question. Such disruptions are time consuming and may even cause the examinee to read more into the item than is actually given. Therefore, we can conclude that implausible distracters are rarely useful and usually interruptive; they should generally be avoided.

Avoid Repeating Key Words in the Stem and the Options

Another problem that occasionally slips in is when key words from the stem also appear in the distracters, thereby providing clues to the correct answer. Care must be taken to avoid this phrasing, because it allows students to answer the item correctly when, in fact, they may not understand the idea and content of the question. Here is an example of this problem:

1. Some tests are used to predict how well prospective college freshmen are likely to do in their first-semester grade point average. The validity that we are concerned with in this instance is:
   a. content validity.
   b. concurrent validity.
   c. predictive validity.
   d. construct validity.

The perceptive student will notice that the word "predict" appears both in the stem and in option c. He can get the item correct on that basis alone.

Another example, this one from an elementary level, is the following:

2. A popular sport fish that is often taken in the Great Lakes region is the:

   a. shark.

   b. tuna.

   c. swordfish.

   d. lake trout.

Here, the word "lake" appears in the stem and then again in the correct option, d. Pickerel or sturgeon may have been better choices than lake trout. A careful review of items, usually by someone other than the item writer, helps spot this kind of problem.

> Multiple-choice items can be improved by following these guidelines:
>
> • Avoid grammatical clues.
> • Keep option lengths uniform.
> • Use plausible distracters.
> • Don't repeat key words from the stem in the options.

Advantages of Multiple-Choice Testing

Measuring Higher Cognitive Levels. Multiple-choice items measure higher cognitive levels very well, much better than true-false items. This is especially true when the items are based on reading passages, charts, maps, or figures. Note how the following items measure cognitive performance at higher levels of the cognitive taxonomy:

1. Lengthening a test would most likely increase the size of which of the following (mark as many as apply):

   a. the mean.

   b. the standard deviation.

   c. the reliability coefficient.

   d. the standard error of measurement.

2. If a test has a standard deviation of 4.5 and a reliability coefficient of 0.84, it has a standard error of measurement of:

   a. 1.80.

   b. 1.60.

   c. 1.40.

   d. none of the above.

3. Aptitude test: Predictive Validity:: Achievement Test:

    (a.) content validity.
    b. construct validity.
    c. concurrent validity.
    d. predictive validity.

Clearly, the multiple-choice item can be written in a wide variety of ways to tap many different kinds of thinking. It is this versatility, in addition to the broad content sampling that can be achieved, that makes multiple choice such a popular format in published tests.

Providing Diagnostic Information.   When the distracters in multiple-choice items are constructed so that they provide information about the kind of mistakes that students are making, the test can provide useful diagnostic information. Note how the incorrect choices in the following items are based on the kinds of errors that students are likely to make:

1. $\frac{1}{4} \div \frac{2}{3} =$ _____ .

    a. $\frac{1}{6}$.
    b. $2\frac{2}{3}$.
    c. $\frac{3}{8}$.
    d. none of the above.

Choice a, $\frac{1}{6}$, is the answer if the student multiplies rather than divides. Choice b, $2\frac{2}{3}$, is the answer if the student inverts the wrong number. The correct response is c, $\frac{3}{8}$. And choice d covers all other errors the student may make.

A test that contains such informative wrong answers can be used to diagnose recurring incorrect procedures being used by the individual student, as well as the class. Constructing such a test is quite a time-consuming process, though.

Multiple-choice items are very versatile:

• They can measure higher cognitive outcomes.
• They can provide diagnostic information.

Other Suggestions
for Writing Multiple-Choice Items

It is also a good idea to alternate the correct response randomly among the options. If the correct answer is too often choice b, the clever student will spot the pattern and adopt the rule "when in doubt, choose option b." Some care is necessary to make sure there is no obvious tendency to place the correct responses in a pattern.

Some multiple-choice items use the options "all of the above" and "none of the above." The "none of the above" response is usually the more useful of the two, since it can be used to lessen the impact of guessing. A weakness of the "all of the above" option is that the student only has to know that two of the several options are correct; if so, "all of the above" is the right answer by default.

There are occasionally items in multiple-choice tests that provide options such as "a and c" or "a but not b." These options introduce more complexity than they are worth. The student's test-taking strategy in this case is, first, to treat each statement individually as a true-false item; he must then combine the statements according to the combinations listed in the distracters. It is simpler and clearer merely to present the parts of such statements as a series of true-false items.

> Correct answers should be randomly ordered across the response option positions. The position of the correct response should not provide a clue about the correctness of the response. Complex options—including "all of the above," "none of the above," or "a and b, but not c"—should be used sparingly, if at all.

General Suggestions for Item Writing

Some additional suggestions for item writing apply to most item formats, including true-false and multiple choice. The first of these concerns guessing. When students are asked to select one or more correct responses from a list of options, it is possible that they may guess a fair number of answers correctly. The odds of guessing correctly on a true-false item are 50:50. The likelihood of guessing correctly on a four-option multiple-choice question is 1:4. Therefore, it is important to include enough items on the test so the guesser—who operates completely at the chance level—can be clearly differentiated from the student with partial knowledge.

A second suggestion for item writing is that the test items should be independent. The information presented in one item should not provide the answers to other questions. Similarly, a student should not have to answer items 1 and 2 correctly as a prerequisite to answering item 3 correctly. Each item should test for a separate piece of information.

A third suggestion is that the reading level of the items should be lower than the grade level of the group, unless it is a reading test. A seventh-grade social studies test should be written at about the fifth-grade reading level so the test results are truly a measure of social studies knowledge, rather than reading ability. Of course, the technical vocabulary covered in the course content must be maintained in the test and not sacrificed to achieve a lower reading level.

The following guidelines apply to most test formats:

- Teachers should be aware of the approximate number of items on an objective test that can be guessed correctly.
- Test items should be independent: The content of one item should not provide the answers to others, nor should correctly answering one question be a prerequisite to correctly answering another.
- Reading levels of items should be kept low.

SUMMARY

This chapter presented the characteristics of true-false and multiple-choice items, as well as suggestions on how to write good test items. Objective test items were described as being objective primarily in terms of how the items are scored. Such objectivity leads to scorer reliability, which is one factor in the reliability of the test. Objective items are also very good in terms of the content sampling that they allow. Many test items can be included per test, so the set of items can be much more representative of the total domain of possible items than would be the case for other item formats, such as essay. However, it was admitted that, without proper planning, true-false and multiple-choice items do tend to measure trivial knowledge.

Possible weaknesses in true-false items were identified and illustrated, as were suggestions for overcoming these problems. Such topics as ambiguity, the use of specific determiners, textbook wording, and the cognitive level tested were among the ideas presented.

Multiple-choice items were presented as a versatile and useful item type. Suggestions for writing good multiple-choice items included avoiding clues in the grammar of the item, having plausible distracters of the same length, using distracters for diagnosis, and measuring higher cognitive levels of performance. Careful use of the "none of the above" and "all of the above" options was also suggested.

The role of guessing in test taking was discussed, as well. Remember that examinees can correctly guess the answers to a fair number of the items on an objective test. The probability of guessing correctly on a true-false test item is 1:2. Thus, it is important to include a reasonably large number of items on the test. Items also need to be independent: The answer to one question should not be dependent upon the correct answer to another. Nor should the information from the stem of one question provide the answers to others. Finally, the reading level of test items should be kept low so that the test does not operate as a reading test when it was designed to measure some other content domain.

KEY TERMS AND CONCEPTS

True-false	Specific determiners
Multiple choice	Options
Objectivity	Distracters
Content sampling	Stem
Scorer reliability	Grammatical clues

REVIEW ITEMS

1. Objective items are objective only in their:
   a. item content.
   b. scoring.
   c. distracters.
   d. wording.

2. Many objective items can be asked in each testing session; thus, they can provide good:
   a. levels of difficulty.
   b. objectivity.
   c. content sampling.
   d. time sampling.

3. One source of measurement error that is minimized by true-false and multiple-choice items is:
   a. scorer unreliability.
   b. fluctuations across time.
   c. examinee fatigue.
   d. guessing the right answer.

4. The tendency for true-false items to measure trivia is a weakness in the item *writer* more than the item *format.*

   T   F

5. The objective scoring of true-false and multiple-choice items enhances the test's:
   a. reliability.
   b. validity.

    c. a and b.

    d. a but not b.

6. Good true-false items must be clearly true or false.

            (T)   F

7. Cleverly worded multiple-choice items often "tease out" more useful information than simple, straightforward items.

            T   (F)

8. Which of the following is *not* a strength of multiple-choice items?

    a. effective testing of higher cognitive levels.

    b. content sampling.

    c. scorer reliability.

    (d.) allowing for "educated guesses."

9. The reading level of the test items should match the grade level of the examinees.

            T   (F)

10. The rules for writing effective multiple-choice questions are:

    (a.) essentially common sense.

    b. precise and scientific.

    c. detailed and structured.

    d. complicated and confusing.

EXERCISES

6.1 Write an instructional objective in American history for an intermediate grade student. In addition:

    a. Write one true-false item that would measure the objective.

    b. Write one multiple-choice item that would measure the same objective.

    c. Contrast the two items in terms of the time it took to construct the item, the relative difficulty of the items, and your judgment of the quality of the items.

6.2 Write two true-false items and two multiple-choice items that measure cognitive performance above the knowledge level of the taxonomy. Which item was harder to write? Which appears to be the better item? Would another item format be more appropriate?

6.3 Correct the blatant flaw in each of the following items:

Major league catchers are never left-handed.

T   F

The number of books in the school library is less than:
   a. 5,000.
   b. 4,000.
   c. 3,000.
   d. 2,000.

"Middle-class flight" refers to:
   a. of middle-class businessmen to use air travel.
   b. encourage people to use stairs rather than elevators.
   c. the middle-class exodus from the city to the suburbs.
   d. from the "snowbelt" to the "sunbelt."

6.4 The item-writing guidelines presented in this chapter have been presented as suggestions, not strict rules. Describe one or two counterexamples that common sense indicates are appropriate exceptions to these guidelines.

6.5 What are the strengths and weaknesses of writing test items of only one format—all multiple choice, for example?

6.6 Explain how scorer reliability is a part of test *reliability,* and content sampling is a part of test *validity.* Then explain the strengths of true-false and multiple-choice tests in these matters.

6.7 Obtain some multiple-choice or true-false tests that you have either administered or taken. Critique these tests according to the suggestions of this chapter, considering longest response, grammar clues, and so forth.

6.8 One could take a multiple-choice question that has four options and break it into four separate true-false items. What are the strengths and weaknesses of this approach?

SUGGESTED READING

Gay, L. R. 1980. *Educational evaluation and measurement.* Columbus: Merrill.

Hopkins, K. D., and J. C. Stanley. 1981. *Educational and psychological measurement and evaluation.* 6th ed. Englewood Cliffs, N.J.: Prentice-Hall.

Thorndike, R. L., and E. P. Hagen. 1977. *Measurement and evaluation in psychology and education.* 4th ed. New York: Wiley.

7

Constructing Other Types of Objective Items

Scoring makes a test objective.

In the preceding chapter, we discussed true-false and multiple-choice items, the most commonly used objective items for both teacher-constructed and published tests. Other types of objective test items include **matching** and **short-answer** items. Although these item formats are not used as extensively as multiple choice and true-false, they can be used effectively to measure learning outcomes. In addition, they provide variety in the test format, for both student and teacher. In the discussion that follows, suggestions for constructing these items are given, along with examples for illustration.

Matching Items

The matching item is exactly what the name implies: an item requiring the student to match, using some association criterion, the words or phrases that represent ideas, concepts, principles, or things. A two-column format is commonly used for the matching item, although variations can be used. The two columns of a matching item are usually called the **premises** (which consist of the item stem) and responses (which consist of the available options). The entire set of premises and responses comprises the item, not just a single premise-response match, since all of the responses must be considered as possible answers to each premise. However, when the item is scored, each individual match is evaluated for correctness; the entire item may be neither all right or all wrong. This is a major difference between matching and multiple-choice or true-false items.

This sort of matching format lends itself well to testing knowledge of relationships or definitions. In addition, the matching item provides the opportunity to compress a considerable amount of content into a single item, which requires a relatively small amount of testing time. In this way, content sampling and validity are enhanced. Finally, the matching format does not require the construction of plausible distracters, which is an advantage over multiple-choice testing.

> Matching items are usually presented in a two-column format: one column consists of premises and the other, responses.

Published tests rarely include matching items, because too many options are required for the answer sheets. Similarly, it is not likely that a teacher-constructed test would consist entirely of matching items. Instead, the test may contain a matching section consisting of a set of related items, such as vocabulary words and their definitions.

Constructing the Matching Item

Matching items oftentimes contain clues to the answer. Therefore, as with any item format, they must be constructed carefully.

A common error in writing matching tests is to include heterogeneous content, thus enabling the student to eliminate certain combinations simply on the basis of lack of similarity between some premises and some responses. Consider the following item:

Column A *(premises)*

____ First president of the United States

____ Inventor of the telephone

____ Founder of Pennsylvania

____ City originally called "New Amsterdam"

____ River on which the Hoover Dam is located

____ River dividing Iowa and Illinois

____ Major southern seaport

Column B *(responses)*

A. Alexander Graham Bell

B. Colorado

C. New York

D. Mississippi

E. Houston

F. Ohio

G. George Washington

H. William Penn

I. Atlanta

This series contains an odd mixture of content: cities, rivers, and famous people. There are only three possible responses—A, G, and H—that fit the first three premises. So, for these premises, six of the nine responses are automatically eliminated because of inconsistent content. This elimination becomes even easier if the student knows that each response can be used only once. For instance, in our example, there are only *three* names of famous people listed, and *three* premises require such names; thus, if any *two* are known, the *third* can be found by elimination.

To avoid this problem, a matching item should contain homogeneous content, usually a single concept or a single basis for classification. For example, it would be ineffective to construct a matching item that contains historical events and book titles in one column and dates and authors in the second column. If these two subject classifications are to be tested, two separate matching items must be constructed. When the matching item is not homogeneous, a student can respond correctly simply through the association of the verbal content. At this point, the test is no longer measuring the knowledge intended.

> Matching items should contain homogeneous content so that all responses must be considered as plausible answers.

Subtle clues as to the correct response may be included inadvertently in a matching item. Consider these examples:

1. The premises make one reference to a famous Chinese person, and only one Chinese name is given in the responses.
2. One premise requires a plural response, and only one plural response is provided.
3. A premise and a response each contain the same word or derivatives of the same word. In the matching series above, premise 3 (the founder of *Penn*sylvania) and response H (William *Penn*) provide such a clue.
4. Incorrect responses may not be plausible, even though they contain homogeneous content. For instance, if premises consist of French cities, and the responses include German cities, all clearly German names can be eliminated. Knowledge of French cities, as described in the premises, is thus not tested.

Matching items must be reviewed carefully for such clues. Otherwise, the student will identify and eliminate incorrect responses based on some technical factor of the test construction, not on his own knowledge.

The numbers of responses and premises should be unequal; usually, the number of responses exceeds the number of premises. There should also be an option of using a response more than once. These conditions make guessing the correct response more difficult and reduce the likelihood of responding correctly by simply eliminating those responses already used.

Matching items are usually structured so that the letter or number designations of the responses are matched to the premises. Nonetheless, students must always be given clear directions as to how the match is indicated and if responses can be used more than once. The responses usually make up the column with the shorter entries; they consist of short phrases, at most. Responses also are commonly arranged in some systematic order, such as alphabetical. This way, students should be able to find the correct answer easily, if they know it.

The optimum length for matching items is between five and eight premises per item, with occasional longer items, but the upper limit of the range is usually set at twelve. Longer items require too many comparisons, and the task becomes tedious and time consuming. Shorter items also tend to have more homogeneous content.

Examples of Matching Items.   Using this background on constructing matching items, consider the following example of a matching item taken from an intermediate-level social studies test.

Directions: Column A lists characteristics or descriptions of cities in the United States. Column B lists names of United States cities. Write the letter of the city in Column B on the line preceding the statement that describes it in Column A. You may use a city name from Column B more than once, and not all of the names will be used.

Column A	Column B
____ A city in the heart of the wheat belt	A. Albany
____ The largest city in the Northwest	B. Birmingham
____ The capital of New York state	C. Chicago
____ A great Southern steel center	D. Denver
____ The largest city in the Rocky Mountain region	E. Detroit
____ The automobile city	F. Kansas City
____ A Lake Michigan seaport	G. New York
____ The largest city in Oregon	H. Portland
	I. Salt Lake City
	J. Seattle
	K. Spokane

Note that there are eight premises and eleven responses. Although the directions state that it is permissible, in this item, no response is used more than once. The content of the item is homogeneous with respect to cities but not geography, which may be a weakness when testing certain knowledge. For example, a student might not know that Portland is Oregon's largest city, but he could respond correctly by recognizing Portland as the only Oregon city listed. To correct this problem, another Oregon city could have been listed with the responses.

The following matching item is taken from a science test. The item is not as clearly homogeneous as the previous one, since the response list consists of terms related to a variety of science concepts.

Directions: List A contains events that happen in everyday life. List B contains words or phrases that are scientific descriptions of the events in List A. Write the letter of the word or phrase in List B on the line before the event it describes in List A.

List A

____ 1. The sun rises.

____ 2. Clothes dry.

____ 3. Wood burns.

____ 4. Spring follows winter.

____ 5. Clouds form.

____ 6. Rain falls.

____ 7. Water freezes.

____ 8. Seeds sprout.

List B

A. Condensation

B. Evaporation

C. Expansion

D. Fusion

E. Germination

F. Oxidation

G. Pollination

H. Precipitation

I. Radiation

J. Revolution of the earth

K. Rotation of the earth

Matching items on teacher-constructed tests are most commonly used to test knowledge of factual information, definitions, use of symbols, and the like. In contrast to multiple-choice items, matching items include several problems in a single item. But, if matching items contain technical deficiencies, they tend to provide superficial measurement, so careful attention must be given to their preparation. Only well-constructed matching items can be used effectively in any test.

Short-Answer Items

Short-answer items consist of items for which the student actually *supplies* the answer, rather than *selects* it from a given set of responses. Thus, such items do not require the development of plausible distracters, as is necessary for multiple-choice items. Short-answer items generally take one of three forms: **question, association,** or **completion.** Each of these forms is illustrated below.

For a short-answer item, the student supplies the answer to a question, association, or completion form.

Constructing Short-Answer Items

Short-answer items should be written so that only a single, unique answer is required. A common weakness of poorly constructed items is that more than one answer may be correct. For example, consider this question:

1. What causes the formation of rain clouds?

Quite clearly, a variety of answers could be provided. To make it an effective test question, the item should be formulated to require a more specific response. Also consider if short-answer is the appropriate format to use. For instance, the intent of this item would probably be met more fully if a short-essay item were used, since an adequate response would likely be longer than a short answer. Nonetheless, if this were retained as a short-answer item, it might be reformulated as:

2. With respect to temperature and upward air movement, describe the formation of cumulus clouds.

The item is now more limited and focuses on a specific response.

The answer to be provided must relate to the main point of the item. For example, if blanks are left in an item, they should require key words. Uniform space for responses should be used, so that the student does not infer the length of the response from the space provided for the answer. Extraneous clues, such as grammar inconsistencies, should be avoided. And, of course, complicated, ambiguous, or confusing wording, such as the use of double negatives, should be avoided, as well.

Question Form. The question form is exactly what the name implies: a question posed in the item. This is the most popular form of short-answer item. Items in mathematics lend themselves readily to this form. For example:

1. Last year, Mr. Jones drove his car 14,112 miles. If he averaged 48 miles per hour, how many hours did he spend driving his car last year?

Answer: _____ hours.

The above item is straightforward; there is no doubt about what form the answer is to take. If there is any question about matters such as the degree of accuracy expected in the answer, this should be explained to the student.

Association Form. In association form testing, the student is given a set of words or phrases and is then required to supply an association—a related idea or term—for each of the words or phrases in the set. The student is given the basis of the association, indicating the type of response that is expected. Consider the following item, which is a partial conversion of the matching item presented earlier to an association item.

Directions: Before each descriptive phrase, write the name of the United States *city* that fits the phrase.

1. _____ Largest city in the Northwest
2. _____ Capital of New York state
3. _____ The automobile city
4. _____ The city of "brotherly love"
5. _____ Capital of Colorado

Note that parts of the original matching item, such as "a Lake Michigan seaport," were not used; these were excluded because they do not have unique answers. Also note that the spaces provided for the responses are the same size, and, of course, they should be adequate for the answer.

Completion Form. The completion form is probably the least popular of the short-answer item formats. In this form, a statement with one or more missing words is presented to the student, who then is to supply the missing words. One common problem with this format is that ambiguous phrasing can easily enter into a completion item. For example, consider this item:

1. John F. Kennedy was a _____ .

This statement clearly does not provide enough direction for the student to realize what kind of response is expected. Any number of correct responses is possible, including man, father, son, American, and president, to name a few. A better phrasing of the item is:

2. The political party to which John F. Kennedy belonged was the _____ party.

When using completion items, the blank should be placed at or near the end of the item. This way the student reads all or most of the item before the blank is presented. In addition only one or two words should be required in the completion. For example, look at this item:

3. _____ was the _____ who led the _____ troops at Valley Forge.

This is what Popham (1981, 274) calls a "Swiss cheese item." Not only does the item lack unique responses, but, with all the missing words, students have difficulty identifying even the intent of the item. The item must retain adequate structure and meaning, even when it contains blanks, so the student can understand the intent and respond in an unambiguous manner. An improved version of the above item is:

4. The general who led the Revolutionary troops at Valley Forge was _____ .

In constructing short-answer items, each item should have a unique, correct answer and be structured so the student can clearly recognize its intent.

Short-answer items require the student to provide his own response, rather than simply select a response, as with the other objective-type items discussed earlier. In this sense, short-answer items are similar to essay items. Since the student must provide the response, short-answer items are less susceptible to guessing than objective items, for which response options are provided. Short-answer items can be effectively used to measure knowledge of facts, definitions, technical terms, and the like. And in mathematics, they can be used to test limited computation and problem interpretation.

The short-answer format is popular with teachers, for several reasons. First of all, short-answer items are relatively easy to construct. In addition, they are efficient in terms of testing time and scoring time. In fact, if numerous short-answer items are included in a test (or even if the entire test is short answer), responses can be placed in blanks along the right-hand side of the page. This arrangement facilitates scoring, as can be seen in the following examples:

5. If apples are priced at 18¢ each, how much would 20 apples cost?

Answer: _____

6. If Jack has 75¢ to spend and candy bars are priced at three for 25¢, how many can he purchase with his 75¢?

Answer: _____

Short-answer items tend to be more popular at the elementary level than the secondary level, but, when constructed properly, they can be used effectively at any level.

Planning the Test

A teacher must consider a number of factors when deciding the content and format of a test, be it a short, ten-point quiz or a two-hour final exam. Ebel (1981, 69) refers to these factors as "test specifications." Namely, these factors include:

1. Content to be sampled.
2. Tasks to be represented.
3. Length of testing time.
4. Item formats to be used.
5. Numbers of items of each format.
6. Item difficulty levels.
7. Directions to the student.

These factors are by no means independent. For example, the length of testing time provided and the item formats used affect the number of items that can be included. And the content sampled and the type of tasks represented will certainly influence the types of items used. So, all of these factors need to be considered simultaneously, at least to some extent. They are separated somewhat below only for discussion purposes.

Content and Tasks
Represented by the Test

Any test consists of a sample of content and/or a sample of one or more tasks expected to be mastered by the student. Of course, a test in algebra samples content from algebra; tasks would consist of solving algebraic problems. But, in order to be useful, the definitions of *content* and *tasks* must be more specific. For example, an algebra test might cover the factoring of binomials or, more generally, the factoring of polynomials. However, the only task represented (and thus required by the students) might be the factoring task.

In chapter 5, we introduced a table of specifications that can be used in connection with content and learning outcomes in designating test coverage. With little modification, similar tables can also be constructed relative to the tasks to be represented on the test. These tables of specifications, covering tasks and content, are probably most useful to teachers when constructing tests.

The value of these tables is twofold: (1) they require the listing of content and tasks, so nothing important is inadvertently missed; and (2) the number of items is specified, thus providing a quantitative picture of that content. The tables do not need to be elaborate and complex; they are valuable only to the extent they are useful: helping the teacher get organized when constructing test items. Because of this preparational use, using a table of specifications also enhances the content validity of the test.

An Example from Elementary Algebra. Suppose a teacher is constructing a one-hour test in first-year algebra, covering a unit on polynomials. The test consists of two types of items: multiple choice and short answer. The short-answer section consists of items requiring the solutions to problems involving operations with polynomials.

Table 7.1.
A Listing of Tasks and Content Areas for a One-Hour Test in Algebra Covering Operations With Polynomials

Item Format	Number of Items	
Multiple Choice (MC)	20	
Short-Answer (SA)	10	
Tasks	**Number of MC**	**Number of SA**
Recall definitions and terminology	4	0
Apply the laws of exponents	3	0
Apply the addition operation	2	2
Apply the multiplication operation	2	2
Apply the subtraction operation	2	2
Apply the division operation	2	2
Develop the polynomial for specific problem	0	2
Identify the factors contained in polynomials	2	0
Apply associative and commutative laws	3	0
Content Areas	**Number of MC**	**Number of SA**
Monomials	2	1
Binomials	4	1
Trinomials	4	4
More complex polynomials	4	4
Commutative law	1	0
Associative law	1	0
Laws of exponents	4	0

Table 7.1 contains a list of the tasks and content areas, along with the numbers of items indicated. (More will be said later about the length of the test.)

The other section of the test is multiple choice. Some of these items deal with recalling terminology, but many deal with application. Such items require the student to solve problems, even though the items are in the multiple-choice format. There is a direct correspondence between tasks and content, but both classifications contribute to specifying the test. For example, several of the tasks deal with applying operations, but the content indicates the types of polynomials for which the applications are made.

Even after having listed the tasks and content, how does the teacher decide on the relative distribution of items? The distribution should be based on two factors: (1) the relative instructional time spent on the tasks/content; and (2) the relative importance of the tasks/content for mastery of the unit. To be sure, the teacher is required to make some subjective judgments about these criteria; however, since most teachers are knowledgeable of the subjects they teach, they are quite capable of doing so.

Length of Test, Item Format, and Number of Items

The length of the test is usually determined directly by the amount of testing time, commonly a class period consisting of fifty minutes or an hour. As was discussed in the chapter on reliability (chapter 4), longer tests tend to be more reliable. But, unless some special testing using published exams is being done, tests in elementary or secondary schools rarely exceed two hours.

Most teacher-constructed tests are **power tests,** not speeded tests. A power test is one for which the student's score would increase little, if any, if the student were given additional time. Thus, most students have adequate time to respond to all the items, working at typical rates.

Considered together, the amount of testing time available and the item format or formats to be used determine the number of items that can be included in a test. As will be discussed in the chapter on essay items (chapter 8), a test consisting entirely of essay questions, can accommodate only a small number of items, especially if the items require extended responses. For this reason, essay tests tend to have poor content sampling. True-false and multiple-choice items usually require the shortest response time, so tests using only these formats can accommodate the greatest number of items for a specified testing time.

> The length of a test is determined by the available testing time; the number of item formats used affects the number of items that can be accommodated.

The complexity of the tasks involved in responding to the items also affects the number of items that can be used. Complex tasks generally require more time; therefore, given a specified testing time, one cannot complete as many complex tasks as simple tasks. Teachers must remember this when deciding the number and difficulty of items to use.

The conclusion here is simple: There is no magic set of numbers of test items that can be specified for all tests of a given time length. A variety of factors must be considered. For instance, a multiple-choice item may require only a few seconds' response time if it involves something simple, like recalling a definition. But, if a complex problem solution is required to identify the correct response, the item may require five minutes or more. Teachers are generally, quite familiar with their course content and their students; thus, they should be able to estimate accurately the number of items to include in tests.

Taking a test should be a learning experience. Pressures about item difficulty or test length cause undesirable test anxiety, which does little to enhance learning. The same is true for excessively easy tests. Students do not necessarily want easy tests—they want fair tests. A fair test is one that represents adequately the instructional content covered and requires appropriate and reasonable tasks of the student.

Directions and the Organization of the Test

Directions for responding to the items should be explicitly written on the test copy. If more than one type of item format is used, directions for each type should be provided. Example directions are as follows.

1. *For true-false items:*

   If the statement below is true, circle the letter T preceding the statement; if false, circle the letter F.

   or

   If the statement below is true, write T in the space provided to the right of the statement; if false, write F.

   (Since the letters T and F are somewhat similar, when written in a sloppy manner, it may be difficult to distinguish between them. To avoid this problem, teachers may have students write out the words *true* and *false*.)

2. *For multiple-choice items:*

   For each of the following questions, circle the letter of the *one* best answer.

   or

   For each of the following questions, write the letter of the *one* best answer in the space provided ahead of the item number.

3. *For short-answer question items:*

   In the space provided following the question, write the word or phrase that best answers the question.

   or

   In the space provided following the problem, provide a solution to the problem, showing the steps you took in solving it. This space should be enough, but if you need more, complete the solution on a separate page, indicating the number of the problem.

4. *For short-answer completion items:*

For each of the following statements, write the missing word in the space provided following the statement at the right side of the page.

or

In each of the following statements, write the missing word or words in the spaces provided.

5. *For short-answer association items:*

For each description listed below, write the name of the European river that best fits. Put the name in the space ahead of the phrase.

or

In the space provided to the left of the phrase, provide the name of the European river that best fits.

   (Note: The directions for a short-answer association item are specific to what is contained in the item, such as European rivers.)

6. *For matching items:*

In the columns below, Column 1 contains characteristics of specific plants, and Column 2 contains the names of plants. Place the letter of the appropriate name from Column 2 in the space at the left of the characteristic in Column 1. You may use the name of a plant more than once, and not all of the names from Column 2 will be used.

In addition to these directions, examples of how to respond may be provided, if this seems necessary. Examples are desirable with younger students, say those in sixth grade and lower. With older students, however, examples are probably not necessary if typical item formats are used.

The directions for each type of item format should immediately precede the items of that format. So, if more than one item format is used, directions will be interspersed throughout the test. Also, students should be informed as to the scoring; the relative weights of the items should be specified. This information may be given at the beginning of the test, or the item value may be specified with each new set of items (for example, "Each multiple-choice item is worth two points"). If there is considerable variability in the point values of items, the points may be specified in parentheses, preceding the item number. Finally, the total points for the test should be given somewhere on the test copy. If all the scoring information is given at the beginning of the test, the total points should be included here as the final bit of scoring information. If scoring information is spread throughout the test, the total points can be given at the end of the test.

If two or more item formats are used in a test, items of similar format should be grouped together. If items vary in level of difficulty, as they usually do somewhat, the easy items should be placed early in the test. Items within a single format can also be grouped by objective or content to enhance the student's continuity of thought.

The order of different item formats should be such that items requiring the *least* response time appear early in the test. For this reason, if essay items are included, they should be placed at the end of the test. If difficult or lengthy items are placed at the beginning of the test or test section, students will get bogged down early in the test and not even attempt items for which the correct answers may be known. In fact, if frustrated at the start, students may not be able to finish the test.

Overall, test items should be numbered consecutively, either throughout the test or within sections. The complete test should have a name and be neatly organized and presented. Finally, for the sake of both student and teacher, test items should be easy to read, easy to answer, and easy to score.

> Explicit and understandable directions should be provided for each section of the test. Items should be arranged according to format, with the least difficult items coming first.

Use of Separate Answer Sheets. It is sometimes advantageous to use separate answer sheets rather than have the answer written directly on the test. This may help reduce scoring time and, in some cases, such sheets are machine scorable. Standardized tests scored by publishers are typically machine scored, and sometimes teachers can create a template of the correct responses for scoring a teacher-constructed test.

Typical machine-scored answer sheets are presented in Figures 7.1 and 7.2. Figure 7.1 is a standard IBM sheet; it can accommodate 148 items, each with up to five options. The answer sheet is intended for use with multiple-choice items; it can also be used for true-false items if the student is instructed to use only options A and B— A for true, B for false. There is space for providing such identification information at the top of the sheet.

The answer sheet shown in Figure 7.2 was designed by the National Computer Systems, which uses optical scanners for scoring. It contains two sides (only side one is shown) and can accommodate up to 240 multiple-choice items with five options. For true-false items, options A and B are used; they are designated T and F on the sheet. Directions for responding, along with an example, are provided at the top of the sheet. The second side of the sheet also contains space for identification.

Figure 7.1.
Example of an IBM Machine-Scored Answer Sheet

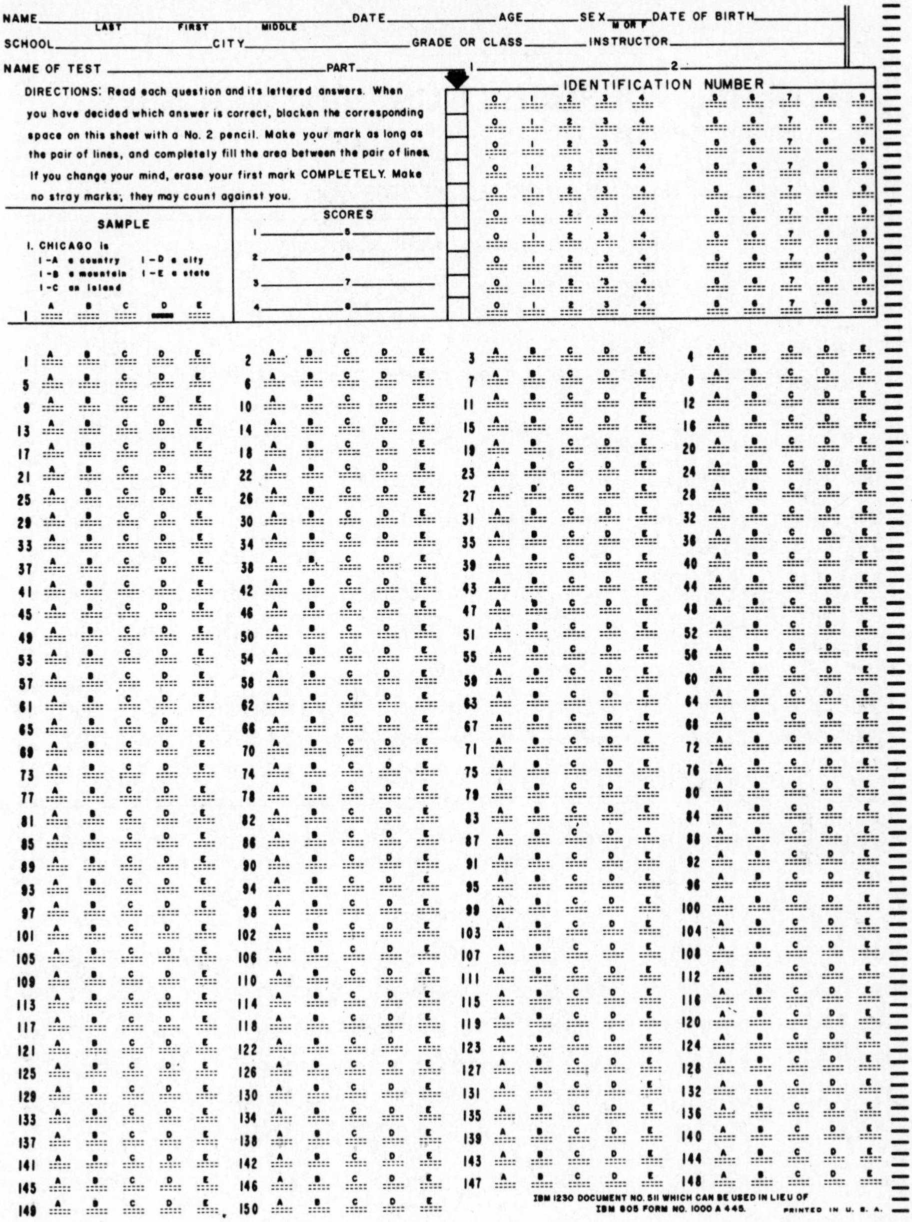

Source: Reprinted with permission of IBM.

Figure 7.2.
Example of an NCS Machine-Scored Answer Sheet

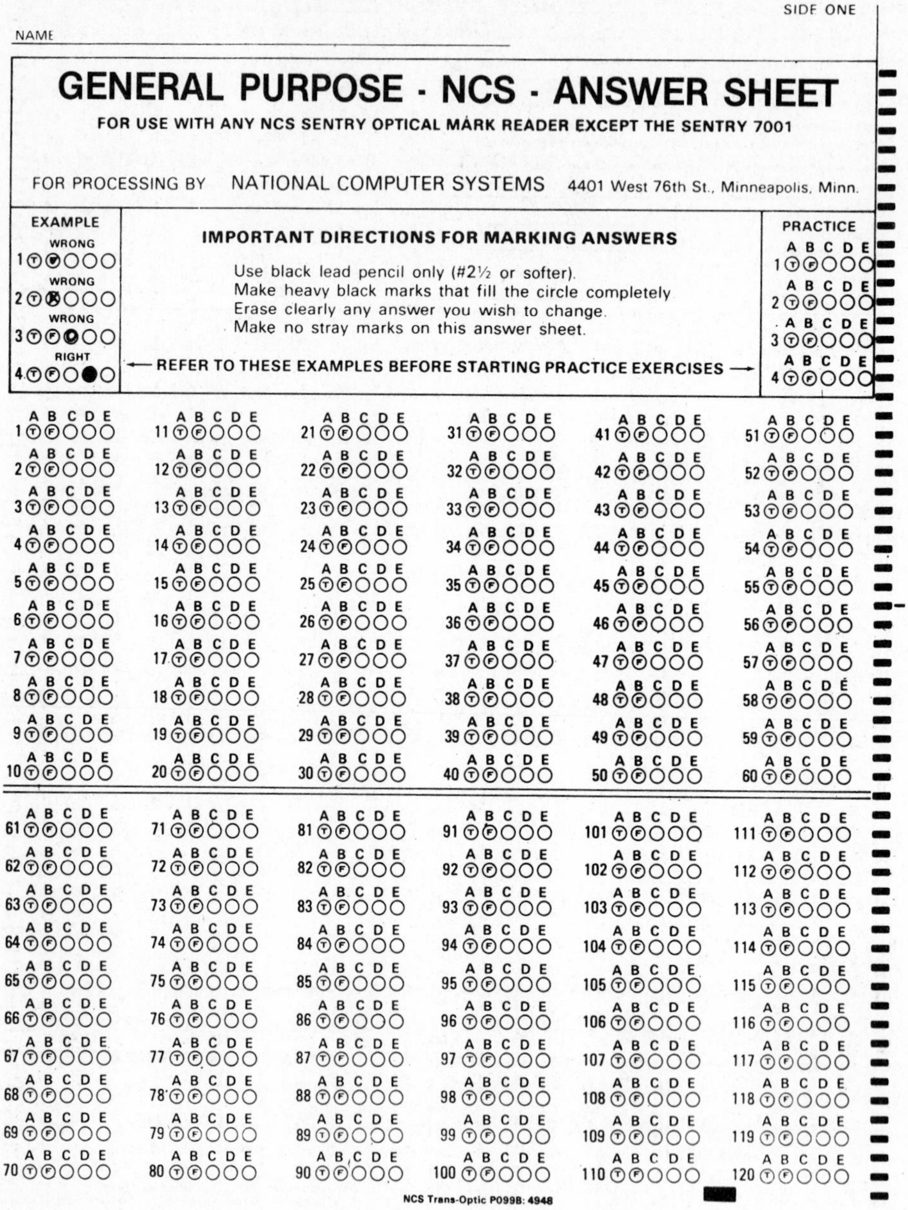

Source: Published by permission of National Computer Systems, Inc., 4401 W. 76th Street, Minneapolis, MN, 55435.

The use of separate answer sheets requires some precautions. Explicit directions about the mechanics of responding must be given to the students orally. For example, all students must use the proper kind of pencil if the answer sheet is to be machine scored. And the answer sheet must not be folded or mutilated. Students should also be cautioned about maintaining the correspondence between the item numbers on the test copy and those on the answer sheet; for example, if a test item is skipped, the corresponding space on the answer sheet must also be skipped. Finally, anytime a test using separate answer sheets is being administered, the teacher should carefully monitor the class to ensure that the sheets are being used properly.

> Separate answer sheets, including machine-scored sheets, can reduce scoring time if large numbers of students are tested. However, their use requires special directions and precautions.

Open-Book and Take-Home Tests

Most tests are conducted in a classroom setting, with students responding individually from memory and the teacher monitoring the process. However, there are two alternatives to this kind of testing: open-book and **take-home** tests.

In an open-book test, students are permitted to use textbooks, notes, and other reference materials. For example, open-book tests may be used if students need to use specialized material that is not memorized, such as formulas or tables of some sort. Open-book tests are also appropriate if students are to apply a process and the emphasis is on *applying* the process, not on *knowing* it from memory.

Open-book tests can be used with any of the item formats. They have some advantages in that they tend to lessen test anxiety and reduce the emphasis on memorization. There may also be less of a tendency to cheat, especially through the use of unauthorized notes. However, the primary reason for using an open-book test should remain clear: to provide the student with the written resources necessary for the purposes of the test.

When open-book tests are used, the students must be instructed on how to use the materials during the test. (This may sound silly, but certain guidelines should be followed.) For example, a book should be opened only when it is needed, and then specifically for the information required. One disadvantage of open-book tests is that students look up answers they already know and are thus diverted in their search for information. Sometimes they are unsuccessful in finding information, and too much time is devoted to a futile search. In the end, considerable time is wasted, and students may not be able to complete the test.

Take-home tests are not used commonly in the elementary and secondary schools. However, they are useful when the task requires too much time for classroom testing or resources are required that are not available in the classroom.

Take-home tests have obvious control disadvantages. For instance, there is no way to ensure that students work individually. There is also no way to control how much time is spent on the test. Usually, take-home tests are to be turned in the next day or very soon thereafter, which introduces inequities in the amount of time different students can devote to the test. Some students may have other commitments, such as jobs, or family responsibilities. This puts them at a disadvantage to those students who can concentrate almost completely on the test until it is time to return it.

One advantage of take-home tests is that they are open-book tests, which are probably less anxiety producing than closed-book tests. But a corresponding disadvantage is that some scorers may set unnecessarily high standards, since there was supposedly ample time to work on the test.

> Open-book and take-home tests are used sparingly in elementary and secondary schools. When they are used, it is because the tasks required of the student cannot be tested using usual, in-class, closed-book tests.

SUMMARY

In this chapter, we have discussed formats for objective items—matching and short-answer. These formats can be used effectively as part of a test, but we would rarely have a test consisting entirely of matching or short-answer items. Procedures for preparing well-constructed items using these formats were presented.

Planning any test is basically a matter of common sense concerning the instructional content covered and the characteristics of the students to be tested. A test is a sampling of content; as such, it should be representative of the content covered. Although planning a test is quite straightforward, it does require the consideration of several factors and attention to detail. A listing of the tasks and content areas is helpful in getting the test organized.

Teachers generally know the capabilities of their students, which is an important factor in deciding the length and difficulty of the test. Unless there is some reason for measuring speed of response, tests usually are power tests in that students have adequate time for completing the entire test.

Many standardized tests are longer than the typical class period. Other factors being equal, longer tests tend to have higher reliability and more extensive content sampling. The importance of these test characteristics is related to the anticipated use of the test results. Teacher-constructed tests may be used for a variety of purposes; the most important one is to measure and evaluate student achievement. But long-term or substantive grading decisions are seldom based on the results of just one test. If several measures are used, sampling error on a specific test is not very serious. On the other hand, if a major, long-term decision, such as admission to college, is heavily influenced by a single test score, that score should contain little error.

Nevertheless, testing—and especially the use of teacher-constructed tests—is an important part of day-to-day instruction. Therefore, tests must be technically well constructed and administered carefully, with adequate directions. Only those tests that students perceive as being fair and challenging are an asset to the learning process.

KEY TERMS AND CONCEPTS

Matching item   Association form
Short-answer item   Completion form
Premises   Power test
Question form   Take-home test

REVIEW ITEMS

1. A matching item includes six events to be matched with nine responses consisting of dates, cities, and states. The error of item construction is:
   a. too many premises.
   b. too few premises.
   c. responses contain heterogeneous content.
   d. responses contain homogeneous content.

2. When constructing a matching item, the numbers of premises and responses should be:
   a. equal, with all responses used only once.
   b. equal, but having the option of using responses more than once.
   c. unequal, with a greater number of responses, and any response being used, at most, once.
   d. unequal, with a greater number of responses and having the option of using a response more than once.

3. For which type of objective item is guessing less likely to occur?
   a. true-false.
   b. matching.
   c. multiple choice.
   d. short answer.

4. In an association form, short-answer item, the spaces for the responses should:
   a. vary according to the length of the correct response.
   b. all be the same size.
   c. vary in size, but not according to any order.
   d. vary in size according to some system of ordering.

5. Completion, short-answer items should have the blank(s) placed:
   a. at or near the beginning of the item.
   b. between the beginning and the middle of the item.
   c. as close to the middle of the item as possible.
   d. at or near the end of the item.

6. A "Swiss cheese" completion item has:
   a. the blanks evenly spaced throughout the item.
   b. too many blanks.
   c. blanks of unequal size.
   d. none of the above.

7. A difference between short answer and other types of objective items, such as multiple choice, true-false, and matching, is:
   a. short-answer items are easier for the student.
   b. the student must supply the response with short-answer items.
   c. short-answer items are more susceptible to guessing.
   d. more complex student outcomes can be measured by short-answer items.

8. In a practical school situation, the length of the test is most directly influenced by the:
   a. amount of content covered.
   b. types of items to be included.
   c. ability levels of the students.
   d. amount of testing time.

9. A power test is a test:
   a. that has time limits per item.
   b. designed for the academically more able students.
   c. for which additional time will have little, if any, effect upon student scores.
   d. requiring the full testing time of all students.

10. The number of items that can be included in a test is affected by:
    a. complexity of the tasks required of the items.
    b. available testing time.
    c. item format.
    d. all of the above.

11. A test contains a number of different item formats, including three essay items. The essay items should be placed:
    a. at the beginning of the test.
    b. near the middle of the test.
    c. at the end of the test.
    d. randomly throughout the test.

12. The primary reason for using an open-book test is:
    a. test anxiety is reduced.
    b. necessary references are provided for the student.
    c. there is less of a tendency to cheat.
    d. the need for memorization is reduced.

13. The item format most appropriate for measuring knowledge of paired associates, such as symbols and their meanings, is:
    a. matching.
    b. multiple choice.
    c. short-answer, question form.
    d. true-false.

14. Increasing the length of a matching item tends to enhance the homogeneity of content.

    T   F

15. Short-answer items are generally easier to construct than matching items.

    T   F

16. There is a tendency for short-answer items to be used more frequently with secondary students than elementary students.

    T   F

17. Most teacher-constructed tests are speeded tests.

T   (F)

18. Multiple-choice items generally require about the same response time per item as matching items.

T   (F)

19. A test contains items with different formats; all written directions for responding to the items should be given at beginning of the test.

T   (F)

20. The use of take-home tests should be increased in the elementary schools in order to lessen test anxiety.

T   (F)

21. The column of a matching item that contains the item stems is called the _____ premises

22. For usual classroom testing, the most desirable length for a matching item is between __5__ and __8__ premises.

EXERCISES

7.1 Give two advantages that matching items have over true-false and multiple-choice items.

7.2 A matching item is constructed that contains a list of the 50 states as premises and the 50 capital cities as responses. Identify the errors made in this item construction.

7.3 Select a subject area of your own interest and construct two matching items. Include eight to twelve premises in each item and a greater number of responses. Check the items for homogeneity of content and inadvertent clues to responses.

7.4 For each of the following short-answer completion items, identify the deficiency in construction:

a. The _____ is the legislative house in which all federal tax legislation originates.

b. An animal that can live both in the sea and on the land is an _____ .

c. _____ measure 90 degrees, while the _____ of the _____ of a _____ measure 180 degrees.

d. _____ is reasoning from the _____ case to the specific situation.

7.5 In a subject area of your own interest, construct six, short-answer items, two of each type: question, completion, and association.

7.6 Select a subject area of your own interest and develop a table of test specifications for a one-hour, classroom test; include a listing of tasks and content and the anticipated number of items for each. Any of the objective-type items we have discussed may be used.

7.7 Describe the difference between a *power test* and a *speeded test.* Why are most teacher-constructed tests power tests?

7.8 Discuss the advantages and disadvantages of using separate answer sheets. Under what conditions would it be worthwhile to use machine-scored answer sheets?

7.9 Describe a situation in which it might be desirable to use an open-book test. What are the advantages and disadvantages of an open-book test?

7.10 Describe a situation in which it might be desirable to use a take-home test. What are the advantages and disadvantages of a take-home test?

REFERENCES

Ebel, R. L. 1979. *Essentials of educational measurement.* 3d ed. Englewood Cliffs, N.J.: Prentice-Hall.

Popham, W. J. 1981. *Modern educational measurement.* Englewood Cliffs, N.J.: Prentice-Hall.

8

Constructing Essay Items

The inclusion of **essay items** on tests, and even the use of tests consisting entirely of essay items, continue to be highly popular among teachers. An essay item is one for which the student is required to structure a response, usually of some detail and length, consisting of up to several paragraphs of narrative. The response is basically an "essay," hence, the name.

The student has considerable latitude of response with an essay item. This is in obvious contrast to objective items, in which the student selects a response from two or more alternatives or produces a short response consisting of a word, phrase, or number.

A number of factors contribute to the popularity of essay items. One is an inherent belief that essay items are more effective than objective items in measuring certain educational outcomes. In fact, some educators would argue that higher-level cognitive outcomes can be measured *only* by essay items. The more common opinion, however, is that higher-level skills can be measured by objective items, as well. Nonetheless, essay testing is an effective means of measuring upper-level outcomes.

Essay items are also considered to be the best approach to measuring writing performance. And there is the notion that essay items require general student skills, as well, including spelling and penmanship; although these skills may not be central to the content of the test, they are important student outcomes that merit evaluation. Finally, essay items indirectly measure student attitudes and values, which are not likely to be reflected in responses to objective items.

Essay tests are usually easier to construct than objective tests, not necessarily because each specific item is less difficult to write, but because fewer items are required for a test of a given time length. Of course, essay items lose this convenience advantage over objective items when it comes to scoring, since grading essays is a time-consuming task. But, for different reasons, even the scoring contributes to the popularity of the essay item. The subjectivity of scoring, definitely a technical disadvantage of essay items, is often viewed favorably, since it provides the scorer with considerable flexibility. For example, the scoring can be adjusted for an item that turned out to be unexpectedly difficult for the students. Despite this benefit, however, the subjectivity of essay scoring is definitely a technical drawback. Still, essay items will continue to appear on tests, and they do serve a useful purpose in educational measurement.

> An essay item is one for which the student structures the response; selecting ideas and then presenting them according to his own organization and wording.

Essay Items and Learning Outcomes

One of the reasons commonly given for the use of essay items is that essay items, when properly constructed, measure learning outcomes of objectives in the higher levels of the instructional objectives taxonomy. By "higher levels" we mean mental processes such as analysis, synthesis, and evaluation outcomes in contrast with the "lower levels" of knowledge, comprehension, and application.

The fact that an item is an essay item does not ensure that the item is measuring a higher-level learning outcome. In fact, one of the most common misuses of essay items is limiting them to the measurement of lower-level and even knowledge outcomes. These kinds of outcomes can be measured more efficiently by objective items.

For instance, essay items should not ask for definitions or lists of information, which require only recall behavior of the students. For example, look at this item:

1. List the major methods of transportation used in the large urban areas of the United States.

This item involves nothing more than factual recall. It should not appear as an essay item; instead, it should be reworked as a short-answer or multiple-choice item.

If essay items are to measure higher-level learning outcomes, the student's response behavior must reflect these outcomes. Synthesis behavior is not obtained by merely having students identify, label, or define. Instead, they must compose, create, or design. Assuming that the instructional objectives are well stated, if essay items are called for, the kinds of student behaviors required should be inferred from the objectives. Thus, a single essay item should call forth more than one type of student behavior or skill.

Keeping with the transportation theme introduced in the item above, a better essay item is:

2. Design and diagram (on the accompanying map) the train, bus, and auto

transportation systems for an urban area of 200,000 population. Contrast the transportation needed and used between Individual A, who lives and works downtown, and Individual B, who lives in a suburban area five miles from the nearest bus or train stop and who works downtown. Consider points such as time spent in transportation, cost, and convenience.

In responding to this item the student is required to synthesize the knowledge of land transportation; he needs to organize the systems and develop a balance between them. The latter part of the item also requires some evaluation of the transportation needs and uses of the two individuals. Here, the student needs to know the meaning of the words defining the task; for example, he must know that *contrast* requires discussing the differences.

Do not infer that essay items should never be used to measure lower-level learning outcomes. In a practical sense, lower-level outcomes are usually necessary prerequisites of higher-level outcomes. But essay items should not emphasize nor be limited to student behaviors that reflect only lower-level learning outcomes. Testing should be more efficient than that.

Essay items are used quite effectively to measure higher-level learning outcomes, such as analysis, synthesis, and evaluation. Essay testing is not, however, an effective means of measuring lower-level learning outcomes.

Characteristics of Essay Items

Practically all teachers—and even all students beyond the third or fourth grades—can identify an essay item or essay test when they see one. The frequent use of essay testing practically guarantees that, in one course or another, the student will be asked to write responses to essay items.

This popularity is not bad or undesirable. When used properly, essay items do serve a very useful purpose in educational measurement. But it is important to understand the characteristics of essay items and what makes some items effective measurement tools while others are practically useless.

Distinctions between Objective and Essay Items

One way to approach the characteristics of essay items is to contrast them with those of objective items. There may be a point of confusion between the descriptive terms *objective* item and *essay* item. Objectivity refers to the scoring—namely, the extent to which equally competent scorers obtain the same results when scoring an item or test.

This implies that essay items are not objective. To some extent, this is true; there is always an element of subjectivity in scoring essay items. However, objectivity is not an either-or characteristic; there are ways to enhance the objectivity of scoring essay items.

When we identify objective items as *matching* or *multiple choice*, we are referring to an item format; this includes but is not limited to the response. *Essay item* basically refers to the format for responding to the item. These are obviously some minor inconsistencies in the descriptive terminology; they may give mistaken impressions if readers are not aware of them.

Students responding to objective items typically check, circle, shade a dot, draw lines, or possibly write a few words. In responding to essay items, students must write, presenting their thoughts in an organized and meaningful way. Responding to an essay item always requires language skills, whether or not it is the intent to test for such skills. For example, spelling, vocabulary, and penmanship are all involved when responding to essay items, much more so than with objective items.

The distinctions between objective items and essay items can be summarized as follows:

1. Although scoring essay items should be as objective as possible, there is always an element of subjectivity, more so than with objective items.
2. Objective items are formatted with the item stem and item response structured according to the type of item; essay items typically have a stem of a short- to medium-sized paragraph.
3. Response time per item is longer for essay items than objective items; so, in a specified time period, fewer items can be included.
4. Responding to essay items always involves writing skills; much more so than responding to objective items, which often do not require writing skills at all.

Advantages of Essay Items

One advantage of the essay item has already been presented: its potential for measuring higher-level or complex learning outcomes. Essay items provide the student with an opportunity to organize, analyze, and synthesize ideas; he must develop his own thoughts and write them in an organized manner. These kinds of behaviors provide useful learning experiences that are not usually developed to the same extent when using objective items.

Examples of higher-level learning outcomes that can be measured by essay items include:

- Organizing ideas in defense of a position.
- Comparing Position A with Position B on an issue.
- Contrasting Position A with Position B on an issue.
- Evaluating Position A on an issue.
- Formulating conclusions, given a set of data.
- Developing a plan for the solution to a problem.
- Explaining the application of biological principles.
- Describing the cause-and-effect relationship between A and B.

These higher-level learning outcomes emphasize information-use skills (such as synthesizing information and solving problems) to a larger extent than lower-level learning outcomes. This is not to say that objective items cannot be constructed to measure higher-level learning outcomes. But *practically,* for the classroom teacher, the essay item is better suited for that purpose.

The essay item is also commonly viewed as a device for measuring and improving a student's language and expression skills. Objective items basically do not provide a medium through which the student can demonstrate self-expression. Nor do they require any technical use of language. The response to an essay item, on the other hand, can be evaluated with respect to English usage, sentence structure, spelling, and penmanship. Whenever the student's response is to be evaluated to this extent, he should be aware of it, and the criteria for evaluation should be identified.

Although good essay items are not easy to prepare, they are more easily prepared than good objective items. Generally, it takes approximately the same amount of *time* to construct a good essay item as an objective item. But the *number* of essay items required for a specified testing time is much less than the number of objective items required for the same period. Hence, the preparation time is reduced when constructing a test for a specified length of time.

Finally, essay items are also helpful in evaluating the quality of the instructional process. If all testing is to be done using objective items, teachers may either consciously or unconsciously bias their teaching in a certain direction. For example, if all tests consist of multiple-choice items, writing skills will be neglected in the testing. This bias will, of course, be reflected in the learning experiences of the students. If this were the case, the development of certain student skills might well suffer if not be neglected altogether.

> Essay items can be used to measure writing and self-expression skills. Although this may not be the primary purpose of a given test, it is certainly worthwhile.

Disadvantages of Essay Items

The disadvantages of essay items are centered in the scoring. Reader inconsistency causes a lack of objectivity in scoring and hence limits test reliability. Reader inconsistency occurs due to a lack of agreement among competent scorers; it occurs when the same scorer is inconsistent in scoring several responses to the same item or items. In fact, the same scorer may be inconsistent in scoring the same response on two different occasions. The result of such reader inconsistency is that a student's score on an essay item or test becomes, to some extent, a function of who does the scoring.

Factors irrelevant to the item content sometimes tend to influence scores on essay items. For example, penmanship might influence the score, even though the item is not intended to measure penmanship. Similarly, neatness and organization of the response may be influential factors, as well.

A serious limitation of the essay exam is its limited content sampling. And, as discussed earlier, poor content sampling causes low content validity. These problems are particularly serious with an essay exam consisting of very few items.

Advocates of essay testing argue that they are not interested in only testing for subject knowledge. However, such knowledge is a prerequisite for demonstrating higher-order cognitive outcomes. In this sense, the essay item overemphasizes the importance of *how* to say something and ignores the importance of knowing *what* to say. For instance, a long, technically proficient response, written in beautiful, neat handwriting, may say *absolutely nothing*. Good writing must have some thought behind it.

> Scoring inconsistencies are the primary disadvantage of essay items. In addition, irrelevant factors, such as neatness and penmanship, may also influence the score.

Writing Essay Items

Like any test format, essay items and tests do have limitations. However, there are guidelines that can be followed to avoid such problems. These guidelines apply to the construction and scoring of items, and they are directed toward improving test reliability.

Restricting the Item and the Response

In general, the use of essay items should be restricted to those learning outcomes that cannot be adequately measured by objective items. Lower-level outcomes, such as knowledge and application, should not be measured by essay items, unless they are prerequisite to higher-level outcomes being measured by the same items. So, the first step in writing essay items is to identify explicitly those outcomes to be measured.

The extent of response to an essay item is basically a continuum, but one that has a wide range. Some writers (Gronlund 1981; Popham 1981) distinguish between a *restricted* response and an *extended* response. Here is an example of a restricted response item:

1. Describe and illustrate, in not more than 75 words, the difference between *grammar* and *syntax* in language.

For comparison, here is an example of an extended response item:

2. Present the arguments for and against the NATO deployment of nuclear weapons in Western Europe. Describe the strengths and weaknesses of each position. Then, take a position of your own and defend it. (Your answer will be evaluated with respect to the inclusion and organization of information, the accuracy of the arguments, and the relevance of information used to defend your position.)

Note that, in the extended response item, providing information about how the response will be evaluated gives the student some direction, as well as information about the item's scope.

Restricted response items tend to focus more directly on the learning outcome being measured. Also, restricted response items are less affected by factors such as spelling and grammar. In a given period, more restricted response items than extended response items can be used, which increases test reliability. For these reasons, restrictive response items are appropriate for testing elementary school students.

> The extent of response is basically on a continuum, from restricted to extended. Writing items with the response geared toward the restricted end tends to provide more focus for the item.

It is important that the item establish a definite and limited framework within which the student responds. Very general, vague items leave the student at a loss about how to respond. Consequently, the teacher will have difficulty in scoring the responses.

There are any number of ways in which a framework can be established for the response to an item. Consider the development of the following item, which, as stated here, is obviously too general:

1. Describe the development of the highway system in the United States.

Why is this item too general? For one thing, it provides no limits to a very extended topic. For instance, no periods of development are indicated: Is the student to begin with the first highway built and continue through the most recent interstate completion? Also, no subset of the highway system is indicated: Are all kinds of highways to be discussed? These are the kinds of points for which the item provides no direction.

In an attempt to restrict the item, we would provide limits, as follows:

2. Describe the development of the interstate highway system in the United States from 1955 to the present.

This revision is an improvement over the original. It indicates both the part of the highway system and the time period to be discussed.

The item also directs the student to one activity only, namely, to *describe*. This may be adequate, but in the context of the item, it may yet be somewhat vague and general. In any event, it would be helpful to provide additional or substitute words that are more descriptive of what the student is to do. Consider this revision:

3. Diagram the development of the interstate highway system in the United States from 1955 to the present. Label all parts of the diagram, indicating the completion times of major segments. Explain why the major segments were placed where they are.

If oral directions are provided, the teacher might define more specifically what is meant by *explain*. With younger students in particular, words such as *contrast, distinguish,* and *generalize* require additional definition in the context of the specific item. Whatever the level of the students, the vocabulary of the item must be words that they understand. For the item above, an illustration, such as a blank map of the United States, may also be helpful to the students in responding.

Directing the Student
to the Desired Response

As an essay item develops, the teacher must attempt to define the students' task as much as possible, directing them to select, organize, and express their ideas. To some extent, restricting the item provides this direction; in addition, the item must be phrased so the task is clearly indicated. It is too easy for teachers to fall into the trap of phrasing the introduction to the item in an ambiguous manner; as a result, the student may well miss what the teacher intends. For example, the following items lack adequate direction:

1. Discuss nuclear disarmament.
2. What are the disadvantages of using coal as a major energy source for generating electricity?
3. Give the causes of the American Revolution.

Another difficulty with such items is that perceptive students recognize such ambiguities and center their responses only on those aspects with which they are most familiar.

Some introductory phrases should be carefully avoided. For example, phrasing items such as "What do you think of ..." clearly calls for an opinion from the student. In this form, it does not require any analysis or synthesis, on the part of the student. Another poor introductory phrasing is "Write all you know about. ..." The response to an item so phrased can easily be limited to simple recall. In accordance, it can be graded only as 100 percent correct. Actually, the student could respond by writing "I don't know anything about. ..." This is a correct response based on the directions of the item, but it is certainly not the response intended by the teacher.

The teacher must identify the student behaviors intended by the item and then explicitly include them. In each of the following examples, a pair of items is given, including: (1) an *original* item, which does not contain adequate direction for the student; and (2) a *revision,* which has been reformulated into an improved item. The student behaviors are underlined for emphasis.

1. *Original:* Compare the political positions of the North and the South just prior to the Civil War.

   Revision: Identify the active political parties of the North and the South during the period 1855–61. Compare the positions of the parties with respect to the slavery issue. Infer how these positions affected the business/commerce and military policies of the parties. Support your inferences with specific examples. (Your answer should not exceed one and a half pages.)

2. *Original:* Analyze the following poems about the seasons of the year. (The student is provided with two poems of about twenty lines each.)

   Revision: Read the following poems about the seasons of the year. Identify the major point made by each author and contrast the perceptions of the authors about the seasons. In contrasting the authors' perceptions, infer what the authors like most and like least about the seasons.

3. *Original:* Describe how a water dam, such as Hoover Dam, produces electricity.

   Revision: A water dam such as Hoover Dam has stored energy as it holds back the water. Then, as gates in the dam are opened, water rushes through the modern water wheels and electricity is produced. Describe when the water does work and identify the kind of energy made by the modern water wheels. List the machines used in the dam to produce the electricity and apply the principle of energy conservation.

The first two items are appropriate for secondary level, and the third item is suitable for elementary science. The anticipated response to the third item would obviously be much shorter than those to the first two items.

> The student must be directed to the desired response. This can be enhanced by identifying the intended student behaviors and including them in the essay item.

Other Considerations

Generally, it is best to include a greater number of essay items with restricted responses, rather than fewer items requiring extended responses. This is especially significant when using essay tests with elementary school students; at this level, a response should rarely require more than one-half page, say not over 120 handwritten words. Length of response should correspond with the cognitive maturity of the students, increasing length with greater maturity.

Designating an approximate time to be devoted to each item is helpful to the students. This not only gives the students some indication of the anticipated length of the response, but it also helps students budget testing time. Designating time per item helps keep students from spending too much time on early items and then being unable to complete the test. Along with the time, it is also helpful to indicate the points allocated to each item.

In an attempt to increase the content sampling of essay items, teachers sometimes provide a number of items and allow the student to select and respond to only a few. Generally, this practice is undesirable for three major reasons:

1. It is difficult to construct items of equal difficulty.
2. Students do not have the ability to select those questions that they answer the best.
3. Good students may be penalized, because they are challenged by the more difficult and complex items.

The inclusion of optional items also introduces scoring difficulties; since students are responding to different items, they are, in fact, taking different tests. Also, as Gronlund (1981, 223) points out, the validity of the test may be jeopardized if students know in advance that optional items will be included. They will prepare accordingly, studying only selected topics, and then choose those test items that correspond to what they have studied. In essence, the test then covers only the limited content the *student* selects, rather than all the content covered by the instruction, as intended by the *teacher*.

> The suggested time for responding to each test item should be provided to the students. This designates the weight or value of each item and also helps students budget their time.

As a concluding suggestion, when preparing an essay test, the teacher constructing the test should have another teacher read the items—in essence, critique the test—before administering it. Such a critique helps uncover any problems, including inappropriate items, ambiguities, and unintended meanings.

Scoring Essay Items

As has been indicated earlier, essay items come under severe criticism because of scoring difficulties—namely, subjectivity—that make the test unreliable. Ideally, scoring is a completely objective task, done within the context of a response structured by the student. But, since scoring essay items is basically a rating process, there will always be some subjectivity. To help reduce this, there are a number of procedures that will increase the objectivity of scoring. However, it should be recognized that scoring essay items is always a demanding and time-consuming task.

Before scoring any response, the teacher should produce an outline of the anticipated answer, identifying the main points that it should include. Preparing a "model answer" may also be done, although this is not necessary; unless used with discretion, a "model" may inadvertently bias the scores on other equally acceptable answers. A scoring outline should also assign values to main points so they have equal influence across the responses being scored. If factors such as penmanship, spelling, and handwriting are going to enter into the scoring, (and it is difficult not to be influenced by such factors), the extent of their influence should be specified and points allotted accordingly.

Approaches to Scoring

Approaches to scoring can be roughly categorized in several ways. Ebel (1979, 105) uses the terms **analytic scoring** and **global-quality scaling,** while Popham (1981, 280) refers to analytic or *holistic* scoring.

In analytic scoring, the essential points of the correct response are identified and, to some extent, scored individually. Global-quality scaling, or holistic scoring, is based more on a general impression of the overall adequacy and quality of the response; in essence, the response is scored as a whole rather than by parts.

Both scoring approaches have their advantages and disadvantages. Analytic scoring tends to be more definitive; thus, it is usually easier to justify the score. However, with complex responses, analytic scoring may become too cumbersome and time consuming. Holistic scoring is usually faster and simpler, but it is more subjective; thus, it may be more difficult to justify the score. Furthermore, initial attempts at holistic scoring are sometimes rather crude; the responses may simply be categorized into two or more categories, such as excellent, good, fair, or poor.

The best approach is to use a combination of the two methods. First, score all responses holistically, to get the feel for their quality and extensiveness; this process orders the responses into relatively broad categories. Then, rescore the responses analytically and focus more on specific points or components. This two-pass method employs the strengths of each type of scoring, avoiding their individual weaknesses.

> Analytic scoring focuses on individual points or components of the response; holistic scoring considers the response in its entirety, as a whole.

Sources of Scoring Inconsistencies

We have already discussed that a student's score on an essay item may be influenced by *when* the item is scored and certainly *by whom* it is scored. When it is scored does not necessarily refer to the time of day (although it, too, may be a factor), but its order of scoring with respect to other responses. Hales and Tokar (1975) found that essays of average quality were rated more highly when preceded by five poor-quality essays than when preceded by five good-quality essays. Hughes, Keating, and Tuck (1980) found similar results in that context effects in essay scoring existed even after a considerable number of essays of varying quality had been read; in addition, these effects were present with both analytic and holistic scoring. Quite clearly, test scores are affected by the quality of those scored previously.

Another source of inconsistency is that teachers are susceptible to becoming more lenient (that is, scoring higher) as they progress through a set of responses. Possibly the teacher begins scoring with certain expectations, only to find that they have not been met, as shown by the student's responses. Unfortunately, those tests scored in the early stages will have been scored more critically than later exams. It is also practically impossible for teachers to ignore what Hopkins and Stanley (1981, 208) refer to as a *language mechanics effects,* which are effects due to errors in spelling, punctuation, and other technical elements. Specifically, it is difficult to ignore these mechanical qualities and consider only the idea being expressed. This is compounded when the response is handwritten.

A number of researchers (for example, Garber 1967) have found that the length of response influences the score, as well. There is a tendency to give the longer response a higher score, even if the shorter response includes the essential content. Teachers can also be influenced by the **halo effect,** which is the tendency to give high scores to those students who are known to be "good," and vice versa. On a given test with two or more essay items, if the response to one item is scored high, there will be a tendency to score the response to the next item high, as well.

Any number of impressionistic factors can influence the score on an essay item. Since scoring essay items involves at least some subjectivity, there is bound to be influence from such factors. This influence can be reduced by following the procedures discussed below, which are designed to enhance the objectivity of essay-item scoring.

Procedures for Scoring

Assuming that responses will be scored by a single teacher or two or more equally competent teachers, and that the essential components of the correct response have been identified and allotted points, the following procedures should be followed:

1. Read a small sample, five or so, of the responses to get a general impression of the quality of response that may be expected.
2. To the extent possible, read the papers anonymously. This is difficult to do with handwritten responses, but at least have students use a number system or put their names on the back of the final test page.
3. Score all of the individual responses to one item before proceeding to score the next item. This enhances the consistency of scoring the item and also enables the scorer to concentrate on one item at a time.
4. Reorder the papers in a random fashion after scoring each item so a given student's paper is not consistently in the same relative position. Reordering papers tends to lessen the chances of a student's score being a function of where the test paper is located in the pile of test papers.

Although it may be desirable to have two or more teachers score an essay test, this option is usually not feasible, due to time demands. However, if two or more teachers are used, it is important that they be equally competent and that they have the same perceptions of the scoring. These perceptions of scoring should include the influence of factors external to content, such as grammar, spelling, and penmanship.

> If possible, responses to items should be scored anonymously. In addition, all responses to one item should be scored before moving on to the next item, rather than scoring an entire test at a time. Also, the papers should be reordered before scoring the next item.

Reliability of Essay Tests

Inconsistencies in scoring affect test reliability. It might thus be inferred that the reliability of essay tests will tend to be lower than that of tests consisting of only objective items.

However, it is important to emphasize that the reliability of an essay exam is *not* only scorer agreement. This is a common source of confusion: to equate scorer agreement or scorer reliability with test reliability. Without scorer agreement, the test could not be reliable, but scorer agreement does not ensure test reliability. For instance, scorers could have near perfect agreement, but the reliability might still be low. Essay test reliability is the correlation between two forms of an exam or an internal consistency estimate.

> Reliability of an essay test should not be confused with scorer reliability or scorer agreement. Reliability is established through usual procedures, such as parallel forms or test-retest stability estimates.

The writing and scoring procedures discussed earlier tend to enhance reliability if they make the task definitive and reduce inconsistencies in scoring. As was seen in the chapter on reliability (chapter 4), increasing test length increases reliability, if all other factors remain constant. This is accomplished by increasing the number of items, not by including items that require longer response time. So, not only will including greater numbers of items with shorter responses tend to enhance the objectivity of scoring, but the test length itself will affect the test reliability.

> Reliability of essay tests can be enhanced by including greater numbers of items, not by including items that just take more time.

SUMMARY

To some extent, essay tests receive "bad press" because of low test reliability. However, essay items do serve an important function in educational measurement: Many teachers use them, and they will continue to use them. The use of essay items can be improved by carefully constructing the items and following procedures that tend to enhance the objectiveness of scoring.

The vagueness of the task may be a weakness of essay items, especially for broad items that require an extended response. Being specific in directing the student to the desired response and identifying the intended student behaviors reduces the indefiniteness of the task. The use of more items with restricted responses usually aids in defining the task and also tends to improve test reliability. Furthermore, essay items can be used as *part* of a test, rather than an *entire* test; this not only improves the objectivity of the test, but it also reduces the scoring time.

When scoring an essay item, the scorer should work from a specific set of important points or topics, possibly an outline of the response. All responses to a specific item should be scored consecutively, rather than scoring across items or scoring an entire test before moving on to the next one. Factors irrelevant to the response, such as penmanship, should not influence the score. If possible, the responses should be read with anonymity.

Teachers are sometimes under the impression that construction of essay items is easy. This is unfortunate, because essay items require careful construction. Individual items must be clearly structured. Also, teachers should check the content sampling, since it may be difficult to obtain adequate sampling with essay items. Finally, consistency in scoring—intra- and interscorer agreement—is important. It is a necessary *condition* for adequate test reliability, but it is not the *definition* of test reliability. The concept of test reliability for essay tests is the same as that for other tests: consistency in measuring what is being measured in the specific application of the test.

KEY TERMS AND CONCEPTS

Essay item
Analytic scoring

Global-quality scaling –holistic
Halo effect - good student

REVIEW ITEMS

1. Essay items are popular in teacher-constructed tests because:
   a. of the subjectivity in their scoring.
   b. they are perceived to be more effective in measuring higher-level outcomes than objective items.
   c. they tend to have greater content validity than objective items.
   d. they tend to have greater reliability than objective items.

2. Subjectivity in scoring responses to essay items tends to affect:
   a. test reliability.
   b. test validity.
   c. both test reliability and validity.
   d. neither test reliability or validity.

3. When scoring essay items, all responses to one item should be scored before scoring the next item, rather than scoring one entire test before scoring the next. This procedure:
   a. increases the test validity.
   b. enhances the consistency of scoring.
   c. reduces bias against individual students.
   d. enhances the objectivity of scoring.

4. The test scorer reads the response to one essay item after already reading several other responses to the same item. The score of this response will tend to be:
   a. higher, if the earlier responses were of poor quality.
   b. higher, if the earlier responses were of high quality.
   c. lower, if the earlier responses were of poor quality.
   d. unaffected by the quality of earlier responses.

5. The halo effect in scoring essay items is a tendency to score more highly those responses:
   a. read later in the scoring process.
   b. read earlier in the scoring process.
   c. of students known to be good students.
   d. that are technically well written.

6. Which of the following is *not* a possible outcome with an essay test?
   a. high test reliability and high scorer agreement.
   b. low test reliability and low scorer agreement.
   c. low test reliability and high scorer agreement.
   d. high test reliability and low scorer agreement.

7. The use of additional essay items with more restricted responses tends to:
   a. increase the content validity of the test.
   b. increase the construct validity of the test.

    c. increase the predictive validity of the test.

    d. have no effect upon test validity.

8. From a measurement standpoint, using classroom tests consisting entirely of essay items is undesirable because:

    a. content sampling tends to be limited.

    b. scoring requires too much time.

    c. it is difficult to construct the items.

    d. structuring model responses is too time consuming.

9. Two forms of an essay test in American history were developed and administered to a group of 35 students. The correlation between the scores on the two forms is a measure of:

    a. predictive validity of the test.

    b. content validity of the test.

    c. test reliability.

    d. reader agreement.

10. A teacher reads all responses to the essay items on a test and then decides the scoring has been too critical. To change this, the scores of each student's essay items are raised five points. This will:

    a. increase test reliability.

    b. decrease test reliability.

    c. have no effect upon test reliability.

    d. have an unknown effect upon test reliability.

11. Anonymous scoring of essay item responses tends to reduce:

    a. reader agreement.

    b. the halo effect.

    c. order effects.

    d. effects due to technical characteristics, such as penmanship.

12. A student receives a high score on an essay item, due, in part, to the quality of responses to the item read earlier. This is:

    a. a context effect.

    b. a halo effect.

    c. a reader-agreement effect.

    d. none of the above.

13. Analytic scoring of essay items tends to be faster than holistic scoring.

          (T)   F

14. Analytic scoring of essay items tends to be more objective than holistic scoring.

          (T)   F

15. There is a tendency to score longer responses to essay items more highly than shorter responses.

          T   (F)

16. A procedure for computing test reliability of an essay test is to compute the correlation between the scores of two test readers.

          (T)   F

17. Essay items provide greater opportunity for student self-expression than multiple-choice items.

          (T)   F

18. Test reliability of an essay test may be low even if reader agreement between two or more scorers is high.

          (T)   F

19. It is possible for scores on an essay test to have low reliability yet high validity.

          T   (F)

20. The use of additional essay items with more restricted responses tends to affect test reliability.

          (T)   F

EXERCISES

8.1 Consider the following essay items, all of which are inadequate. Identify the deficiencies and reformulate them into acceptable items.

    a. Discuss the development of railroads in the United States.

    b. List the causes of the stock market crash of 1929.

    c. Analyze the processes used in developing the first atomic bomb.

    d. Write all you know about the development of New Orleans as a seaport during the nineteenth century.

e. Contrast the economic conditions of the 1920s just prior to the Depression with those of the period 1973–81.

8.2 In your educational area of interest, identify five learning outcomes that probably could be measured more effectively by essay items than objective items.

8.3 Suppose an essay item directs the students to read and evaluate a short story of about four pages dealing with the life of a ten-year-old boy in a small Texas town during the 1960s. Provide some example directions for responding, including intended student behaviors if: (1) the students are sixth-graders in a language arts class; and (2) the students are in a high school senior honors class in American literature.

8.4 Summarize the reasons for avoiding the use of optional items on an essay test.

8.5 An essay exam has two forms, each consisting of six items. The reliability coefficient for each form singly is around 0.50. Estimate the reliability of an exam consisting of the two forms combined.

REFERENCES

Ebel, R. L. 1979. *Essentials of educational measurement.* 3d ed. Englewood Cliffs, N.J.: Prentice Hall.

Garber, H. 1967. The Digital computer simulates human rating behavior. In *Assessing behaviors: Readings in educational and psychological measurement,* by J. T. Flynn and H. Garber. Reading, Mass: Addison-Wesley.

Gronlund, N. E. 1981. *Measurement and evaluation in teaching.* 4th ed. New York: MacMillan.

Hales, L. W., and E. Tokar. 1975. The effect of the quality of preceding responses on the grades assigned to subsequent responses on an essay question. *Journal of Educational Measurement* 12:115–17.

Hopkins, K. D., and J. C. Stanley. 1981. *Educational and psychological measurement and evaluation.* 6th ed. Englewood Cliffs, N.J.: Prentice-Hall.

Hughes, D. C., B. Keating, and B. F. Tuck. 1980. The influence of context position and scoring method on essay scoring. *Journal of Educational Measurement* 17:131–35.

Popham, W. J. 1981. *Modern educational measurement.* Englewood Cliffs, N.J.: Prentice-Hall.

9

The Use
of Standardized
Achievement Tests

Standardized achievement tests are given in most schools in the United States. Strictly speaking, a *standardized* test is one that is given under standard conditions so that the basis for interpreting the scores extends beyond the site and group of examinees used in a specific test administration. Most standardized tests are created by test publishing companies or agencies such as the Educational Testing Service.

Standardized achievement tests were developed to provide a measure of individual student achievement. In norm-referenced standardized tests, an individual's score is compared to those of other individuals or groups who took the same test under similar conditions, using the same directions and time limits. These comparison groups, or *norm groups,* may be national, state, or local, depending on how extensive the sampling procedures have been.

Standardized achievement tests are also frequently used for other purposes, purposes for which they were not really designed. For instance, sometimes standardized achievement tests are used to evaluate teacher effectiveness, to decide who is eligible for compensatory services, to certify successful completion of a grade, and to accredit schools.

Our development of standardized achievement tests will not include these ulterior purposes. Instead, we will limit their use in assessing achievement of individual students. Those who are interested in the use of achievement tests for these other purposes are referred to the *Journal of Educational Measurement,* Summer 1983. Much of this issue focuses on the psychological procedures involved in answering test questions. In addition, tests are discussed in terms of their relation to learning theory in addition to the domain of content.

> Standardized achievement tests are given under standard conditions so there will be a broader basis for interpreting the scores than is provided by the specific test administration characteristics. The primary purpose of standardized achievement tests is to measure the level of achievement of individual students.

Standards for Standardized Tests

Publishers of standardized achievement tests have a set of criteria that lists guidelines for the kind of information they should provide to potential test users. *Standards for Educational and Psychological Tests* (1974) is a product of a joint committee made up of persons from selected professional organizations that use published tests. The standards, or criteria, describe the technical adequacy of the tests. Major topics include Test Selection and Administration, Validity, Reliability, Norms, and Score Interpretation. The standards describe the information that should be in the test manuals, so that the tests' users or consumers can properly evaluate the appropriateness of the test for their specific purposes.

One important distinction that was made in *Standards* was that the tests can be divided into three categories, based on the levels of training required for interpreting the scores from various tests. These three categories are:

A. *Tests that can be adequately administered, scored, and interpreted with the aid of the manual and a general orientation to the kind of institution or organization in which one is working.*

B. *Tests that require some technical knowledge of test construction and use and of supporting psychological and educational fields, such as statistics, individual differences, psychology of adjustment, personal psychology, and guidance.*

C. *Tests that require substantial understanding of testing and supporting fields, together with supervised experience in the use of these devices. (1974, 10–11)*

The achievement tests described in this chapter fit into category A. Aptitude tests and psychological adjustment inventories (category B) and projective tests and individually administered mental tests (category C) are discussed in chapter 11.

Standards also describes what information should be provided in the test manual:

A.2 The test manual should describe fully the development of the test: the ration-

ale, specifications followed in writing items or selecting observations, and procedures and results of item analysis or other research. (1974, 11)

Additionally, there are standards on the technical information about the tests; for instance:

F.1 The test manual should present evidence of reliability, including estimates of the standard error of measurement, that permits the reader to judge whether scores are sufficiently dependable for the intended uses of the test. (1974, 50)

E.1 A manual should present the evidence of validity for each type of inference for which use of the test is recommended. If validity for some suggested interpretation has not been investigated, that fact should be made clear. (1974, 31)

D.2 Norms presented in the test manual should refer to defined and clearly described populations. These populations should be the groups with whom users of the test will ordinarily wish to compare the persons tested. (1974, 20)

These standards provide guidance to the publishers of standardized tests, enabling them to produce manuals that contain enough relevant information so test selection and use can be based on complete and appropriate information. Of course, not all published tests are of high quality. In that respect, these standards are also helpful in judging the adequacy of a test.

Note that a test is never "validated." A test that has worked well with one particular group on one specific occasion may not necessarily work well with a different set of examinees at another point in time. Therefore, one should not expect that a validity coefficient (or even a reliability coefficient) reported for one norm group will also be found in each subsequent administration of the test. Whether a test is appropriate must be based on the merits of the particular situation, not on how the test has worked in other situations.

Standardized achievement tests vary in quality. *Standards for Educational and Psychological Tests* (1974) provides criteria for judging the adequacy of these tests.

Selecting Standardized Achievement Tests

The responsibility of choosing a standardized achievement test includes facing a potentially baffling array of decisions. In fact, the complexity of the choice may appear to be overwhelming.

The variety of standardized achievement tests makes it likely that there is a test available for most purposes. However, there are several factors that should be considered when selecting a test. We will address three central factors: (1) **relevance,** which is essentially content validity; (2) **technical adequacy,** which is concerned with reliability and norms; and (3) **usability,** which refers to the practical considerations of testing.

Relevance

Perhaps *the* most important factor in judging the appropriateness of an achievement test is whether the items are relevant to the content and emphasis of the school's curriculum. To be appropriate, the test items must be concerned with the skills and knowledge actually taught in the classroom.

The test manual should also provide adequate information about the source of the item content. The decision about the relevance of a specific test can be made only by inspecting the actual test items. Test publishers sell specimen sets that allow potential users to review the actual items. Test selection committees or individuals should examine the specimen sets of those tests being considered to see whether the items match the knowledge and skills taught in their particular school.

Technical Adequacy

The test selection should be based in large part on whether the test is reliable and valid. If norm-referenced score interpretations will be done, there is also a concern about the adequacy of the norms. The test's manual will provide sufficient information on these issues.

Often test selectors feel that they are not quite capable of judging these matters. Fortunately, there is a resource available for help: the *Mental Measurements Yearbook* (*MMY*) (1978). This reference is published every few years and contains descriptions and reviews of most available standardized achievement tests. In addition, it includes tests of other constructs, such as aptitude, personality, and interests.

The first part of an *MMY* entry describes the publication date of the test, the subtests, and the available scoring services, along with a number of other characteristics. An example of this information is given in Figure 9.1.

The second part of an *MMY* entry is a review of the test by someone knowledgable about that particular area of testing. Each review contains comments on the reliability, validity, and norms of the test. In fact, the test review is often based on *Standards for Educational and Psychological Tests* (1974), which was discussed earlier. Test selectors should not defer their decision to the test reviewers, but the information and opinions from the review should be considered.

Figure 9.1.
A Sample Entry of an Achievement Test Description from the *Mental Measurements Yearbook*

Iowa Tests of Basic Skills, Forms 5 and 6. Grades 1.7–2.5, 2.6–3.5, 3–9; 1955–75; ITBS; postage extra; E. F. Lindquist, A. N. Hieronymus, and others; NCS scoring stencils and services for Levels Edition available from NCS Interpretive Scoring Systems; Houghton Mifflin Co.

A. PRIMARY BATTERY: LEVELS 7–8. Grades 1.7–2.5, 2.6–3.5; 1972–75; 2 forms; 2 levels; 2 editions: standard, basic (a battery of 6 subtests from the standard edition); administrator's manual ('75, 56 pages); percentile norms booklet for large cities, Catholic schools, ('75, 16 pages); profile ('73, 2 pages); profile chart for averages ('73, 1 page); report to parents ('72, 4 pages); practice test ('72, 4 pages); practice test guide ('72, 7 pages); $2.40 per 35 profiles; $1.80 per 25 parents' report; $3.90 per 25 practice tests; $1.95 per teacher's manual; $1.80 per administrator's manual; $4.50 per specimen set.

  1) *Level 7.* Grades 1.7–2.5; 3 editions; Form 5 manual ('72, 63 pages), Form 6 manual ('72, 43 pages).
  (a) Standard Edition. 16 scores: listening, vocabulary, word analysis, reading comprehension, language skills (spelling, capitalization, punctuation, usuage, total), work-study skills (maps/graphs and tables, references, total), mathematics skills (mathematics concepts, mathematics problems, total), composite; Forms 5, 6, ('72, 28 pages, MRC scorable); $17.10 per 25 tests; scoring service, 73¢ and over per test ($33 minimum); (260) minutes in 5 sessions.
  (b) Basic Edition. 8 scores: vocabulary, word analysis, reading comprehension, spelling, mathematics skills (mathematics concepts, mathematics problems, total), composite; for Canadian adaptation, see *Canadian Tests of Basic Skills;* Forms 5, 6, ('72, 15 pages); 2 editions: MRC scorable, hand scorable; $12.30 per 25 MRC scorable tests; $8.76 per 25 hand scorable tests; $3.30 per set of hand scoring stencils; MRC scoring service, 62¢ and over per test ($27.50 minimum); (150) minutes in 4 sessions.

  2) *Level 8.* Grades 2.6–3.5; 3 editions; Form 5 manual ('72, 65 pages), Form 6 manual ('72, 44 pages).
  (a) Standard Edition. 16 scores: same as for level 7; Forms 5, 6, ('72, 28 pages, MRC scorable); prices same as for 1*a*; (270) minutes in 5 sessions.
  (b) Basic Edition. 8 scores: same as for level 7; Forms 5, 6, ('72, 16 pages); 2 editions: MRC scorable, hand scorable; prices same as for 1*b*; (160) minutes in 4 sessions.

Source: O. K. Buros, ed., *Mental Measurements Yearbook,* 8th ed. (Highland Park, N.J.: Gryphon Press, 1978), 53.

Usability

Usability refers to those practical considerations that affect the convenience and effectiveness of a test. The importance of these factors is likely to vary from one situation to another.

Score-Reporting Options. The standardized achievement test that is finally selected should provide results that are useful to all potential users, including local and national norms. There may also be a need for school building averages, as well as individual student norms.

The specificity of the test results is always a concern. Are scores in reading comprehension and arithmetic computation specific enough, or do the users want the results printed for each detailed objective? Finally, do the users want norm-referenced or criterion-referenced interpretations of the results? If criterion-referenced results are desired, are locally developed performance criteria available?

Test results may be used in many ways. Therefore, it is important that they are reported in a format that is usable by most, if not all, persons interested in the test results. Test publishers offer a variety of ways to report the scores, so this may not be a difficult problem.

Utility and Cost. Utility considerations include the ease of administration, the amount of testing time, and the details of ordering and processing test answer sheets, including machine or hand scoring.

Another related factor is the cost of the test. Generally, it will vary, reflecting the extent of services ordered, such as different reporting formats or the development of local norms. Cost factors are usually considered in terms of the local testing budget.

> Selecting appropriate standardized achievement tests can be very involved. Test selectors should be concerned with relevance, technical adequacy, and usability.

Types of Standardized Achievement Tests

Standardized achievement tests can be classified into several types: Some focus on a single content area, while others have subtests that cover a range of content. In this section, we will examine three types of achievement tests that include several content areas: (1) the norm-referenced survey, which usually examines reading, mathematics, and at least one other content area; (2) the criterion-referenced examination, in which items are keyed to specific instructional objectives; and (3) the criterion-referenced **item-bank test,** in which items are generated in response to preselected objectives.

Each of these basic types will be discussed in detail, first in terms of its general use and then in terms of score reporting.

> Standardized achievement tests follow several basic formats. Some test scores are interpreted in either a norm-referenced or criterion-referenced manner. There are also tests that are made-to-order, based on the preselection of specific objectives.

Norm-Referenced Achievement Tests

General Use.   Several excellent norm-referenced achievement tests are available. The one that we present as an example is the Iowa Test of Basic Skills (ITBS). (This test may also be used as a criterion-referenced test, which is explained in the ITBS manual [Hieronymous, Lindquist, and Hoover 1982].)

The ITBS was selected because it is used by a large number of school districts and has a very thorough documentation. Although the ITBS is popular, there are also other fine tests available.

The ITBS has several purposes, including:

1. *To determine the developmental level of the pupil in order to better adapt materials and instructional procedures to individual needs and abilities.*
2. *To diagnose specific qualitative strengths and weaknesses in a pupil's educational development.*
3. *To report performance in basic skills to parents and patrons in objective, meaningful terms. (Hieronymous, Lindquist, and Hoover 1982, 1)*

These purposes illustrate several different yet related uses for the test results. The overall perspective provided by the norms clearly serves these purposes more effectively than the limited perspective provided by teacher-made measures. Note also how this information relates to *Standards,* as was mentioned earlier.

The *Early Primary Battery* of the ITBS is appropriate for children with an average developmental level of 5 and 6 years. This battery has subtests in Listening, Vocabulary, Word Analysis, Language, Mathematics, and Reading.

The *Primary Battery,* for ages 7 and 8, contains the following subtests:

- Listening
- Vocabulary*
- Word Analysis*
- Reading Comprehension
    Pictures*
    Sentences*
    Stories*
- Language Skills
    Spelling*
    Capitalization
    Punctuation
    Usage
- Work Study Skills
    Visual Materials
    Reference Materials

- Mathematics Skills
    Mathematics Concepts*
    Mathematics Problems*
    Mathematics Computation* (Hieronymous, Lindquist, and Hoover 1982, 2)

(The asterisks [*] denote that this battery is available in both the complete test and the basic test.)

The *Multilevel Battery* is available for ages 9–14. The skills that are measured include:

- Vocabulary
- Reading
- Language
    Spelling
    Capitalization
    Punctuation
    Usage
- Work-Study
    Visual Materials
    Reference
- Mathematics
    Mathematics Concepts
    Mathematics Problem Solving
    Mathematics Computation (Hieronymous, Lindquist, and Hoover 1982, 4)

A Social Studies/Science supplement can be used in addition to the regular ITBS battery to broaden the scope of the tested content.

The content emphasis of the ITBS items comes from a variety of sources, including current instructional materials (such as textbooks), continuous interaction with users, independent reviews by professionals from diverse cultural groups, recommendations from specialists and national curriculum committees, and empirical studies. Such a variety of sources assures that the items cover relevant content, are free from bias, and have appropriate technical characteristics (Hieronymous, Lindquist, and Hoover 1982, 65–66). Note how this information addresses criterion A.2 of *Standards,* which was listed earlier.

Evidence about the reliability of the ITBS is also presented. For example, the KR20 reliability coefficients that were found on the Reading Subtest of the Multilevel Battery ranged from 0.90 for grade 4 to 0.93 in grade 6 and grade 9. Several different reliability coefficients are reported, including internal consistency, equivalent forms, and longitudinal stability. In addition, the standard error of measurement for each of three kinds of scores—raw, grade equivalent, and standard—is presented for each subtest at each grade level. Note that this addresses criterion F.1 of *Standards.*

Of course, the key component of a norm-referenced achievement test is the norm group used as the basis for interpretation. The sampling procedures used in the norming of the ITBS were very complete, as described below.

School districts were classified on three variables: district enrollment, geographic region, and community socioeconomic status. Then, within all combinations of those three variables, school districts were randomly selected. This sampling procedure produced:

1. a national probability sample representative of the nation's pupils;
2. a sample of the nation's school buildings to provide the basis for school building norms; and
3. the data on which to base special regional, large-city, high- and low-socioeconomic, and Catholic school norms. (Hieronymous, Lindquist, and Hoover 1982, 8)

Note that this addresses criterion D.2 of *Standards.*

The ITBS scores can be reported in several different formats, including status measures, raw scores, percentile ranks, stanines or normal curve equivalents, as well as developmental scores (grade equivalents and expected standard scores).

Score Reporting. The ITBS test manual provides much information on the interpretation and use of test results. One example is the *List Report of Pupil Scores,* which lists the names of the pupils in a classroom along with each person's grade equivalent and national percentile rank on each of the subtests. Classroom averages for each subtest and the composite are given, as well.

Another type of record is the *Profile Narrative Report* that is prepared for each pupil. This report presents each student's grade equivalent, stanine, and percentile rank on each subtest. There is also a narrative report that provides a written description of the pupil's performance. Thus, there are really three ways of presenting the results on this report: as a set of norm-referenced scores, as a set of bar graphs, and as a narrative report. Although all three formats provide the same information, some test users may understand one format better than another.

The information in Figure 9.2 is for a sixth-grade boy tested in October. His highest levels of performance are on the language tests; his total score for the language area was at the 88th percentile, better than 88 percent of the national sample of sixth-graders. His lowest performance was on the math concepts test, where his percentile rank was 33, better than only 33 percent of the national sample. The narrative part of the report presents a description of his performance that can be used to assist teachers in interpreting the results for parents.

Clearly, the Iowa Test of Basic Skills is an impressive standardized achievement test, one that was carefully designed, developed, and analyzed. The standardization samples (norm groups) are reliable, so the score interpretations will be as meaningful as possible. In addition, the content of the tests reflects the current emphases

Figure 9.2.
Profile Narrative Report for the ITBS

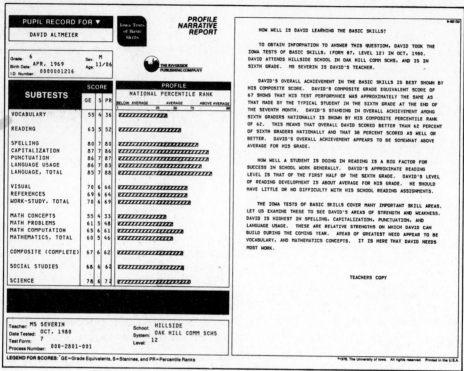

Report Facsimile—Names and data presented are fictitious.

Source: Hieronymous, Lindquist and Hoover 1982, 35. Copyright © by the University of Iowa. Reproduced by permission of the Publisher, The Riverside Publishing Company, 8420 Bryn Mawr Avenue, Chicago, IL 60631.

in textbooks and other instructional materials, the views of content specialists and curriculum committees, as well the feedback from school districts that use the test. Finally, the technical information on the reliability and validity of the scores is complete, as are the instructions on how to use the test scores for various practical purposes.

Criterion-Referenced Achievement Tests

General Use. The *Tests of Achievement and Proficiency* (TAP) (Scannell 1982) is an example of a widely used criterion-referenced achievement test. This set of tests was designed to measure the achievement of secondary school students in the following areas:

- Reading Comprehension
- Mathematics
- Written Expression
- Using Sources of Information
- Social Studies
- Science

The purposes of the TAP are defined for several types of school personnel:

1. *for teachers, as they plan instruction for a specific class, select topics for remedial or enrichment activities, and revise courses of study;*
2. *for counselors, as they develop plans for group counseling activities, help students plan specific enrollments and work with individual students in developing future educational and vocational plans;*
3. *for administrators, as they review curriculum content and organization, developmental progress of students toward academic and basic skill goals of the school, and resource allocations both by levels and across subject fields; and as they report successes and continuing needs to parents, school board members, and the general public. (Scannell 1982, 5)*

The TAP does use norm-referenced interpretations, such as standard scores and percentiles. However, it also can be used with criterion-referenced interpretations. The *Student Criterion-Referenced Skills Analysis Report* lists the number of items attempted, the number correct, and the number of such items on the test. The report also includes the percentage of items answered correctly by each student, as well as the class and national norm group averages. This kind of criterion-referenced reporting is available at both the student and the school building levels.

The actual prespecified criteria used to judge test performance adequacy are determined locally. Teachers can enter an *expectation index*, which indicates their estimate of the percent of students who will answer an item correctly.

Of course, the TAP manual also presents extensive information on the item content sources, reliability coefficients and standard errors of measurement, and validity coefficients, as suggested by *Standards for Educational and Psychological Tests.*

Score Reporting. Reporting test performance for a criterion-referenced interpretation is somewhat different than that discussed earlier for the norm-referenced example. The *Student Criterion-Referenced Skills Analysis* of the TAP (see Figure 9.3) provides some norm-referenced information, but it also lists the number of items for each content area, the number of items the student answered correctly, and the

Figure 9.3.
Student Criterion-Referenced Skills Analysis Report, TAP

NAME PATTERSON, DEBBIE   FORM T   TEST LEVEL 16
DATE TESTED 11/80   TEACHER MS RITA GARRISON   GRADE 10
SCHOOL LINCOLN SENIOR HS   SCHOOL CODE

	READING COMPREHENSION	MATHEMATICS	WRITTEN EXPRESSION	USING SOURCES OF INFORMATION	BASIC COMPOSITE	SOCIAL STUDIES	SCIENCE	BATTERY COMPOSITE	APPLIED PROFICIENCY
SS	220	196	203	201	205	213	204	206	44 MED
PR	94	81	81	76	85	91	84	86	

SS = STANDARD SCORE   PR = PERCENTILE RANK

Houghton Mifflin Company
Tests of Achievement and Proficiency
STUDENT CRITERION-REFERENCED SKILLS ANALYSIS
9-75051
PROCESS NO. 000-0335-000
PAGE 19

SKILLS	NUMBER ATTEMPTED	NUMBER CORRECT	NUMBER OF ITEMS	PERCENT CORRECT FOR THIS STUDENT	CLASS AVERAGE PERCENT CORRECT	NATIONAL AVERAGE PERCENT CORRECT
READING COMPREHENSION (N= 23)	61	55	62	89	54	62
Textbook	33	30	33	91	53	63
Everyday	28	25	29	86	55	61
Fact	22	20	23	87	56	63
Inference	26	23	26	88	52	59
Generalization	13	12	13	92	54	66
MATHEMATICS (N= 23)	48	34	48	71	47	51
Operations	6	5	6	83	61	66
Equivalent Forms & Order	5	3	5	60	34	41
Common Applications	11	6	11	55	49	53
Algebra	5	4	5	80	45	48
Geometry & Measurement	7	7	7	100	45	46
Statistics, Graphs & Tables	7	5	7	71	47	55
Basic Mathematical Principles	7	4	7	57	46	46
Computation	9	8	9	89	58	62
Concepts	20	14	20	70	46	49
Problem Solving	19	12	19	63	44	48
WRITTEN EXPRESSION (N= 23)	62	42	62	68	48	51
Spelling & Capitalization	7	3	7	43	37	47
Punctuation	8	4	8	50	45	51
Grammar & Usage	18	12	18	67	50	54
Organization	30	22	30	73	52	52
Forms	3	3	3	100	38	41
Factual Identification	5	2	5	40	35	46
Comprehension & Application	26	20	26	77	52	55
Analysis & Synthesis	19	11	19	58	45	46
Evaluation	12	9	12	75	51	52
USING SOURCES OF INFORMATION (N= 22)	67	54	67	81	57	65
Map Reading	8	6	8	75	64	62
Determining Direction, Distance, & Elevation	3	1	3	33	47	45
Interpreting Data & Inferring Conditions	5	5	5	100	74	72
Reading Graphs & Tables	22	17	22	77	51	59
Determining Amounts & Comparing Quantities	14	11	14	79	55	66
Interpreting Relationships	8	6	8	75	45	49

SKILLS	NUMBER ATTEMPTED	NUMBER CORRECT	NUMBER OF ITEMS	PERCENT CORRECT FOR THIS STUDENT	CLASS AVERAGE PERCENT CORRECT	NATIONAL AVERAGE PERCENT CORRECT
Knowledge & Use of Reference Materials	37	31	37	84	59	68
Using Tables of Contents & Indexes	18	15	18	83	63	71
Using the Dictionary	11	10	11	91	56	69
Using General Reference Materials	8	6	8	75	53	61
Identification	18	15	18	83	64	74
Comprehension	23	17	23	74	54	61
Application	18	14	18	78	54	63
Inference	8	8	8	100	56	60
SOCIAL STUDIES (N= 23)	60	50	60	83	45	51
Historical Perspective	19	17	19	89	46	53
Patterns & Systems	41	33	41	80	44	50
Economic	16	13	16	81	43	51
Geographic	8	8	8	100	52	60
Political						
Social & Anthropologic	16	12	16	75	43	47
Related Social Sciences	4	4	4	100	49	57
Knowledge	11	11	11	100	54	58
Understanding	24	18	24	75	43	50
Generalization	22	19	22	86	44	49
Evaluation	3	2	3	67	38	51
SCIENCE (N= 23)	62	44	62	71	46	50
Nature of Science	18	14	18	78	45	47
Biology	23	17	23	74	50	52
Earth & Space Science	17	12	17	71	45	51
Chemistry & Physics	4	1	4	25	35	48
Knowledge	29	20	29	69	45	50
Application	10	7	10	70	42	50
Explanation	12	9	12	75	53	54
Experimental Methods & Techniques	11	8	11	73	45	47
APPLIED PROFICIENCY SKILLS (N= 22)	55	44	55	80	58	64
Obtaining Information	35	30	35	86	61	68
Primarily Verbal Materials	16	15	16	94	56	65
Visual Materials	13	10	13	77	63	69
Reference Materials	6	5	6	83	65	75
Communicating Ideas to Others in Writing	9	7	9	78	47	48
Applied Mathematics	11	7	11	64	56	62

* = Strongest skill areas   - = Weakest skill areas
NA (not available) indicates that the student did not take this test

Report Facsimile — Names and data presented on this report are fictitious.

Source: Scannell 1982, Copyright © 1982 by Riverside Publishing Company. Reproduced by permission of the Publisher, The Riverside Publishing Company, 8420 Bryn Mawr Avenue, Chicago, IL 60631.

number of items attempted. The percent correct is listed, so this percentage can be compared to a locally determined criterion of acceptable performance.

The student in the example answered 15 of the 18 test items correctly, which is 83 percent correct. If the school had established a standard of 75 percent as the acceptable level of performance, this student would have surpassed that mark. However, the student answered only half of the punctuation items correctly, and 50 percent is probably below the standard of performance on that test.

This kind of information indicates the areas in which the student needs to improve, relative to the locally established criteria. The *Student Criterion-Referenced Skills Analysis* report also gives the average percent correct for the class and national norm group. Although these numbers are irrelevant to a criterion-referenced interpretation, they are significant to a norm-referenced report.

> The Tests of Achievement and Proficiency (TAP) can be used to perform criterion-referenced test interpretations, but the criteria must be specified locally.

Item-Bank Achievement Tests

General Use.   Item-bank standardized achievement tests, a form of criterion-referenced tests, have become increasingly popular. This new approach employs a catalog of objectives, each of which is linked to a test item stored in an item bank, usually a computerized list of items or item-generating rules.

To create a test, a school district selects specific, relevant objectives from the general catalog. A list of these selected objectives is sent to the test publisher. Test items associated with the chosen objectives are then selected from the item bank, and specialized test booklets are printed for that school district. Standard instructions and answer sheets are used in the test administration.

Examples of the kinds of objectives available are listed below. These were taken from the *SCORE* tests (Houghton-Mifflin Company).

1. Reading and Language Arts Objectives—The student:
    *   selects the word having the same /o/ sound as the letter(s) underlined in the stimulus word.
    *   selects the appropriate affix for a root word to complete a sentence.
    *   identifies the number of syllables in a given word.
    *   selects the possessive form of the given singular norm.
    *   selects the plural verb to complete a sentence with a compound subject.

2. Mathematics Objectives—The student:
    *   identifies the largest object in a group of objects.
    *   solves a word problem that involves subtraction of one- or two-digit numbers without regrouping.
    *   solves a word problem dealing with percent of increase.
    *   adds measures in gallons, quarts, and pints and renames the sum in gallons, quarts, and pints.
    *   reads temperature on a Fahrenheit scale. (Ferney 1982)

Clearly, these selected objectives indicate that a wide range of skills and abilities is available. The SCORE tests cover grade levels 1–6 for the reading and language arts tests and levels 1–8 for the mathematics objectives. The objectives are specific enough that the catalog of objectives is understandable and the corresponding test items will, in fact, match the objectives.

Score Reporting. Although item-bank tests are criterion-referenced, the criteria of adequate performance are locally determined. For instance, the test results indicate what percentage of the class answered an item correctly, but whether that percentage is satisfactory is a local decision. Similarly, the test results indicate the number of items the student answered correctly for each objective, but the decision whether the student has mastered the objective is left to the local teachers and administrators.

> Item banks allow the creation of standardized achievement tests that are tailored to the specific objectives of an individual school district.

Single-Subject and Diagnostic Tests

Not all standardized achievement tests span several content areas. Some are focused on a single subject and many provide very specific rather than global information.

Standardized achievement tests are available for almost every subject (see Table 9.1). The most commonly used are those in reading and mathematics for children in the primary grades. Several "readiness" tests are also available; they have been designed to identify children who possess the prerequisite skills for some cognitive task and thus can be predicted to profit from instruction. Other tests in reading and mathematics measure components of certain skills, such as vocabulary, comprehension, speed, and accuracy.

Single-subject achievement tests are quite relevant to the elementary curriculum, which consists of an ordered hierarchy of skills and knowledge. The secondary school curriculum is typically less standard and ordered; thus, an achievement battery at this level may be inappropriate.

Diagnostic tests differ from achievement surveys in that they provide a very specific description of the weak areas in a person's performance. For example, reading performance can be broken down so that errors in pronunciation, omissions, and reversals are noted. Teachers find this kind of information more useful than a global measure of reading achievement.

Diagnostic tests are usually given only to those students experiencing learning difficulty, not all students. These tests are often long, detailed, and time consuming, since they need to assess accurately a number of specific skills. For these reasons, they are only used in special situations.

Table 9.1.
A Sample of Standardized Achievement Tests

- Adult Basic Learning Examination
- California Achievement Test
- Comprehensive Test of Basic Skills
- Durrell Analysis of Reading Difficulty
- Gates-MacGinitie Reading Tests
- Gates-McKillop Reading Diagnostic Tests
- Iowa Silent Reading Tests
- Iowa Test of Basic Skills
- Lee-Clark Reading Readiness Test
- Metropolitan Readiness Test
- Metropolitan Achievement Test
- Prescriptive Mathematics Inventory
- Prescriptive Reading Inventory
- SCORE
- Sequential Tests of Educational Progress
- SRA Achievement Series
- Stanford Achievement Test
- Tests of Academic Progress
- Tests of Achievement and Proficiency
- Wide Range Achievement Test

> Single-subject standardized achievement tests are available for most content areas. They measure general levels of achievement and readiness for instruction and can also diagnose specific weaknesses.

Limitations
of Standardized Achievement Tests

Standardized achievement testing has generated a major educational industry. Millions of tests are given every year. Quite obviously, this would not be the case if standardized tests did not provide useful information.

Historically, the major purpose of these tests has been to assess an individual's achievement level compared to some average, such as a national norm. Recently, however, this purpose has expanded to include measuring the performance relative to specific instructional objectives.

Carefully constructed achievement tests have served these purposes well. In fact, such commonly used terms as "achieving at-grade-level" have evolved from our use of standardized achievement tests, where "grade level" is defined as the average performance of some well-defined national norm group.

However, standardized tests are not without limitations. Some of these limitations are serious, while others are relatively unimportant. In addition, some limitations are due to the unrealistic expectations placed on tests. In the following sections, we will examine some of the most frequently cited limitations.

Testing Time and Disruptions

One common complaint, especially among students, is that standardized achievement tests take up a large amount of class time and disrupt the school schedule. These tests do take time to administer; some batteries may take the majority of a week's class time.

The relevance of this complaint depends on two things; (1) the value of the information gained from the tests; and (2) the extent of opportunity lost during the testing time. We have seen the kind of information that such tests provide. The amount of information produced—in terms of both the number of content areas tested and the accuracy of each score—is directly related to the length of the test. Thus, to produce accurate scores over several content areas, lengthy testing is required. In terms of opportunity costs, giving up part of one week in a school year for testing hardly seems like a critical loss of instructional opportunity.

Timing of Test Administration

Some teachers feel that a fall administration of a standardized achievement test will provide information in sufficient time to make individualized student instructional plans. Unfortunately, this is a great misconception. Teachers wait weeks for test results to be returned, upset with the fact that this important information was not available when it would have been most useful.

This is a case of an unrealistic expectation. Teachers should be aware of what information the test scores will provide and when they can expect to receive the results. Standardized test results can supplement other information about students' performance, but they cannot be expected to do more than they were designed to do.

Test Scores—Specific or Global?

Some people believe that standardized test scores are either too global or too specific to be useful. This complaint often emerges when there are competing uses for test scores. A test that is selected because it provides useful information regarding broad content areas may not provide the detailed information that teachers find useful. On the other hand, a test that provides scores on very specific objectives may not serve the purpose of an administrator who needs an overall measure for a content area.

It is unrealistic to expect that a single test can do all things for all people. Ideally, a test is designed to do a specific job well; it may not (even should not) do other jobs equally well. If different kinds of scores are needed, more than one achievement test must be used.

Accuracy of Test Scores

When standardized achievement test scores are used as the basis of decisions, there is a tendency to treat the scores as infallible, as though they had no error component. The standard error of measurement reported for each subtest gives some idea about how much a test score may fluctuate from one occasion to the next. In essence, the standard error of measurement indicates how accurate the test score is. Of course, decisions that are based on test scores should also consider their relative accuracy.

Test Scores in Isolation

Achievement test scores are but one indicator of student performance. They are most useful when considered along with other measures of student performance. When they are used as the sole criterion in decision making, there is bound to be some dissatisfaction with the outcome. Achievement tests are good measures of *what they are intended to measure,* but they do not include all aspects of student performance.

Item Content

Critics of standardized achievement tests remark that the test content determines what is covered in the curriculum, rather than the curriculum determining what is included in the test. The procedures used in determining the content emphasis of test items (including the description from the ITBS described earlier in this chapter) suggest that this fear is unfounded.

Teachers and administrators decide what is taught in the schools. If they use standardized achievement tests to help them know what is commonly taught around the country, then the test may help shape the curriculum, but in a positive way.

Norms versus Standards

A final concern of norm-referenced standardized achievement tests is that norms are sometimes interpreted as standards. Achieving "at-grade-level" becomes a standard of performance that is sought for all students. But this level of achievement is, by definition, *average* for the students in a particular grade. Since about half of the students are, by definition, below the average, it is impossible for them all to achieve at-grade-level.

This kind of misinterpretation of standardized tests should in no way diminish the value of these tests. However, it does point out the need to educate the public about what test scores do and do not mean. Unfortunately, this type of misinterpretation is sometimes done by educators, as well as the general public.

Another related problem is that average performance is a measure of *actual* performance, not necessarily *good* performance. The average performance may be quite high or quite low, very poor, or very good. Being below a very high average may still indicate a high level of performance. On the other hand, being above a low average may actually represent an inadequate level of performance. For example, a seventh-grade student who performs at the 99th percentile on a French test may still be unable to order a meal at a French restaurant. "Good" performance is relative.

> Standardized achievement tests do have limitations. However, some of these limitations are due to unreasonable expectations, and misunderstanding what the test can provide.

SUMMARY

Standardized achievement tests are widely used in our schools. There are many tests on the market, available in a variety of forms, including norm-referenced and criterion-referenced tests, as well as tests built from selected objectives that are linked to banks of items.

Test results can be reported for individual students, classrooms, or even school buildings. In addition, local and national norms are available for many tests.

Publishers of standardized achievement tests are guided by *Standards For Educational and Psychological Tests* (1974). These guidelines can also be used by consumers to evaluate the test information that publishers provide.

Despite their popular use, standardized achievement tests do have certain limitations. Some of these deal with the time required for the test administration and the processing of test scores. Other limitations concern the usefulness and accuracy of the reported scores. Some people worry that the *average* performance has become a *standard* of performance and that achievement tests may have too much influence over school curricula.

High-quality standardized achievement tests are available; they do the job that they were designed to do. However, when tests are used for other purposes, their effectiveness will be limited. Therefore, those who select standardized achievement tests must do a careful and complete job of comparing alternatives.

The major determinant of the appropriateness of a standardized achievement test is the match between the items and what was actually taught in the schools. Technical adequacy and cost are factors, as well.

Standardized achievement tests are perhaps our best example of high-quality testing in education. Careful item preparation, extensive reliability and validity studies, well-designed norm groups, and clear reporting formats combine to make standardized achievement tests useful, accurate measures of student performance.

KEY TERMS AND CONCEPTS

Standardized achieve-
   ment test
Relevance

Technical adequacy
Usability
Item-bank test

REVIEW ITEMS

1. *Standards for Educational and Psychological Tests* divides tests into three major categories based on:
    a. the test content, attitude, aptitude, and achievement.
    b. the age range of the examinees.
    c. the degree to which adequate validity data is presented.
    d. the level of training needed to interpret the test scores.

2. The thing that is most "standardized" about standardized tests is:
    a. the scoring of the test.
    b. the testing conditions.
    c. the training of the test administrator.
    d. the format in which the scores are reported.

3. Once a test has been thoroughly validated, there is no need to revalidate it.

       T   F

4. A major purpose of norm-referenced standardized achievement tests is to:
   a. provide accurate predictions of subsequent performance.
   b. report present levels of performance in objective terms.
   c. diagnose school and community factors that affect achievement standards.
   d. determine whether the performance levels of particular students or schools are adequate.

5. The criterion of adequate performance on criterion-referenced standardized achievement tests is usually set:
   a. locally.
   b. by the test publisher.
   c. at the state level.
   d. in accordance with each student's level of ability.

6. If a standardized achievement test lacks relevance, it does not have adequate:
   a. predictive validity.
   b. reliability.
   c. norm groups.
   d. content validity.

7. The complaint that standardized achievement tests take up too much class time is legitimate if:
   a. the test scores go unused.
   b. the test requires more than one-half day of class time.
   c. the test cannot be used as a teaching tool.
   d. the students complain about the test length.

8. A test that is useful for the purposes of school administrators is very likely useful for classroom teachers, as well.

   T   F

9. The complaint that the content of standardized achievement tests often shapes the schools' curriculum is:
   a. true in a large number of schools.
   b. evidence that tests are more influential than textbooks.
   c. a strong reason to limit testing.
   d. largely unfounded.

10. Which of the following resources would be helpful to a school committee charged with selecting a standardized achievement test?

    a. Buros' *Mental Measurements Yearbook*.

    b. *Standards for Educational and Psychological Tests*.

    c. specimen sets of each test considered.

    (d.) all of these would be helpful.

EXERCISES

9.1 Read reviews of two or three standardized achievement tests in Buros' *Mental Measurements Yearbook*. Compare the reviewers' comments on reliability, validity, and norms.

9.2 Suppose one of your pupils scores at the 52d percentile, which is the 5th stanine nationally but the 38th percentile or 4th stanine locally. Explain how you would describe test performance to his parents using local and national norms (percentiles and stanines).

9.3 Would you expect teachers to prefer norm-referenced or criterion-referenced standardized achievement tests? What about school principals? Explain your response.

9.4 Compare actual test items from a specimen set of an achievement test to the knowledge and abilities called for in an arithmetic textbook. Discuss whether that test is relevant for that text.

9.5 Review the *Profile Narrative Report* in Figure 9.1. Then describe which test users would probably prefer the narrative description to the bar graphs. Which test users would prefer the columns of stanines and percentiles to the narrative report?

9.6 Describe the advantages and disadvantages of creating a unique test for a school district using the item-bank approach as opposed to using a test that is the same for all districts.

REFERENCES

Buros, O. K., ed. 1978. *Mental measurements yearbook*. 8th ed. Highland Park, N.J.: Gryphon Press.

Ferney, G., ed. 1977. *SCORE criterion referenced testing service: Reading and language arts objectives*. Iowa City: Houghton-Mifflin.

————. 1977. *SCORE criterion referenced testing service: Mathematics objectives.* Iowa City: Houghton-Mifflin.

Hieronymous, A. N., E. F. Lindquist, and H. O. Hoover. 1982. *Manual for administrators, Iowa Test of Basic Skills.* Chicago: Riverside.

1983. *Journal of Educational Measurement* 20 (Summer): 2.

Scannell, Dale P. 1982. *Manual for tests of achievement and proficiency.* Chicago: Riverside.

1974. *Standards for educational and psychological tests.* Washington, D.C.: American Psychological Association.

10

Performance Tests and Work Samples

Many of the learning outcomes intended from elementary and secondary school instruction can be measured by paper-and-pencil tests. Certainly, such tests—teacher-constructed and published—are used widely, especially for measuring outcomes in the cognitive domain.

However, in areas such as vocational and laboratory skills, learning outcomes commonly must include the *process* in order to obtain meaningful measurement. And in some areas, a *product* (other than something put on paper) receives the emphasis of the measurement. Areas such as auto mechanics involve *both* process and product outcomes; that is, the process for fixing a defective car is measured along with the end product—whether or not the car operates properly after the repair is completed.

Process is important in areas other than vocational skills. For example, the procedure of conducting a scientific experiment involves process. The organization and manipulation of scientific apparatus might, in part, be measured by a paper-and-pencil test, but it would also require a demonstration. Tests of typing speed and accuracy also require a demonstration. This type of test is commonly called a **performance test**.

Even in typical academic areas, not all measurement is conducted through tests. Students complete reports, problem solutions, and projects of various sorts, all of which are evaluated. And, if they are evaluated, some measurement must be done. This type of nontest product is called a **work sample,** because it represents a sampling of student performance. Most importantly, this sample is not obtained through a typical testing situation, providing an alternative form of measurement.

Characteristics of Performance Tests

Performance tests are available in a variety of forms. They may be simple and of short duration, or they may be complex and extended. For instance, a teacher may observe a student conducting some process and evaluate what he has done on one or more criteria. Perhaps the sequence in which various parts of the process were done is considered important. Or maybe the efficiency of the process, in terms of the time required or the number of errors, is to be evaluated.

Typically, performance tests elicit a subjective judgment from the teacher that serves as a measurement of student achievement. The scoring system may be a simple dichotomy—satisfactory or unsatisfactory—or perhaps a more complex method may be used. In some situations, a relatively extensive system of points may be involved, leading to multiple levels of performance scores. However, the length of the performance does not necessarily influence the number of possible performance levels. For example, in medical school, a student may spend two or three months in a specialty clerkship (such as pediatrics or surgery), which is basically an extended performance test. However, the final grade may be nothing more complex than satisfactory or unsatisfactory, or possibly not pass, pass, or honors.

Some type of written performance record is usually maintained; this may be a **checklist** or another form specifically developed for the performance. The written record contains important aspects of the performance, criteria by which the performance is evaluated, and perhaps even space for comments. **Rating scales,** which provide ordinal scale measurement, are often used on such forms. Whatever the case, there should be specific points by which to evaluate the performance.

In elementary and secondary schools, performance tests tend to be short, from a few minutes to a class period in length. The tests may be regularly scheduled, such as assigning students to give speeches at designated intervals. Or performance tests may be included in a sequence of instructional activities, such as conducting laboratory experiments in science. Whatever the case, performance tests are used extensively in the measurement of student achievement.

> Performance tests are non–paper-and-pencil tests that require the student to engage in some process, to produce a product, or both.

Examples of Performance Tests

In order to illustrate performance tests, we will review examples from elementary and secondary schools, as provided below. Of course, required performances cannot be reproduced through the written page, but their descriptions should be adequate for illustration purposes.

Elementary School Science Example

Aho et al. (1974) have published an evaluation program for the *Elementary Science Study* (ESS), an openended, activity-centered science program. The program has five major overarching goals, summarized as:

1. Rational thinking processes
2. Manipulation
3. Communication
4. Concepts
5. Attitudes (Aho et al. 1974, iv)

These major goals have varying levels of subgoals. For example, rational thinking processes also contain observation, classification, and measurement. In the evaluation program, each ESS unit deals with specific unit objectives, related to the overarching goals, and observable student behaviors are identified for meeting the unit objectives.

There are 56 ESS units, each of which contains unit objectives. Teachers select unit objectives relevant to the instruction in their classrooms. ESS units are appropriate for more than one grade, and a student may encounter a unit several times while in elementary school. In fact, some units have content that is applicable in various forms across grades K–9, while others are limited to use in only two or three grades. Although ESS materials suggest grade levels, the emphasis is on student needs and individualization. Specifically, the evaluation program states:

> Because of the multi-age design and provisions for individualizing instruction in each ESS unit, evaluation objectives are designated by levels:
>
> A. Basic (B)
> *Evaluation objectives at a lower level of achievement. Almost every student in the class should be able to achieve at this level.*
>
> B. Intermediate (I)
> *Evaluation objectives at a higher level of achievement. The majority of the students should be able to achieve at this level.*
>
> C. Advanced (A)
> *Evaluation objectives at a still higher level. Students achieving at this level will have outperformed the majority of their classmates. (Aho et al. 1974, v)*

The evaluation objectives are performance based, and, in this sense, they comprise performance tests. We will consider three unit objectives, each having more than one evaluation objective. The level of the evaluation objective is identified above: basic (B), intermediate (I), and advanced (A). The overarching goals (called *goal areas*) are also specified for the evaluation objectives.

Table 10.1.
Example Performance Test from Elementary Science
Involving Small Animals and an Activity Wheel

UNIT OBJECTIVE 2.   The student will observe an animal's use of the activity wheel.

Evaluation Objective	Goal Area
B. The student will observe and describe orally how an animal uses the activity wheel.	Rational thinking process (Observation), Communication
I. The student will observe and write a descriptive statement about how an animal uses the activity wheel.	Rational thinking process (Observation), Communication
I. The student will describe how different animals use the activity wheel.	Rational thinking process (Observation), Communication
I. The student will observe and describe the behavior of an animal when the activity wheel is made difficult to turn.	Rational thinking process (Observation), Communication

---

B = basic; I = intermediate; A = advanced
   Source: From Elementary Science Study unit involving small animals and an activity wheel, with permission of Education Development Center, Inc., Newton, MA.

Animal Activity Example.   The first example includes four evaluation objectives, one at the basic (B) level and three at the intermediate (I) level. This performance test requires that the students have access to small mammals (such as hamsters or mice) in cages, as well as an activity wheel (see Table 10.1). Note that all objectives relate to the goal areas *rational thinking process* and *communication*. This performance test is applicable for grades 4–6.

Budding Twigs Example.   The next example contains three evaluation objectives, all of intermediate level. The required equipment for this performance test is quite minimal: a small twig (approximately ¼" in diameter), water in a container, and food coloring (see Table 10.2). The evaluation objectives are directed to the goal area *rational thinking process*. In addition, the first objective is also directed to *manipulation* and the third objective to *communication*. This performance test would apply for intermediate grade levels, primarily grades 4–6; it may also be useful for testing accelerated third-grade students.

Optics Example.   The three evaluation objectives in this example are at the basic, intermediate, and advanced levels (see Table 10.3). Students require a number of mirrors and a probe stick in order to do the tasks of this performance test. All evaluation objectives are directed to the goal areas of *rational thinking process* and *communication*. This performance test is appropriate for the intermediate grades, 4 through 6.

Table 10.2.
Example Performance Test from Elementary Science
Involving Budding Twigs Placed in Water

UNIT OBJECTIVE 9. Given one or more twigs, the student will investigate water conduction.	

Evaluation Objective	Goal Area
I. The student will devise and conduct a test with a twig, container, and food coloring, to identify how water is carried to the buds.	Rational thinking process (Making and Testing Hypotheses), Manipulation
I. The student will remove various parts of the stem and observe the effect on the buds when the twigs are placed in water.	Rational thinking process (Observation)
I. The student will describe the results of his water-stem investigation with a picture story or written report.	Rational thinking process (Data Collection and Organization), Communication

B = basic; I = intermediate; A = advanced
Source: From Elementary Science Study unit involving budding twigs placed in water, with permission of Education Development Center, Inc., Newton, MA.

Table 10.3.
Example Performance Test from Elementary Science
Involving an Experiment on the Reflection of Light

UNIT OBJECTIVE 5. Given sufficient opportunity to observe the reflection of a beam of light onto a screen, the student will test to determine whether or not the light he sees on the screen is truly being reflected by his mirrors.	

Evaluation Objective	Goal Area
B. Using two mirrors to reflect a beam of light onto a screen, the student will move either mirror and observe and report the simultaneous movement of light on the screen.	Rational thinking process (Making and Testing Hypotheses), Communication
I. Using three or four mirrors to reflect a beam of light onto a screen, the student will move any of the mirrors and observe and report the simultaneous movement of light on the screen.	Rational thinking process (Making and Testing Hypotheses), Communication
A. Using four mirrors and a probe stick, the student will observe and report the casting of a shadow on the screen when the probe stick is placed directly in front of any of the mirrors.	Rational thinking process (Making and Testing Hypotheses), Communication

B = basic; I = intermediate; A = advanced
Source: From Elementary Science Study unit involving an experiment on th reflection of light, with permission of Education Development Center, Inc., Newton, MA.

Evaluation of Performance.   To evaluate these performance tests, the teacher uses a checklist indicating the tasks of the evaluation objectives that have been completed successfully by students. The checklist then becomes a record of the student's performance, which may be used for grading and feedback purposes. The ESS materials do not provide specific checklists. Thus, the teacher has considerable flexibility in constructing specialized checklists and establishing criteria for acceptable performance. An example checklist for evaluating the performance test involving small animals and an activity wheel is given in Figure 10.1. This checklist deals with the student's observation and oral description. If a written statement were required, those additional points expected in the statement would be included in the checklist. With a relatively short checklist (such as the one in Figure 10.1), the criterion for satisfactory performance might be quite simple, such as receiving checkmarks under yes for all items.

It is also possible to maintain an **anecdotal record** for each student, if this is desirable. For instance, the third evaluation objective of Unit Objective 9 (Table 10.2) requires a product—a picture story or written report—that would be evaluated using appropriate criteria. For instance, one of the criteria would be that all steps of the process be listed in the report.

Vocational Example: Plumbing

Vocational courses—including areas such as secretarial, plumbing, food services, and auto mechanics—are usually found at the high school level and are highly performance oriented. The performance test described in Table 10.4 is from a plumbing course. A performance objective is specified for the test, and the performance guide lists the activities of the task in sequence. This performance test also has a criterion-referenced measure that refers to the evaluation of the performance.

This evaluation is conducted through the use of the Instructor Checklist (given in Figure 10.2), which contains eight items. The criterion for satisfactory performance is to receive yes for all eight items. An unsatisfactory score (no) on one or more of the items (which represent subtasks of the overall task) would result in an unsatisfactory test performance.

The establishment of standards always involves some arbitrary decisions. Vocational areas derive their standards from one or a combination of four sources:

1. Codes, local or state, that apply to work or products in the vocational area.
2. Accepted practices within the business or industry.
3. Criteria set by the instructor.
4. Manufacturer's recommended standards.

Thus, with specifications and suggestions from these sources, the identification of criteria for satisfactory test performance is usually quite straightforward.

Figure 10.1.
An Example Checklist for Evaluating Performance Test from Elementary Science

Evaluation Checklist

UNIT OBJECTIVE 2. The student will observe an animal's use of the activity wheel.

Based on student observation of the animal and the description provided by the student:

The student:	*Yes*	*No*
1. described the forward motion of the animal in using the wheel.	————	————
2. commented on the animal's desire (motivation) in using the wheel.	————	————
3. identified a minimum of two similarities in the activities of two or more different animals as they use the activity wheel.	————	————
4. identified a minimum of two differences in the activities of two or more different animals as they use the activity wheel.	————	————
5. identified the animal's behavioral change when the wheel was made more difficult to turn.	————	————

Table 10.4.
An Example Performance Test from a Plumbing Course

TASK: Secure with hangers horizontal and vertical lines of pipe to masonry surfaces.

PERFORMANCE OBJECTIVES:
Given an assortment of hangers, necessary tools and equipment, and lengths of pipe of different kinds and sizes, hang one pipe horizontally and one vertically to a masonry surface. The correct hanger must be chosen for the selected pipe. Work will be gauged by checklist with all items to be rated yes for satisfactory performance.

PERFORMANCE GUIDE:
1. Select pipe, position, and needed hanger.
2. Locate hanger points on surface.
3. Prepare surface (if needed).
4. Secure hanger or hanger section (whichever needed) to surface.
5. Attach hanger clamp portion to pipe (if needed).
6. Hoist pipe into position for hanger acceptance.
7. Secure pipe to hanger.

CRITERION-REFERENCED MEASURE:
Placement and attachment with hangers, horizontal and vertical lines of pipe to masonry surfaces, using the materials furnished with satisfactory completion of all items on the Instructor's Checklist.

Source: Vocational-Technical Consortium of States (V-TECS). Used with permission.

Figure 10.2.
Evaluation Form used with the Performance Test of the Plumbing Example

---

Instructor Checklist

INSTRUCTIONS: If the performance is satisfactory, write YES in the space provided. If the performance is unsatisfactory, write NO in the space. Each item must be rated yes for satisfactory task performance.

- _____ 1. Were hangers properly selected for each pipe and working surface?
- _____ 2. Were hangers affixed correctly?
- _____ 3. Are vertical pipes secured at 90 degrees to the floor surface?
- _____ 4. Are overhead pipes at proper angle to the floor surface?
- _____ 5. Are distances between hangers correct for pipe used?
- _____ 6. Is the pipe or tubing secure?
- _____ 7. Is work neatly done?
- _____ 8. Does installation comply with local codes?

Source: Vocational-Technical Education Consortium of States (V-TECS). Used with permission.

Vocational Example: Secretarial

Business-related education areas, such as secretarial training, are heavily performance oriented; thus, performance tests are commonly used. Students are required to perform in areas such as typing, shorthand, and the use of dictating equipment. A number of performance tests are available, corresponding to specific materials and programs.

The example discussed below (Lessenberry et al. 1972) involves typing at a somewhat advanced level, specifically, typing business letters. It is appropriate for use in a secondary-level, advanced course for secretarial training (see Table 10.5).

The directions for the test are given in Numbers 1 and 2 under "DO"; the specifications for each of the three business letters are given in the "Problem" statement preceding the letter. Students are given a specified amount of time to type the three letters. The time factor is part of the evaluation in that the total word content is divided by the number of minutes (usually 20–30) the student types.

The performance evaluation is based on a "Mailable Copy Rate," which is a words-per-minute rate at which mailable copy is produced. It involves both the quantity and quality of copy produced; it is not simply limited to gross words per minute, a commonly used measure of typing output.

The criteria for judging the quality of the produced copy (letters) are given in Table 10.6. Descriptive criteria are listed as items: M indicates mailable; NM, not mailable; and F indicates completely unacceptable performance—in essence, a

Table 10.5.
An Example Performance Test from a Secretarial Training Course: Typing of Business Letters

DO: For each of Letters 1, 2, and 3:

1. Study the appropriate style letter in the Reference Guide, page v.
2. Determine margins and dateline position for the letter length indicated. (See Reference Guide, page vii.)

Problem 1: Block Letter with Open Punctuation

	Words
Miss Patricia M. Sheridan 1603 Britton	11
Road, N.W. Oklahoma City, OK 73120	18
Dear Miss Sheridan (¶ 1) Thank you very	25
much for your application for a Howe's charge	34
account. We value your patronage. (¶ 2) We	42
are very sorry that there has been a delay in	51
processing your application. This delay is due	61
to the unusual number of requests for our	69
charge cards, and we are making every effort	78
to provide you with this shopping convenience	87
as soon as possible. (¶ 3) You can expect to	95
hear from us in a few days. Sincerely B. J.	104
Clark New Accounts Department (xxx) (78)	111/126

Problem 2: Block Letter with Mixed Punctuation

	Words
Mr. Donald Jones 1548 Maple Street York,	11
PA 17403 Dear Mr. Jones (¶ 1) Your	18
letter of May 16 addressed to our main office	27
in Chicago has been forwarded to me for reply.	36
(¶ 2) Complete repair services for your SUN-	44
BURY Electric Mixer are available in our	52
Lancaster store, which is located at the corner	62
of Broad and Vine Streets. The store is open	71
Monday through Friday from 8 a.m. until	79
5 p.m. and on Saturday from 8 a.m. until 1 p.m.	88
If you do not wish to visit our store personally,	98
you may mail your SUNBURY mixer to us.	106
We will repair it promptly and return it to you	116
free of any charge. Sincerely yours Alexander	126
C. Billingsley Manager (xxx) (103)	131/141

Problem 3: Modified Block Letter
with Indented Paragraphs and Mixed Punctuation

	Words
National Department Stores, Inc. 4500 Michi-	12
gan Boulevard Chicago, IL 60615 Atten-	19
tion Mr. John L. Schmitt, Purchasing Officer	28

Table 10.5.
Continued

Gentlemen Subject: Your Order #4729A	36
(¶ 1) Thank you for your order for 5,000 of	44
our Model T6145 transistor radios to be mar-	52
keted under your brand name, "NATCO." We	61
know you will find our transistor radio a qual-	70
ity item that will please your customers. (¶ 2)	79
In our conversation last week, you indicated	88
that you were satisfied with the terms of sale	97
we offered with the exception of the delivery	106
schedule. After discussing this matter with our	116
chief of production, I am pleased to say that	125
we can deliver the radios as you requested.	134
Production on the radios will begin as soon as	144
you send us the design of the crest to be em-	152
bossed on the carrying case. (¶ 3) It has been	161
a great pleasure working with you on this	169
order. We hope that it marks the beginning of	179
a mutually satisfactory and profitable associa-	188
tion. Sincerely yours Ralph C. Henderson	196
Director of Marketing (xxx) (158)	201/216

Source: Century 21 Typewriting, Lessenberry, Crawford, Erickson, Beaumont, and Robinson. Copyright 1972, South-Western Publishing Co. Used by permission of South-Western Publishing Co.

disaster. Again, there is some subjectivity in evaluating the performance. However, the criteria are quite descriptive of the completed product and typing errors that are deviations from the criteria can be identified. Standards of acceptable perform- ance are usually set by the teachers, but acceptable minimum performance stan- dards for employment may be used when available.

The recent addition of sophisticated equipment (such as word processors) to the office has extended the typist's role to include knowledge of such machines. Com- panies that manufacture this equipment provide detailed manuals for its operation; using these manuals, students can learn to operate the various machines available in the business classroom. Subsequently, they can be tested by performing the pro- cedures outlined in the manuals.

For example, the CPT Corporation word processor has a procedure for adding text, which is described in the manual:

To add text or space:
1. Position the line requiring additional text or space on the typing line.
2. Position the pointer exactly where the first character or space should be added.
3. Touch the HOLD key once to turn HOLD on.

Table 10.6.
Criteria for Evaluating Performance
on the Secretarial Training Performance Test

M+ Item: (Weighted as 100 percent of the word count of an item)

1. Typed without error of any kind.
2. Very few corrections, all neatly made.

M Item: (Weighted as 90 percent of the word count of an item)

1. Enclosure notation omitted.
2. Less than ideal placement.
3. Minor deviation from given directions.
4. Neatly made but an excessive number of corrections.
5. Acceptable but undesirable division of words.
6. Acceptable but not the most desirable capitalization rules followed.
7. For shorthand transcription, minor deviations from exact dictation but with the same meaning.

NM Item: (Weighted as 0 percent of the word count of an item)

1. Poorly made corrections.
2. Incorrect salutation.
3. Errors due to lack of knowledge (excluding errors of punctuation, spelling, and grammar).
4. For shorthand transcription, deviation from exact dictation with changed meaning.

F. Item: (Weighted as 0 percent of the word count of an item)

1. Uncorrected typographical errors.
2. Uncorrected, obvious strikeover errors.
3. Misspelled words.
4. Essential punctuation violations.
5. Basic grammar violations.
6. Omissions from typed or dictated material which are obvious when proofread.

Only mailable work earns any mailable-word-count credit. The small penalty of 10 percent of word count assessed against the mailable letter is easy to calculate and differentiates the M letter but slightly from the higher quality M+ product.

Source: Developed by Ester Anderson, Professor of Business Education, University of Toledo. Used with permission.

4. Type the additional characters or space.
5. Touch the HOLD key once to turn HOLD off.

To add missing text to a page:
1. Position the line that is missing text directly below the margin scale.
2. Touch the RETURN key to create a blank typing line.

3. Adjust the existing text to the point where the missing text should be added.
4. Type the missing text.
5. Repeat steps 3 and 4 until all missing text has been added to the page.
6. Adjust the remaining text. (Westreich et al. 1983, 3–19)

A student can be tested on this procedure by demonstrating the addition of text to a line. For example, this sentence:

> The committee meeting will be held prior to the meeting of the Board of Directors.

might be changed to:

> The committee meeting will be held June 20, 1985, in Suite A of the Plaza Hotel, prior to the meeting of the Board of Directors.

Additional items could be included. Performance would be judged either correct or incorrect.

> Designating performance levels for tests in vocational areas is often influenced by minimal acceptable performance standards of potential employers. Such standards are helpful in establishing realistic criteria for evaluating performance.

Constructing Performance Tests

The construction of performance tests requires attention to detail, as does the construction of any test. However, performance tests introduce additional considerations not relevant to typical paper-and-pencil tests. A primary factor is that performance tests must approximate the real situation and natural performance conditions. This may introduce problems of equipment and facilities and thus complicate administration of the test. To help alleviate some of these problems, Gronlund (1982) has specified the following four-step procedure for constructing performance tests:

1. Specify the performance outcomes to be measured.
2. Select an appropriate degree of realism.
3. Prepare instructions that clearly specify the test situation.
4. Prepare the observational form to be used in evaluating performance. (1982, 87–90)

The specific performance test under consideration determines the amount of attention each step requires. For example, the performance tests of the elementary school science example discussed earlier do not require a great degree of realism. The experiments of the tests can be conducted easily within the typical classroom, provided the necessary equipment is available.

The objectives of a performance test typically include action verbs. They may focus on process or product outcomes but, more commonly, both are implied. For example, in chemistry, this objective might be used:

The student will assemble, in the appropriate sequence, apparatus for an oxygen release experiment.

This objective emphasizes process, although a correctly assembled apparatus is certainly an implied outcome, as well.

Here is an objective for secretarial skills training:

The student will type three mailable business letters within a maximum of 20 minutes.

The three mailable business letters comprise the product, but they are produced through the typing process.

> Performance tests commonly involve both process- and product-type outcomes.

Generally, the degree of realism associated with a performance test depends upon two factors: (1) how much is required in order to adequately test the intended performance; and (2) how much is feasible within the educational setting. With respect to the first factor, for knowledge-level outcomes, paper-and-pencil tests may be adequate, requiring little simulation of the real situation. But as students advance in the sequence of instruction, more realism is required. In an auto mechanics course, for example, a knowledge level of tools can be measured using a paper-and-pencil test. But to measure performance in auto repair requires a realistic situation with tools, an auto, and appropriate space and facilities.

The auto mechanics shops found in most vocational schools come quite close to simulating real working conditions. Performance tests in business education courses are often conducted in a classroom setting with considerable equipment, but the physical trappings of a business office are seldom present, especially those of a private secretary.

In some areas of study, performance testing is conducted in the real situation. This is essentially what happens when student teachers are observed by their supervisors. Testing in the real situation may also occur in some secondary-level work-study programs when student workers are evaluated by their teachers or employers. Overall, the extent of realism for performance testing varies considerably from area to area, and even within an area, as instruction progresses.

> The extent of realism in performance testing is determined by two factors: how much is required to test the intended performance and how much is feasible in the given situation.

The test instructions for a performance test must be detailed and complete so there is no confusion about what is expected of students. Directions for performance tests usually require more specification of conditions (such as required equipment) than is necessary for paper-and-pencil tests. Instructions may be in written form or read orally to the students, depending upon the specific situation. If possible, it is best to provide written instructions and then review them with the students prior to the test. This is often done when a performance test is administered to an entire class.

The observational form or checklist that contains the performance criteria should be carefully developed before any performance is scored. Not even the first performance should be observed or scored without using carefully constructed criteria. Otherwise, that performance may become the basis for scoring subsequent performances. Simple rating scales, often with scores from 0 to 4 or 1 to 5, and yes/no-type checklists are commonly used.

Ratings are qualitative judgments about a process or product. As indicated before, standards for satisfactory performance are quite often arbitrary; some subjectivity is always involved. Anyone using rating scales should be aware of these limitations, since they may cause error in the measurement. However, it is important that some prepared evaluation form be in hand to guide the measurement of performance.

In summary, constructing performance tests requires much effort: effort focused on obtaining an appropriate task with adequate realism, clear directions for the students, and a means by which the performance can be evaluated. Curriculum materials often contain performance tests or information about tasks that can be used in developing such tests. Sometimes tests may need to be individualized or administered on an individual basis. The nature of the performance being tested determines the specific test conditions.

Work Samples

Testing is by no means the only method that provides information for evaluating student learning. A good deal of information is obtained through the daily contact between students and teachers. One method of obtaining information is through work samples.

The use of the term *work sample* is not entirely consistent among writers. For example, Gronlund (1982, 84) uses work samples to indicate the highest degree of realism in performance testing. However, we will use the term to mean a sample of student performance not obtained through a typical testing situation. In other words, a work sample is a nontest product of student learning.

Samples might represent any number of products—handwriting, spelling, drawing, report preparation, problem solutions, and science projects, to mention a few examples. And since work samples are done under nontesting conditions, time restrictions, freedom of movement, use of reference materials, and the like are not involved. For instance, everyday homework, handed in and graded, is a work sample.

Work samples are usually written, but nonwritten work can also be assessed. Examples of nonwritten work include oral reading and demonstrating a science experiment. For the latter, a student would be observed while conducting the experiment; in addition, the result of the experiment also may be some product that can be evaluated.

> Work samples consist of student products generated in nontesting situations.

Written Reports as Work Samples

In areas such as social studies and science, students are often required to prepare reports on a specified topic, such as a country or industry. An extensive report would require student behaviors that relate to several objectives. Language arts skills are required, as well as knowledge and comprehension of the topic. Synthesis behaviors may also be required in order to pull the report together. Before evaluating this type of report, a list of criteria should be prepared by the teacher and then explained to the students. There should be no mystery about the nature of these criteria. Students must know what is expected of them.

The criteria by which a report is evaluated may vary somewhat, depending upon the objectives that the report is to meet. However, there are criteria of organization, neatness, spelling, and grammar that are relevant to practically any report. Additional criteria might be used in a combination, such as:

1. Inclusion of relevant points.
2. Comprehensiveness of the coverage of the topic.
3. Continuity of the ideas in the report.
4. Relating the major points in the report.
5. Recognizing major and minor points.

Teachers may find it useful to sample pages from each report and carefully check such routine things as spelling and punctuation. Of course, the entire report will need to be read for content.

It is not feasible for us to include an entire report as an example work sample. However, Figure 10.3 contains a sample page from a report on woodland animals prepared by an elementary school student.

The criteria by which a report is evaluated are important, but it is very unlikely they will produce a mastery-nonmastery dichotomy of evaluation. For example, consider the criteria of "having correct punctuation." Teachers can identify and count punctuation errors, but it is doubtful that a criterion such as "fewer than six punctuation errors in a report indicates mastery of punctuation skills" will be used. Rather, the criterion of "correct punctuation" is used as a quality for which students should strive. For instance, if a student who usually makes an excessive number of punctuation errors is able to reduce that number with each new report, progress is being made toward attaining the criterion. Although the student may still not be a master writer, he is moving in that direction.

The primary value of this sort of work sample evaluation lies in the learning experience it provides for the student. The teacher can show the student the errors he has made and how they can be corrected. The student and teacher should also discuss major weaknesses, such as sentence structure or organization, and how these things can be improved upon. Overall, it is important that the teacher not concentrate entirely on the errors or weak points of the student's performance; evaluation should include the strong points, as well. The student should be praised for the things he has done well and encouraged to set new goals.

Comments About Observation

The teacher's day-to-day classroom activities include a lot of observation. Observation may be more or less formally structured. For example, a student taking a performance test in conducting a science experiment will probably be observed using a checklist or rating scale. On the other hand, teachers often observe students' impromptu behaviors, which reflect achievement, learning styles, and attitudes. The information obtained from such observation is usually quite subjective. It may not provide a measure of student performance, but it does reflect how the student and class are managed and how instruction takes place.

Numerous systematic observation inventories are available for providing a record of teacher behavior, student behavior, and student-teacher interaction. Many of these inventories were developed in a research context in the 1960s and 1970s, for which it was necessary to have an objective record of classroom interaction. Early examples of such inventories include Observation Schedule and Record Form 5 Ver-

The first shot is the most power-ful, but there is enough ammunition for six succesive "shots." After the "magazine" is empty it is a little while before it is reloaded.

The skunk uses it's ammunition only as a last resort.

A direct hit at close range will cause tears to flow freely and may cause temporary blindness.

Easy Going ways of the Skunk.

Perfectly aware of it's power of defense, the skunk is slow and deliberate in it's actions. If not bothered, it walks along good-naturedly. Now and then it will stop to dig up a nest of wasps, with it's sharp claws and eat the grubs, for insects are a staple in their diet. Or it may speed up and catch a fleeing mouse, snake or frog. All kinds of creeping things are food for the skunk, as well as berries, fruits and grain. A skunk is active mostly at night. He is a nocturnal animal.

bal (OScAR 5V) (Medley 1973) and the Spaulding Teacher Activity Recording Schedule (STARS) (Spaulding 1976). A more recently developed inventory is the Classroom Observations Keyed for Effectiveness Research (COKER), which is described in a number of publications, including Coker (1982). Some observation inventories focus on the behaviors of individual students, while others examine groups of students.

The typical classroom teacher is not likely to use such inventories. Why? For one thing, their use requires special training, which teachers may not have. They are also time consuming to use on any regular basis. Furthermore, it is difficult to relate the results of such observation to student achievement without sophisticated analysis of extensive data.

The Anecdotal Record

One type of informal observation is the anecdotal record: a description of an observed event, usually one that takes place in the classroom. Anecdotal records consist of specific information about behavior; the total record does not exceed a couple of paragraphs. Observations should be recorded as soon as possible after the behavior has occurred in order to enhance objectivity. This is particularly important, since anecdotal records invariably involve some subjectivity. Teachers must strive to report and interpret objectively, avoiding personal comments.

Accumulated observations taken over time provide the teacher with useful information about individuals and how instruction might be enhanced for them and the class. An example of quite an extensive anecdotal record is given in Figure 10.4. Note how the pertinent information about when the incident occurred is provided along with the description and interpretation of the incident. The incident was recorded very soon after it occurred, and the interpretation was also made at that point. Recalling incidents from memory tends to lessen the accuracy of both the description and the interpretation.

Anecdotal records do have disadvantages. First of all, they are time consuming to record, organize, and synthesize; thus, teachers should use them sparingly so that they do not become a paperwork burden. Also, the subjectivity of anecdotal records may introduce inadvertent personal biases that may persist. If anecdotal records are passed along from one teacher to another, incorrect impressions about a student may be fostered. Because of this subjectivity, anecdotal records must be used with discretion.

Anecdotal records do provide useful qualitative information about student ability and behavior. However, this information is quite subjective in nature, perhaps to a fault. To help avoid bias and preconceptions, the teacher should provide an objective description of the event.

Figure 10.4.
An Example Anecdotal Record

Student	John Doe	Date	1/25
Observer	A.J.	Grade	7
		Subject	Science

Description of Incident:

As the science experiment got underway, John was very active in assembling equipment and assisting with necessary preparations. He knew how to approach the experiment and how to perform the necessary steps in sequence. When other students asked for explanations, John was willing to explain what he was doing and did a good job of explaining the mechanics of the experiment. When asked to read the description of the experiment from the text, John became hesitant and read it with some difficulty. Following the reading, John sat down and failed to participate in the remainder of the experiment.

Interpretation of Incident:

John tends to be mechanically inclined and enjoys manipulating things. When he can manipulate things, he is "confident" in what he is doing and confident in explaining his actions. He becomes insecure when asked to read because he has some difficulty with reading. His sensitivity about reading difficulty overshadowed the confidence he showed early in the experiment.

Thus, observation in the classroom may take on a variety of forms, formal and informal. Often, it is part of performance testing and may be the best approach to evaluating certain types of work samples, such as a student making a speech or presentation. Observation is an everyday part of teaching, but for most teachers, the information provided is qualitative and quite subjective.

Reliability and Validity of Performance Tests and Work Samples

To be useful, the results from performance tests and work samples must be valid and reliable. Usually, the validity of concern is content validity—the extent to which the knowledge and skills intended are covered by the performance test or work sample.

On occasion, we must assess predictive validity—the extent to which performance on tests or work samples predicts later success in the corresponding vocation. This is important in vocational training at the secondary level. Some published performance tests provide predictive validity information. We establish predictive validity by correlating scores on a test or work sample with later measures of job performance. However, this performance information may be difficult to obtain. For one thing, upon graduation, students scatter to various employers and no consistent measures of job performance are available. In reality, validity is often more implicit than explicit: It is assumed that performance on tests and work samples is positively related to later job success. At the very least, performance tests and work samples should be content valid.

If a performance test or work sample contains several items, internal consistency reliability can be estimated using the usual methods. When it is practical to use more than one form, reliability can be estimated using parallel forms. Published observation inventories usually contain reliability information.

It is practically impossible to establish the reliability of anecdotal records. Generally, it is inferred that the teacher observing the incident would provide the same description and interpretation if the incident occurred at another time. But, considering the subjectivity involved in recording anecdotal records, this may not be a valid inference.

> The most common validity concern of performance tests and work samples is content validity—the extent to which the knowledge and skills stated in objectives are, in fact, the basis for measurement.

SUMMARY

The use of performance tests is an important part of measurement and instruction in both elementary and secondary schools. They are used in the typical cognitive and skills areas, as well as specialized areas, such as vocational training. Performance tests introduce unique characteristics into the testing process, such as special equipment and the simulation of a real work situation.

Work samples are a day-to-day part of instruction in most elementary and secondary schools. They may take on a variety of forms, but, in general, they are produced under nontesting conditions. A good example is homework, which makes up a vast array of work samples. Although there is considerable emphasis on test results in the schools, results based on work samples also make a valuable contribution to the measurement of student performance or achievement.

The anecdotal record is an example of informal observation being used as an evaluative tool. However, most teachers use these records sparingly because they are time consuming. Nonetheless, if they are used, teachers must make certain that their observations are as objective as possible and that the records themselves are used with discretion.

KEY TERMS AND CONCEPTS

Performance test   **Rating scale**
Work sample   **Anecdotal record**
Checklist

REVIEW ITEMS

1. Performance tests in the elementary and secondary schools:
   a. are limited to measuring process.
   b. are limited to measuring product.
   c. may measure a process, a product, or both.
   d. measure neither a process nor a product.

2. Which of the following would likely be measured using a performance test?
   a. knowledge of the periodic table of the elements in chemistry.
   b. an experimental procedure in physics, illustrating the use of the basic machines.
   c. writing style in a short story written for an English class.
   d. accuracy of spelling of technical terms in medicine.

3. In which area would performance testing be least likely to be used?
   a. plumbing.
   b. cosmetology.
   c. carpentry.
   d. history.

4. Which of the following would most likely not be considered a work sample:
   a. a written report for biology class.
   b. a model of molecular structure for chemistry class.
   c. a speech given for speech class.
   d. a drawing for drafting class.

5. Anecdotal records may provide information about students, but they are not measures of student performance because they:
   a. are too subjective.
   b. are used by some teachers but not others.

c. do not result in numerical values being assigned.

d. may contain teacher bias.

6. The degree of realism for performance tests is:

   a. of more concern in vocational areas than academic areas.

   b. of more concern in academic areas than vocational areas.

   c. always of concern, regardless of the area.

   d. of little concern in either academic or vocational areas.

7. Which of the following can best be measured through a work sample?

   a. clarity of handwriting.

   b. ability to solve word problems in mathematics.

   c. accuracy in identifying examples of geometric shapes.

   d. sequence in assembling a mechanical model.

8. Among teachers, the use of observation inventories for recording student-teacher interactions are more appropriate than anecdotal records.

   T   F

9. For each of the following, indicate in the space provided on the left whether student performance would best be measured by a paper-and-pencil test (T), a performance test (P), or a work sample (W).

   W sewing project in home economics.

   W poem written for a creative writing unit.

   P applying intravenous feedings in medicine.

   T proficiency in solving algebra problems.

   W model of a building in architecture class.

   W program for the solution of a problem in a computer class.

   T proficiency in identifying individual American states in an elementary school geography unit. T

   P reading with expression in a dramatics class. P

   T readiness for advanced placement in college French. T

   P administration of physical therapy. P

10. List three possible sources for information about the establishment of standards for performance tests in vocational areas.

EXERCISES

10.1 Identify a text or set of curriculum materials in an area of your interest, and develop an appropriate performance test. Then identify criteria to be used in evaluating the performance.

10.2 Using curriculum materials from a vocational area, select a performance test. Critique the test in terms of: (1) adequate directions; and (2) adequate scoring information.

10.3 Develop a checklist of criteria for evaluating a five-page written social studies report assigned at the sixth-grade level. Then develop a similar checklist for a five-page senior high school history report. How are the criteria similar and how are they different?

10.4 Suppose an engine repair performance test is given in an auto mechanics class. Identify possible *sources* of criteria (not the criteria themselves) that will be helpful in evaluating whether or not the performance is satisfactory.

REFERENCES

Aho, William et al. 1974. *The McGraw-Hill evaluation program for ESS.* New York: McGraw-Hill.

Coker, Joan G., and Homer Coker. 1982. *Classroom observations keyed for effectiveness research, Observer training manual.* Rev. ed. Atlanta, Ga.: Georgia State University, Carroll County Teacher Corps Project.

Gronlund, N. E. 1982. *Constructing achievement tests.* 3d ed. Englewood Cliffs, N.J.: Prentice-Hall.

Lessenberry, D. D. et al. 1972. *Century 21 typewriting.* Cincinnati: South-Western Publishing Company.

Medley, Donald M. 1973. *Observation schedule and record, Form 5 verbal.* Charlottesville, Va.: University of Virginia.

Sanders, J. R., and T. P. Sachse. 1975. *Problems and potentials of applied performance testing.* Portland, Oreg.: Northwest Regional Educational Laboratory.

Spaulding, Robert L. 1976. *Spaulding Teacher Activity Rating Schedule (STARS).* San Jose, Calif.: San Jose State University.

Westreich, A. et al. 1983. *CPT 8500 series reference manual.* Minneapolis, Minn.: CPT Corporation.

11

Scholastic
and Other Aptitude Tests

In addition to cognitive achievement tests, many other tests are given in the schools. Achievement tests provide information about the student's *present level* of performance. **Aptitude tests,** on the other hand, provide information about a student's *probable level* of future performance.

Aptitude tests can be used to estimate whether a student will profit from some specific instructional programs, or they can be useful in helping a student identify career areas for which he may have special aptitudes. A measure of **aptitude** also provides a context in which to interpret achievement test scores. For instance, if a student's achievement is well below his aptitude, there is probably a need for corrective action.

Aptitude tests are useful parts of a school's testing program when they are used appropriately. This chapter presents an overview of aptitude tests, along with specific examples. We will also discuss the problems and weaknesses of aptitude tests. Again, as with achievement tests, many of these problems are the fault of the test user, not the test itself.

Our focus is on tests that help us understand those student talents and abilities related to future success in school, as well as other aspects of life. Thus, we are concerned with **scholastic aptitude** much more than **intelligence.** Figure 11.1 presents a continuum of the various purposes of tests. Basic research on the nature of intelligence is at one end, and identifying special aptitudes is at the other; predicting scholastic success from general intellectual ability is found midway. A continuum is used to suggest that tests cannot be distinctly categorized: There is always overlap, and some of the same kinds of items are used across the continuum.

An intellectual factor runs through all of these tests, sometimes as the primary construct and sometimes as one of several components; thus, these tests are usually

continuum - One extreme to the other with no definite dividing line.

231

Figure 11.1.
Continuum of Aptitude-Intelligence Tests

| Basic research on the nature of intelligence | Predicting scholastic success from general intellectual ability | Identifying special aptitudes |

thought of as cognitive measures. Nonetheless, an overlap of **cognitive, affective, and psychomotor** factors operates in any test.

The division into cognitive, affective, and psychomotor areas is basically one of convenience. Measures are not strictly cognitive nor strictly affective. Imagine an essay question on the economic factors that influenced the French Revolution. To answer such a question, the student must first understand the various social and economic forces at work in France at that time. In addition, he must be motivated to do his best and must have the motor skills to write a legible response to the question. Similarly, a student's performance on a half-mile run in physical education is dependent not only on physical abilities; knowledge of how to pace oneself and a positive attitude toward the task and physical fitness in general are also significant.

The point is simple: Large components from all three areas—cognitive, affective, and psychomotor—are involved in most testing situations. Our separation is based on the primary focus of the measurement. It is done to make the array of tests more manageable, not to subscribe to some theoretical position.

> An overlap of cognitive, affective, and psychomotor variables exists in any test. For instance, cognitive performance depends on affective and psychomotor variables and vice versa.

Scholastic Aptitude Tests

We will include intelligence and aptitude tests in a single category, because their use in the schools tends to be for the same purpose: assessing the student's likely success on school-related tasks. Intelligence tests were created to predict which children were likely to benefit from schooling. This occurred in France around 1900, when Alfred Binet tested many children to see what intellectual skills and abilities differentiated the age groups. Children that performed substantially lower than their agemates were judged to be unlikely candidates for formal schooling.

The purpose of these "intelligence" tests was not really to measure how much intelligence one had, as though this was some fixed amount. Rather, it was a means of predicting subsequent performance on school tasks. Thus, it is reasonable to classify intelligence tests as a kind of aptitude test and treat them together in this chapter.

The Purposes of Scholastic Aptitude Tests

There are several reasons why scholastic aptitude tests are given in schools. One of the major reasons is to measure a student's present level of cognitive functioning to help place him into programs that provide special services. For example, the decision to place a student in a class for the mentally retarded must include a review of scores from such tests. Legal decisions have established that scholastic aptitude tests cannot be the sole basis for such a decision, but their use in the decision process has been affirmed by the courts.

A second purpose of scholastic aptitude tests is to help interpret students' levels of achievement. When an aptitude test and an achievement test are given to the same group of students, the test scores can be correlated. This correlation allows one to predict the expected range of achievement test scores for students with varying aptitude scores. When a student's achievement level is substantially below his expected level of performance, parents and teachers may need to change the motivation or instructional program for that student.

A third purpose of scholastic aptitude tests is to identify special talents and skills that the student may possess. Some aptitude tests provide detailed subtests that can serve as the basis for suggestions about courses of study and even career possibilities. An understanding of the student's areas of strength helps counselors and teachers to work better with students.

Aptitude and intelligence tests are given for several reasons:

- to help in placement decisions;
- to provide a context for interpreting achievement performance; and
- to identify special talents and skills.

Theories of Intelligence and Aptitude

The kinds of items used on scholastic aptitude tests reflect the test developer's beliefs about the nature of intelligence and aptitude. In fact, whether the test provides one score or more than one score probably depends on the test author's theoretical position about the nature of intelligence. It is not our intention in this chapter to develop the major theories of intelligence, but some overview may be helpful in understanding the diversity of available tests.

Binet. The measurement of intelligence or scholastic aptitude became prominent in the early 1900s when Alfred Binet and Theodore Simon began testing children in France in order to distinguish between normal and retarded children. These early tests assessed attention span, recall of a series of digits, vocabulary, and comprehension. The idea of **mental age** was developed by comparing the test performance of people of different ages.

The Binet Scales were translated into English by Henry Goddard in 1908; Lewis Terman revised the scales in 1916. This work led to the development of the **intelligence quotient (IQ),** the ratio of mental age to chronological age × 100 (Terman 1916).

Spearman. Later, around 1927, Charles Spearman proposed a **g-factor,** or general factor of intelligence, after observing an intercorrelation among the separate measures of the components of intellectual performance (Spearman 1927). In 1938, the lack of extremely high correlations among the tests led L. L. Thurstone to suggest that the study of intelligence should focus on the independent factors in intellectual tasks, rather than on their overlap. He identified the **primary mental abilities** of number facility, verbal meaning, inductive reasoning, perceptual speed, spatial relations, memory, and verbal fluency (Thurstone 1938).

Guilford. Clearly, the tests that were designed to measure these various definitions of intelligence differed according to theorized components. One of the later (1967) and more complex theories of intelligence was J. P. Guilford's structure of the intellect. He saw the need to measure different mental operations and categorized them on three dimensions: operations, products, and contents (see Figure 11.2). Each combination of these dimensions was seen as a different intellectual task that required a different set of test items (Guilford 1967).

Piaget. Other popular approaches to measuring intellectual development are based on the developmental theories of Piaget and the information-processing models from experimental psychology. The Piagetian approach is to divide the development into stages as follows:

1. *Sensorimotor Stage* (0 to 24 months)
   This stage contains only motor actions, such as reflexes, thumbsucking, kicking an object, or shaking a rattle to hear it. The development is ordered in terms of typical developmental sequence.

2. *Preoperational Stage* (2 to 7 years)
   This stage has increasing verbal performance and the beginnings of symbolic play. The preconceptual phase includes the use of symbolic language and

Figure 11.2.
Guilford's Structure of the Intellect

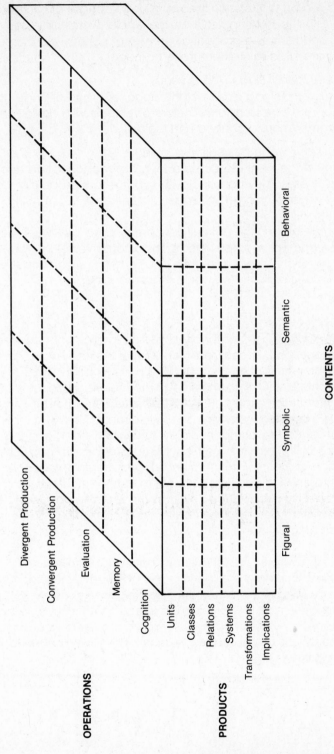

OPERATIONS

Divergent Production
Convergent Production
Evaluation
Memory
Cognition

PRODUCTS

Units
Classes
Relations
Systems
Transformations
Implications

CONTENTS

Figural
Symbolic
Semantic
Behavioral

Source: Adapted from Guilford, *The Nature of Human Intelligence* (McGraw-Hill, 1967). Used with permission.

thought and reason that is very egocentric. In the phase of intuitive thought, the child deals with the parts rather than the whole, words are used but not fully understood, and there is a gradual awareness of conservation (amount remains the same if transferred to a different size or shape).

3. *Concrete Operational Stage* (7 to 11 years)
   Concrete problem solving occurs at this stage, one can arrange objects on an ordinal scale, and one can form a class of objects with similar characteristics. Thought becomes more organized and logical.

4. *Formal Operations Stage* (12 years and older)
   Persons at this stage begin to comprehend abstract concepts and to develop and test hypotheses. They can deal with hypothetical propositions and use abstract rules to organize problems. (Gage and Berliner 1979, 141–52)

The developmental explanation of intelligence espoused by Piaget requires testing specific to each stage. For example, the ability to conserve volume or weight, a part of the preoperational phase, would require one set of questions, and the serialization or quantification along a dimension would require another.

Information Processing. Another theory of testing intellectual development is that of **information processing.** Recent research on the intellective processes has given new insights into the nature of memory and cognitive functioning.

The Atkinson and Schiffrin model defines three major components: (1) the sensory register, where information enters; (2) short-term memory, where information is next transferred; and (3) long-term memory, where information is stored. In addition, control processes govern these components by influencing the organization of the information and mediating or retrieving the information (Atkinson and Schiffrin 1968).

The implication of the information-processing model for intelligence assessment is that the measures must tap both structures of memory—short-term and long-term—as well as the control processes. Tasks such as the repetition of given sequences of digits may measure the short-term memory component, while vocabulary items may tap the long-term memory and coding systems or control processes used to retrieve this information.

The point of this overview is to show how theories of intelligence have changed over the years and thus how intelligence and aptitude tests have changed in a corresponding way. There is no universally agreed-upon measure of intelligence or scholastic aptitude. The tests that are available represent the various theories of test developers and the array of purposes for which each test was designed. Some of the most commonly used standardized tests are described below to illustrate the variety that is available.

> The variety of intelligence and scholastic aptitude tests reflects the changing theories about the nature of intellectual functioning. Early tests were designed to predict who would benefit from schooling, while more recent measures are concerned with the psychological processes required in intellectual tasks.

Individually Administered Tests   *More accurate*

The two most commonly used individually administered intelligence tests are the Stanford-Binet (Terman and Merrill 1972) and the Wechsler Intelligence Scale for Children (Wechsler 1974).   *WISC*

The Stanford-Binet is appropriate for persons above the age of 2. Intelligence is seen as general mental ability and is comprised of items from the following seven areas: language, memory, conceptual thinking, reasoning, numerical reasoning, visual-motor, and social intelligence. Months of mental age are added to the person's score for each correctly answered item. IQ scores with a mean of 100 and a standard deviation of 16 are also reported. The Stanford-Binet takes about an hour to administer, and the person administering the test needs considerable training. Thus, this test is usually given by a school psychologist.

The Wechsler Intelligence Scale for Children-Revised (WISC-R) is used more extensively than the Stanford-Binet, because it provides more information. In addition to reporting an overall IQ, it provides subtest scores, as well. The *Verbal* portion of the WISC-R has subtests in information, similarities, arithmetic, vocabulary, and comprehension. The *Performance* part has subtests in picture completion, picture arrangement, block design, object assembly, and coding. There are also supplementary subtests in digit span and mazes. The WISC-R is intended for children between the ages of 6 and 17.

The WISC-R provides Verbal, Performance, and Full Scale IQ scores with a mean of 100 and standard deviation of 15, as well as scaled scores on each of the subtests, which are standard scores with mean of 10 and a standard deviation of 3. This test, like the Stanford-Binet, is typically administered by a school psychologist.

Group-Administered Tests

The Stanford-Binet and Wechsler tests are administered individually, usually by school psychologists, which involves time and expense. There are other tests that are more convenient and less expensive, because they can be administered in larger groups and by individuals other than psychologists. However, these tests are often thought of as approximations of the scores provided by individually administered tests. In fact, a part of the test development includes the correlation of the group test scores with scores from individual assessments such as the Stanford-Binet or Wechsler.

The need for group testing was recognized during the induction of draftees in World War I. The Otis Group Intelligence Scale was developed at that time to assist in sorting men into various job and training categories. The tests developed for this purpose were valuable enough to prompt the development of other group-administered intelligence tests for school-aged children. Two of these tests, the Lorge-Thorndike Intelligence Test (Lorge, Thorndike, and Hagen 1966) and the California Test of Mental Maturity (Sullivan, Clark, and Tiegs 1963), are briefly described below.

Lorge-Thorndike. The Lorge-Thorndike Intelligence Test is designed to test students from kindergarten through grade 13. It has two major parts: verbal and nonverbal. The verbal subtests are word knowledge, sentence completion, verbal classification, verbal analysis, and arithmetic reasoning. The nonverbal subtests are oral vocabulary, cross-out, and pairing on the lower level of the test, and figure analysis, figure classification, and number series on the higher level. The test scores are reported as IQs, as well as grade percentiles, grade equivalents, and age equivalents.

California Test of Mental Maturity. The California Test of Mental Maturity is available in both a long form and a short form; the short form is used more often in schools. Seven scores are reported: logical reasoning, numerical reasoning, verbal concepts, memory, language total, nonlanguage total and total. Mental ages and IQs are available for the language, nonlanguage, and total scores. The different levels of the test span from preprimary to adult.

These group intelligence tests have reliability coefficients in the 0.80–0.90 range. Since they are designed, in part, to be predictive of success in school, it is not surprising that scores on these tests correlate around 0.70 or so with those on standardized achievement tests.

> Both individual and group-administered intelligence tests are available. Scores may be reported as IQs, percentiles, grade equivalents, and age equivalents, depending on the test.

Testing Other Aptitudes

Standardized tests have also been designed to assess many other specific aptitudes. However, few of these are given on a regular basis in schools. One exception is the multifactored assessment required of special students for the basis of Individual Educational Plans (IEPs). Many students do not encounter tests of specific aptitudes or interests until high school, when some of these tests are used in career development programs. A very brief description of some of the commonly used tests is given below to show the range of available aptitude tests. Also note that the nature of these tests clearly shows that not all aptitude tests are intelligence tests.

Job Selection and Placement. There are several aptitude tests that have been developed to assist in career development programs and job placement. One such test is the General Aptitude Test Battery (GATB), provided by the U.S. Department of Labor (1970). The GATB measures nine aptitudes: (1) general learning ability; (2) verbal aptitude; (3) numerical aptitude; (4) spatial aptitude; (5) form perception; (6) clerical perception; (7) motor coordination; (8) finger dexterity; and (9) manual dexterity. The GATB is a group test that takes over two hours to complete. It is appropriate for students as young as the ninth grade.

Another widely used battery is the Differential Aptitude Test (DAT) (1974). The DAT is designed to assist the vocational counseling of students in grades 8 through 12. The subtests on the DAT are: Verbal Reasoning; Numerical Ability; Abstract Reasoning; Clerical Speed and Accuracy; Mechanical Reasoning; Space Relations; Spelling; and Language Usage. The DAT manual is very thorough and numerous studies report high validity coefficients for the total test score. A *Career Planning Questionnaire* is also available so that both the student's interests and abilities can be used in career counseling.

A great deal has been written about aptitude tests used for job selection and placement. Most of the guidelines for constructing these tests have been established through court decisions. When such tests are used for personnel decisions, the content of the test items must be clearly related to the job and there must be empirical evidence about the test's predictive validity. However, when these tests are given in the schools, it is usually for assisting students, parents, and guidance counselors in discussing possible career choices. No irrevocable decisions are being made.

Creativity. The Torrance Tests of Creativity (Torrance 1974) measure four components of creativity: fluency; flexibility; originality; and elaboration. Both verbal and figural scores are available for each of these components. This test can be administered in group settings in less than an hour. The *Thinking Creatively With Pictures* form takes thirty minutes; it includes subtests on picture construction, picture completion, and lines. This form is appropriate for those in kindergarten and above. A second form, *Thinking Creatively with Words,* is available for those in fourth grade and above. This form takes forty-five minutes and allows for divergent responses.

Musical Aptitude. A musical aptitude test, Seashore Measures of Musical Talents (Seashore 1938) is mentioned to illustrate the variety of special aptitude tests available. The *Seashore* has six subtests: (1) discrimination of pitch; (2) discrimination of loudness; (3) discrimination of time interval; (4) judgment of rhythm; (5) judgment of timbre; and (6) tonal memory. There are not many standardized aptitude tests available in the arts, and this list of subtests may show why: These are difficult things to measure. Furthermore, when the total is more than the sum of the separate parts, measuring just the separate parts may not be sufficient. These *Seashore* subtests certainly are narrowly focused on the separate parts of musical aptitude.

The aptitude tests we have discussed are merely a small sampling of available tests; there are aptitude tests for many ages and in many content and vocational areas. For reviews of these and other similar tests, consult Buros' *Mental Measurements Yearbook* (1978). (For a review of this reference, see chapter 9.)

> A variety of aptitude tests is available. Many of these tests measure scholastic aptitude, while others examine special aptitudes, such as musical ability and creativity.

Issues Concerning Aptitude Tests

Every kind of test has specific problems and weaknesses. This is also the case for aptitude tests. Some of these problems stem from inherent weaknesses in the tests, while others result when the tests are misused. A number of common issues are explained below.

Reliability and Validity

Since the purpose of an aptitude test is to predict the likelihood of success in school or in some vocation, predictive validity is of primary concern. Aptitude tests usually have adequate reliability coefficients, often in the 0.90 range. However, predictive validity can be another matter.

In chapter 5, we stressed that a test has predictive validity if it is significantly correlated with some criterion of interest. Since an aptitude test is used to help individuals make decisions, it should provide accurate predictions for *each person.* Many tests predict well enough for groups yet are not accurate predictors at the individual level.

Another problem is that the subtests of an aptitude battery may not predict as accurately as the total score. For example, the Abstract Reasoning test on the DAT may not have adequate predictive validity by itself. But it is an important part of the total score, which may have adequate predictive validity.

Overall, the aptitude test is a useful counseling tool. However, interpretations are limited by several weaknesses, including inaccuracies in predicting individual aptitudes and the lack of a direct cause-and-effect predictive relationship. In conclusion, the aptitude test score provides a guideline, not a prescription.

Labeling and Stability

One problem with aptitude tests is that once a student has been tested, he may be "stuck" with that test score. **Labeling** occurs when an individual is assigned a description such as "delayed," "disabled," "slow," or "below average." This is also true for children who are labeled as "geniuses" and then are expected to excel. Each label masks a wide range of individual qualities, positive and negative. When these qualities are ignored and only the label is recognized, all individuality is lost. People are grouped by label and treated as such. Test scores must thus be interpreted carefully, acknowledging that many different factors are involved. Labeling is an improper and unfair use of aptitude scores.

A similar problem occurs when the child is "stuck" with a particular test score for an extended length of time. In a test-retest sense, aptitude test scores are quite reliable. However, the long-term stability of aptitude test scores is something else again. Individual IQ scores can be reasonably expected to fluctuate by twelve or more points over five- and ten-year periods. Therefore, a single scholastic aptitude test score should not haunt a child for years. Such aptitudes need to be reassessed periodically to provide current and accurate scores.

Bias

Another potential problem of aptitude tests is bias, which results when a test is systematically rather than randomly inaccurate. For example, the XYZ aptitude test might predict that short people make terrific electrical engineers. If, in fact, one's height has no bearing on his ability to succeed as an electrical engineer, then the test is biased.

Charges of test bias are sometimes made when entire groups of people score substantially lower or higher than other groups on the same test. This, in itself, does not constitute bias; the test may be accurately measuring group differences. Nonetheless, a test is biased if it under- or overpredicts the actual level of performance of one or more groups.

More will be said about test bias in chapter 14. Note, though, that evidence about an aptitude test's bias must establish that the test is a systematically inaccurate predictor of subsequent performances.

> Weaknesses of aptitude tests include limited predictive validity, labeling, and bias. These weaknesses can be alleviated, at least in part, by using aptitude tests in an appropriate, objective manner. In short, use the tests as they are designed to be used.

SUMMARY

Although most of the testing done in schools today is achievement testing, aptitude testing can also provide valuable information about students. Aptitude tests indicate the likelihood of future success in both school- and nonschool-related tasks. Such tests can be useful in placing students into specialized school programs and in helping students explore careers in which their interests and abilities can be combined.

Much of scholastic aptitude testing is grounded in the developing theories of intelligence, which were outlined in an overview. Specific tests were also described to illustrate the components of scholastic aptitude.

Tests of special aptitudes, such as creativity, are also available. Details about these tests are available in test manuals and Buros' *Mental Measurements Yearbook* (1978).

Finally, several limitations of aptitude tests were described. The major weaknesses included: (1) the limited levels of predictive validity; (2) problems with labeling and long-term stability of the scores; and (3) possible test bias.

KEY TERMS AND CONCEPTS

Aptitude test

Aptitude

Scholastic aptitude

Intelligence

Cognitive

Affective

Psychomotor

Mental age

Intelligence quotient

 (IQ)

g-factor

Primary mental abilities

Information processing

Labeling

REVIEW ITEMS

1. Scholastic aptitude tests are designed to:

   a. measure present levels of achievement.

   b. measure future levels of performance.

   c. estimate present levels of performance.

   d. estimate future levels of achievement.

2. Tests that assess cognitive, affective, and psychomotor outcomes usually contain elements from all three domains.

    T   F

3. The original purpose of intelligence testing was to:
   a. identify the brightest or most talented school children.
   b. sort individuals into career paths.
   c. discover what constituted "intelligence."
   (d) identify those who might benefit from schooling.

4. Spearman's g-factor measures:
   (a) the general overlap of cognitive abilities.
   b. the gestational development of congenital idiots.
   c. the growth factor of developing intellect.
   d. the gradient of abilities among intelligence test items.

5. The items on an intelligence or scholastic aptitude test reflect the author's theory about the nature of intelligence.

   (T)   F

6. Which of the following viewed intelligence in terms of developmental stages?
   a. Spearman.
   (b) Piaget.
   c. Guilford.
   d. Binet.

7. The information processing theory contains:
   a. the primary mental abilities.
   (b) both short-term and long-term memory.
   c. distinct stages of processing development.
   d. the g-factor.

8. Results from vocational aptitude tests are best used as:
   (a) counseling guidelines.
   b. vocational selection criteria.
   c. sources of prescriptions for remediation.
   d. substitutes for longer achievement tests.

9. Scores from scholastic aptitude tests are:
   a. relatively invariant across the elementary grades.
   (b) likely to fluctuate quite a bit for most people.

c. so erratic that they are of limited usefulness.

d. extremely stable after age 7.

10. If Hispanics scored significantly lower than blacks on an aptitude test, that test would probably be biased against Hispanics.

T   (F)

EXERCISES

11.1 Obtain specimen sets of two or more intelligence or scholastic aptitude tests. Then compare the test items on the basis of the intellectual skills they require.

11.2 Describe the differences and similarities in test items designed to assess scholastic aptitude and those used to assess intelligence or intellectual functioning.

11.3 Compare the different procedures used in establishing the validity of aptitude tests versus achievement tests?

11.4 Identify at least two purposes for which intelligence and scholastic aptitude tests are used that differ from the purpose for which they were designed. How well have they served these additional purposes?

11.5 Read the manuals of at least two published aptitude tests. Compare the thoroughness of the item development and norming procedures to that of achievement test batteries.

11.6 Read reviews of at least two special aptitude tests in Buros' *Mental Measurements Yearbook*. Describe the adequacy of the reliability and validity information the tests provide.

11.7 *Mental Measurement Yearbook* entries also cite studies that reflect the validity of the tests. Peruse two or three of the journal articles to see what information is provided.

11.8 Give an example of an instance in which two children might have equal aptitude test scores but different long-range expectations of success. How does this relate to labeling and predictive validity?

11.9 Identify possible consequences of biased aptitude tests for primary-aged schoolchildren and for high school students exploring possible careers.

11.10 How much aptitude testing should be an integral part of a school district's testing program? What aptitudes should be tested? At what age levels should testing be done?

REFERENCES

Atkinson, R., and R. Schiffrin. 1968. Human memory. In *The psychology of learning and motivation.* Vol. 2, ed. K. Spence and J. Spence. New York: Academic Press.

Buros, O. K., ed. 1978. *Mental measurements yearbook.* 8th ed. Highland Park, N.J.: Gryphon Press.

1974. *Differential Aptitude Tests.* New York: The Psychological Corporation.

Gage, N. L., and David C. Berliner. 1979. *Educational psychology.* Chicago: Rand McNally.

Guilford, J. P. 1967. *The nature of human intelligence.* New York: McGraw-Hill.

Lorge, Irving, Robert L. Thorndike, and Elizabeth Hagen. 1966. *Lorge-Thorndike Intelligence Tests.* Boston: Houghton Mifflin.

Seashore, C. E. 1938. *Psychology of music.* New York: McGraw-Hill.

Spearman, C. 1927. *The abilities of man.* New York: MacMillan.

Sullivan, E., W. Clark, and E. Tiegs. 1963. *California Test of Mental Maturity.* Monterey, Calif.: California Test Bureau/McGraw-Hill.

Terman, L. M. 1916. *The measurement of intelligence.* Boston: Houghton Mifflin.

Terman L. M., and M. Merrill. 1972. *Stanford-Binet Intelligence Scale.* Chicago: Riverside.

Thurstone, L. L. 1938. Primary mental abilities. *Psychometric Monographs* 1.

Torrance, E. P. 1974. *Torrance Tests of Creative Thinking.* Princeton, N.J.: Personnel Press.

United States Department of Labor: Manpower Administration. 1970. *Manual for the U.S.E.S. General Aptitude Test Battery.* Washington, D.C.: U.S. Employment Service.

Wechsler, D. 1974. *Wechsler Intelligence Scale for Children-Revised.* New York: The Psychological Corporation.

12

Affective and Psychomotor Measures

Most of the tests given in schools are concerned with cognitive variables. For instance, achievement and aptitude tests focus on the student's knowledge and skills, assessing many levels of understanding. However, other tests are important, too. In this chapter, we will examine **affective** and **psychomotor** tests. These measures are important in their own right, as well as in how they relate to cognitive performance.

Affective measurement addresses beliefs, attitudes, opinions, and values. A student's feelings and emotions are known to be important correlates of achievement, as well as significant factors in overall development. For this reason, they warrant attention as worthwhile targets of accurate measurement.

Psychomotor development is the remaining domain of educational measurement. We may think that psychomotor measurement is limited to physical education applications, but there are also measures that deal with the physical development of young children and the elements of coordination and manipulation necessary for learning cursive handwriting or performing other motor tasks.

Affective Measures

Affective measurement is concerned with individual values, beliefs, interests, attitudes, and personalities. Teachers, parents, and administrators talk a lot about these variables, but they seldom formally assess them. Standardized measures of many affective variables are available, but few are given in schools on a regular basis. They are used primarily as psychological profiles in placement decisions regarding candidates for special education services. And sometimes they are used as outcome measures when parts of an instructional program are evaluated.

In many situations, information about student attitudes and opinions would greatly help teachers. Affective measures can be constructed in these instances. Actually, the process is not too different from that used in constructing cognitive tests.

This section will describe some of the available standardized affective measures, as well as the procedures for creating one's own measures. It is hoped that such an awareness will lead to a comprehensive assessment program that includes both affective and cognitive outcomes. Unfortunately, most testing programs emphasize cognitive outcomes, which are thoroughly measured and documented, while only a few subjective comments are made about affective outcomes.

Purposes of Affective Measures

There are several purposes for assessing affective variables. One of these reasons is that some instructional objectives may be written about affective outcomes. For instance, educational intervention may attempt to change a student's self-concept or perhaps assess his level of stress. The effectiveness of the program would best be established by providing evidence that students' scores on these variables did in fact change as a result of the intervention. Thus, there is a need for accurate measurement of the affective outcomes of intervention.

Another purpose of affective assessment is to assess students' interests and personality characteristics and assist counselors in helping identify appropriate vocational goals. The initial exploration of various careers can be guided somewhat by matching a student's characteristics with specific job characteristics.

Many research studies deal with affective variables and therefore require measurement instruments. For example, there is some evidence that boys and girls have similar attitudes toward mathematics in the early grades, but after junior high, girls have more negative attitudes toward math than do boys. The attitude measures used in such research are examples of useful affective instruments.

The Taxonomy
of the Affective Domain

There is a taxonomy of educational objectives for the affective domain, just as there is a taxonomy for the cognitive domain. The central theme of this taxonomy is the internalization of a value. Figure 12.1 contains the levels of the **affective taxonomy** that was developed by Krathwohl, Bloom, and Masia (1964).

An illustration of the various levels of the affective taxonomy may be helpful. Suppose we are concerned with one's attitude toward environmental issues. If someone is only aware of these issues but is willing to accept new information, he is at the *receiving* level.

Figure 12.1.
Levels of the Affective Taxonomy

When the individual seeks out information about environmental issues and shares his thoughts with others, he is at the *responding* level.

When one feels more than a mere interest and appreciation and actually forms a value or commitment, he has reached the *valuing* level.

The next level—*organization*—is reached when the person integrates these new values into his belief system. At this point, his feelings are very strong, and the concern with environmental issues has become a part of his lifestyle.

Finally, the *character* level requires a complete lifestyle adjustment to accommodate this new belief and value. In our example, this person's life might now center on active involvement in environmental issues.

The affective taxonomy shows very clearly how the strength of an attitude, opinion, or belief can vary. The importance of the taxonomy may be (as was the case for the cognitive taxonomy) that it alerts us to measuring the full range of internalization. Both the published tests and the self-constructed tests described in this chapter attempt to measure several levels of this taxonomy. Unfortunately, the items may not be as clearly linked with the taxonomic levels as was the case for the cognitive taxonomy, because there is not a qualitatively different product that reflects the taxonomic level.

Examples of Affective Tests

Tests are available on most psychological constructs, including guilt, anxiety, need for achievement, self-concept, locus of control, sex role, and moral development. Consider the following examples.

Locus of Control. The *Nowicki-Strickland Locus of Control Scale* (Nowicki and Strickland 1973) is one of several measures of this construct. It consists of forty questions that are answered yes or no. The scale measures whether the student is more *internal,* such that he controls what happens to him, or more *external,* such that other forces and people control what happens to him. A sample question from this scale is: If you find a four-leaf clover, do you believe that it might bring you good luck? Clearly, one's answer would reflect what he believes has control of his fortune.

Self-Concept. The *Tennessee Self Concept Scale* (Fitts 1965) is a one hundred-item test that can be used with persons who are 12 or older. Several scores are derived, including an overall level of self-esteem, a variability score of one's consistency from area to area, a measure of extreme response style, a true-false ratio, a conflict score, and a number of deviant signs score. The overall self-esteem score is usually the score of principal interest.

Self-Image. The *Draw-A-Person* (Urban 1963) test is a projective technique. First, the examinee is told to draw a person; then he is told to draw a person of the opposite sex. Clinical judgments are made about the order in which the body parts are drawn, the aggression and perseverance of the drawer, the characteristics of the drawing, the behavior of the drawer, and the subject matter of the drawing itself. Evidence about the validity of such projective measures is sparse, but the approach is unique and less easily faked than most self-report measures.

Training test administrators and scorers of affective tests may be somewhat more involved than was the case for achievement tests. Certainly, the users of these test results need to be competent in many areas of developmental psychology. For further review of these tests and others, consult the *Mental Measurements Yearbook* (1978).

> The users of affective tests need to be well trained in various areas of developmental psychology, since the interpretation of these tests is somewhat involved.

Constructing Affective Measures

On occasion, student attitudes or opinions need to be measured, but no suitable published test is available. In these situations, teachers must construct their own measures using item formats that create scales for the specific occasion. For example, suppose a teacher wanted to assess students' attitudes toward arithmetic homework. She could create some simple self-report scales that include questions about various aspects of the arithmetic homework. This report can be constructed in one of several ways, as discussed below.

Yes-No Format. To assess feelings about arithmetic homework, the teacher could give the student a number of statements and ask him to disagree or agree with the comment, marking yes or no. For example:

1. The arithmetic homework helps me understand the assignments.
2. The arithmetic homework takes too much time.
3. I can seldom finish the arithmetic homework on my own.

A total score can be determined by giving one point for each positively worded statement (such as 1, above) that is *agreed* with and one point for every negatively worded statement (2 and 3) that is *disagreed* with.

Agree-Disagree Format. Similar items can be written using a five-point response scale, as follows:

1 Strongly agree

2 Agree

3 Undecided

4 Disagree

5 Strongly disagree

This kind of format is called a **Likert scale.** Individuals mark how strongly they agree or disagree; one's score is the sum of the marked answers on a set of items. Of course, the scoring has to be reversed on negatively phrased items. A three-, five-, or seven-point scale is used so that the midpoint (3, above) will be a neutral response, such as "undecided." The number of possible choices depends on the age of the persons tested and the specificity that is desired in the answers. Consider these example items:

SA A U D SD   The arithmetic homework takes too much time.

SA A U D SD   I learn a lot by doing the arithmetic homework.

SA A U D SD   The arithmetic homework is generally pretty reasonable.

Semantic Differential Format. Another simple method for assessing attitudes is the **semantic differential.** The subject to be rated is given along with a set of bipolar adjectives separated by a seven-point scale. For example:

Arithmetic Homework

Hard	—	—	—	—	—	—	—	Easy
Valuable	—	—	—	—	—	—	—	Not Valuable
Boring	—	—	—	—	—	—	—	Challenging
Reasonable	—	—	—	—	—	—	—	Unreasonable

The student responds by marking a choice along the seven point continuum be-tween each pair of adjectives. For example, if the student thinks homework is really boring, he marks the leftmost choice on the boring-challenging line. The scoring assigns high marks to positive responses and low marks to negative responses (for example, Valuable = 7; Not Valuable = 1). A student's final score is the sum of his responses to the adjective pairs.

Scores from any of these item formats can be used in a manner similar to those from cognitive achievement tests. Means and standard deviations can be com-puted, different classes or groups can be compared, and individual scores can be related to group averages. Even criterion-referenced interpretations are possible, including statements such as "90 percent of the students will give positive responses to 90 percent of the items on the attitude scale." (Keep in mind that the responses will probably be a function of how strongly the statements are worded.)

Reliability and Validity of Affective Measures

Students' attitudes and opinions are harder to define than their cognitive achieve-ments. They also tend to be more unstable and impressionable from day to day. Thus, the reliability and validity of affective measures tend to be somewhat lower than for measures of cognitive performance.

The reliability of the attitude shown toward arithmetic homework could be as-sessed by seeing how consistent the scores are from one day to the next. The pro-cedures and concerns would be very much like those discussed in the chapter on the reliability of cognitive tests (chapter 4). One difference is that there may be a *preferred* response to an affective question, but there is probably not a *correct* re-sponse. Therefore, there is no scoring key of right answers for items on a five- or seven-point scale.

A modification of the Kuder-Richardson formula for internal consistency was done to accommodate this difference. The coefficient alpha reliability is:

$$r_\alpha = \frac{J}{J-1}\left[1 - \frac{\Sigma s_j^2}{s^2}\right],$$

(12.1)

where J = the number of items,
s_j^2 = the sum of the variances of the items, and
s^2 = the variance of the set of total scores.

This is similar to the KR-20 formula that was presented in the reliability chapter (chapter 4). The only difference is that pq has been replaced by s_j^2, the sum of the separate item variances.

The validity considerations of these affective measures are precisely the same as those of cognitive items. Content validity is assessed by judging whether the items on the scale adequately represent the construct or concept being measured. For example, do the items on the attitude-toward-arithmetic-homework scale adequately cover the dimensions of the issue?

Predictive or concurrent validity is established by correlating scores from the attitude scale with scores from some future or present measure of another variable, perhaps achievement levels. Construct validity can also be established through the same means used for cognitive measures.

The reliability coefficients for affective scales and cognitive measures are both found in the same way. The only difference is a small change in the internal consistency formula.

Weaknesses of Affective Measures

The weaknesses of affective measures tend to be general problems that are not restricted to particular item formats. Each of these weaknesses can lessen the reliability and/or the validity of any type of measure. However, some of the problems are more controllable than others.

Definition Weakness. The definitions of the psychological constructs assessed are often debatable. There can be reasonable alternative definitions of characteristics such as anxiety, stress, optimism, and the like. Even attitudes toward school and family can be defined in several different ways. This looseness of definition certainly can affect the content validity of the measures, since the items reflect the definition. This is not an extensive problem with cognitive measures.

Socially Acceptable Responses

Many items on affective measures are quite transparent: What is being tested for is quite obvious. In response, people may "tell you what you want to hear," which often means giving a **socially acceptable response,** rather than an accurate one. A question about prejudice, for example, may be answered to imply that there is no prejudice when, in fact, actual behavior shows quite the opposite. Paper-and-pencil self-report measures are quite easily faked, but behaviors are not.

Acquiescence and Role Playing

Some problems are unique to affective measurement. Since these measures address typical behavior rather than maximum performance, both intentional and unintentional distortions can taint the answers.

Suppose an interest inventory contains an item on sailing. A student who has never sailed, has never seriously considered sailing, and will probably never sail in her lifetime can very easily respond positively about an interest in sailing. Granted, she has never really considered sailing before, but seeing it on the interest inventory prompted her to think, "Yes, that might be interesting," so she endorsed the item. This kind of acceptance or agreement with the item is called the **acquiescence set.**

Problems with **role playing** can be either intentional or unintentional. A person may fake responses in a way that is consistent with a particular role. For instance, a boy might strike an overly masculine pose in his responses, but another person may not even be aware of his role playing. This can occur with people that have psychological problems, even very mild ones.

The limitations of affective measures are quite different from those of cognitive testing. Perhaps the best suggestions for controlling the problems of affective testing is to have clear and precise definitions of the characteristics being measured and to establish some degree of credibility and rapport with the examinees. When you know what you want to measure, you can select or create appropriate items. And when the examinees respect and trust the tester, they will respond honestly and accurately.

> The weaknesses of affective measures are due largely to inadequate definitions of the characteristics measured and the problems of fakeable and inaccurate self-reports.

Psychomotor Measures

Psychomotor abilities are measured only slightly more often than affective variables. Classroom teachers may measure psychomotor skills in penmanship or physical education, but not in many other areas. Teachers do, however, recognize that motor ability plays a significant role in the student's classroom performance. For example, teachers often express concern that young children do not possess the physical skills needed to write answers on a separate answer sheet rather than in a test booklet without making a substantial number of errors. Teachers also recognize the practical limits that physical development imposes. For example, cursive handwriting is introduced only after the student's hand coordination is adequately developed.

Purposes of Psychomotor Measures

Psychomotor measures are given for two major purposes. The first of these is to assess any developmental lags that might limit a student's performance in school. Most measures of psychomotor development are designed for preschoolers, so this testing responsibility is not usually the responsibility of the classroom teacher.

The second purpose of psychomotor assessment is to measure achievement levels on learned motor skills. Performance data on classroom variables (such as handwriting) and physical education skills (such as running, striking an object, or gymnastic techniques) are collected so that judgments can be made about the adequacy of performance and the possible need for continued or revised instruction.

Taxonomy of the Psychomotor Domain

Harrow (1972) developed a taxonomy of objectives in the psychomotor domain. This **psychomotor taxonomy** contains six major classification levels, which are divided further into subcategories. The six major categories include:

1. Reflex movements
2. Basic fundamental movements
3. Perceptual abilities
4. Physical abilities
5. Skilled movements
6. Nondiscursive communications (1972, 3)

This taxonomy is hierarchical in that it is ordered from the least to the most sophisticated types of movements, with respect to learner concentration. For instance, reflex movements are involuntary; they are functional at birth and develop as the individual matures. On the other hand, nondiscursive communication—at the other end of the taxonomy—includes behaviors that are both innate and learned. However, innate behaviors are combinations of reflexes and, as communications, represent types of emotional expression. Learned behaviors are those composed of movements performed for the purpose of conveying a message. (Note that the higher levels of this taxonomy contain major affective and cognitive components.)

> Psychomotor measures are used to identify children with developmental delays and to assess performance on physical achievements. A taxonomy of objectives in the psychomotor domain ranges from involuntary, reflex movements to emotional expression and communication through movement.

Examples of Psychomotor Measures

Many kinds of apparatus can be used in psychomotor assessment, including timers, dynabalometers, and dynamometers, to name a few. These are calibrated instruments that are much more precise than human judgments or paper-and-pencil devices. However, these instruments usually measure basic movements, rather than complex motor abilities, so measures to rate the adequacy of performance must be developed.

The simplest type of **checklist** merely requires a yes-no judgment from the observer (see Figure 12.2). Nonetheless, since a judgment is required, observers must be trained and their consistency must be established.

The example in Figure 12.2 deals with running. Thus, scoring is rather simple: Either the student does or does not exhibit the behavior, yes or no. The teacher (most likely the physical education teacher) may even have several students do the exercise simultaneously. However, the measurement must be on individual students. As individuals do or do not demonstrate the behavior, appropriate instruction can be provided, reviewing both separate-item and total scores.

Psychomotor assessment is certainly not limited to physical education. It can also include activities that take place in the day-to-day instructional setting. A checklist appropriate for such assessment appears in Figure 12.3.

This checklist requires considerable interpretation by the observer. The list consists of only ten items, taken from the *Rhode Island Pupil Identification Scale* (Novack, Bonaventura, and Merenda 1972). Notice that words like *difficulty* require more inferences about the behavior than were required of the behaviors in Figure 12.2. Similarly, although the five-point scale provides a measure of degree, it also requires the observer to make additional judgments. Observers must have adequate training so their ratings are consistent. It is helpful to have a practice session, in which all observers rate the same student and then discuss how to use the points on the scale.

Teachers may use an available scale, like the Rhode Island one, or they might find it useful to develop a scale of their own. This type of scale is helpful in identifying chronic psychomotor problems or lack of expected development. In addition, the systematic use of an instrument assures a good data base and uniform interpretation of the data.

A final example (see Figure 12.4) is from one part of the *Williams Gross Motor Coordination Test Battery* (Williams 1974b). This instrument provides normative data, in contrast to the instruments of the previous example. For these kinds of data, criterion-referenced measurement is clearly arbitrary and inappropriate.

Figure 12.2.
Behavioral Checklist for Psychomotor Measurement

Running

Name _____ Age _____ Sex _____

1. Trunk inclined slightly forward.

   Yes _____ No _____

2. Arms and legs used in operation.

   Yes _____ No _____

3. Arms swing freely; close to the body (large arc in sagittal plane).

   Yes _____ No _____

4. Arms bent (slightly) at elbows.

   Yes _____ No _____

5. Head erect; facing forward.

   Yes _____ No _____

Source: Williams 1974a. From *Motor characteristics of perceptual motor development: Process descriptions and evaluations* (Toledo, Ohio: University of Toledo) (mimeo).

Figure 12.3.
Items from the Rhode Island Pupil Identification Scale

Psychomotor Skills

Name _____ Age _____ Sex _____

1. Has difficulty cutting.

   ☐ never ☐ rarely ☐ occasionally ☐ frequently ☐ always

2. Has difficulty pasting.

   ☐ never ☐ rarely ☐ occasionally ☐ frequently ☐ always

3. Bumps into objects.

   ☐ never ☐ rarely ☐ occasionally ☐ frequently ☐ always

4. Trips over self.

   ☐ never ☐ rarely ☐ occasionally ☐ frequently ☐ always

5. Has difficulty catching a ball.

   ☐ never ☐ rarely ☐ occasionally ☐ frequently ☐ always

Source: Novack, Bonaventura, and Merenda 1973, 100. From "A scale for early detection of children with learning problems, *Exceptional Children* 40 (2): 98–106.

The detail provided in the scale is necessary so that all observers follow the same rules for judging performance. Such precision of definition ensures the validity of the measurement and facilitates the identification of specific meaning for each score. The Williams scale was included because it is a model of the behavioral definition

Figure 12.4.
Item from the Williams Gross Motor Coordination Test Battery

    I. Balance

        A. Static Balance—Eyes Closed

            The child is first asked to stand on one foot (the preferred foot) with hands on hips, then asked to close the eyes and to try to balance for as long as possible. The child is considered to be "out of balance": (a) if hands are removed from hips; (b) if the nonsupport foot touches the ground; (c) if there is excessive movement of the body and/or support foot. The source for a single trial is the number of seconds (to the nearest tenth) that the child remains in a controlled balance position. The performance measure is the average of four consecutive trials. NOTE: if the child remains in balance continuously for 60 seconds on any given trial, that trial is automatically terminated.

        B. Balance Beam Walk—Time and Number of Falls

            The child is asked to walk (forward) the length of a two-inch balance beam in a heel-to-toe fashion. The heel of one foot must be placed on the beam in such a way that it touches or comes in contact with the toe of the other foot. The child who steps or falls off the balance beam is instructed to step back onto the beam at the point at which the child stepped off and to continue walking (as before) to the end of the beam. Each step off the beam (with either one or both feet) is counted as one "fall." Two scores are recorded for each trial: (a) the total number of falls and (b) the time (to the nearest tenth of a second) required to complete the balance beam walk. Four trials are given. The measure of the child's performance is the average of four trials.

Source: Williams 1974b. From *Williams Gross Motor Coordination Test* (Toledo, Ohio: University of Toledo).

that could be used in many other scales. Defining outcomes in this way avoids the value-laden inferences required of some rating scales. Furthermore, data from a scale like this are much less apt to be over- or underinterpreted, because everyone is clear about what the numbers represent.

Developing Psychomotor Measures

The procedures used to develop effective psychomotor measures are essentially the same as those used for cognitive and affective measures. First, one must define very specifically what is to be measured. It doesn't matter whether the construct is intelligence or javelin throwing: One must still define the dimensions of the task or attribute clearly.

    Second, items that adequately cover the dimensions of the construct must be written, that is, content validity must be established. Additionally, precise directions for both the examinee and the rater or scorer must be provided.

Third, it must be determined whether the test or rating scale provides consistent, reliable information. Again, the procedures for assessing the reliability of psychomotor measures are essentially the same as those for cognitive or affective measures. Both stability and internal consistency reliability coefficients may be appropriate.

Fourth, one must determine whether the measure adequately serves the purpose for which it was designed. Namely, is the test useful in discriminating between groups of performers? Is the measure predictive of future performance? And does the measure provide useful information for decisions about students?

These steps are really a general procedure for developing any measurement instrument. That the procedures are similar for cognitive, affective, and psychomotor measures should be comforting. Overall, the distinctions between these areas of measurement are important, but they are not fundamental.

SUMMARY

This chapter presented an overview of affective and psychomotor measures. The presentation was decidedly less detailed than the chapters on cognitive assessment. We feel that teachers need an awareness of these measures but will use them less often than cognitive measures.

Some affective tests need to be administered and interpreted by persons with extensive training, such as a school psychologist. Other measures can be created, given, and used by classroom teachers for a variety of purposes. Measures of attitude and opinion, as well as psychomotor achievement, can be very useful, even when they are locally created and administered.

Both published and teacher-constructed affective measurements were described. Published tests are most often measures of psychological constructs, such as self-concept or locus of control. The item formats presented as suggestions for teacher-devised measures focused on student attitude assessment.

Finally, psychomotor measures were shown to be applications of general test construction principles to physical and motor performance. Thus, there is an overlap in the measurement of cognitive, affective, and psychomotor performance. Although distinctions exist, the basic measurement concepts apply across the domains.

KEY TERMS AND CONCEPTS

Affective
Psychomotor

Socially acceptable response

Affective taxonomy
Yes-No format
Agree-Disagree format
Likert scale
Semantic differential

Acquiescence set
Role playing
Psychomotor taxonomy
Checklist

REVIEW ITEMS

1. The underlying dimension of the affective taxonomy is:
    a. salience.
    b. internalization.
    c. affectivity.
    d. valuing.

2. The most important thing to do when developing an affective measure is to:
    a. define the characteristic that is to be measured.
    b. identify the level of the taxonomy at which the items should be written.
    c. use a variety of item formats.
    d. create two forms of the measure so that validity and reliability can be established.

3. The reliability coefficients of affective measures tend to exceed those of cognitive measures.

    T   F

4. Which of the following had bipolar adjective pairs?
    a. Likert scales.
    b. semantic differential.
    c. affective continuum.
    d. rating scales.

5. The procedures for developing affective and psychomotor measures are quite different from those used for cognitive measures.

    T   F

6. The greater the inferences required in a rating scale, the lower the reliability.

    T   F

7. Which of the following is *not* a weakness of affective measures?
   a. fakeability.
   b. role playing.
   c. socially acceptable responses.
   (d.) unreliable scoring.

8. Affective measures are used to:
   a. show that instruction or intervention is effective.
   b. provide information to teachers about the correlates of cognitive achievement.
   c. provide feedback to students to help them understand their performance.
   (d.) all of the above.

9. Which of these is more concerned with typical performance than optimal performance?
   a. cognitive measures.
   (b.) affective measures.
   c. psychomotor measures.

10. Which of the following is the best way to get accurate self-reports from affective measures?
    a. impose a penalty for falsifying data.
    b. have clear directions about how to answer questions.
    (c.) establish rapport with the examinees.
    d. use only low inference, yes-no questions.

EXERCISES

12.1 Create several items for measuring attitudes toward reading using yes-no items, strongly-agree-to-strongly-disagree ratings, and a semantic differential.

12.2 Compare affective and cognitive measurement in terms of reliability and the student's ability to play a role and fake answers.

12.3 What procedures are needed to provide evidence about the reliability and validity when measuring a psychological construct such as depression?

12.4 Most student grades are based on an assessment of cognitive performance. Discuss the concerns that must be addressed when grading students on the basis of affective and psychomotor performance?

12.5 Design a rating scale for measuring a psychomotor performance such as handwriting. What should be done to increase the agreement among scorers on this scale?

12.6 Look up reviews of two affective measures in Buros' *Mental Measurements Yearbook* (1978). Are any of the criticisms concerned with those problems unique to affective measurement?

12.7 Interview an elementary teacher and a high school teacher to see the extent to which affective and psychomotor variables influence their grading policies. What are their concerns with measuring these variables?

12.8 Explain how the amount of judgment required of an observer using a checklist of psychomotor behavior influences the reliability of the scores.

12.9 Contrast psychomotor and affective measurement in terms of the adequacy with which the variables can be defined. What implications does this have for the item writer?

12.10 Review the manuals of several published affective measures to see what is included concerning problems such as role playing and faking.

REFERENCES

Buros, O. K., ed. 1978. *Mental measurements yearbook.* 8th ed. Highland Park, N.J.: Gryphon Press.

Fitts, W. H. 1965. *Tennessee Self-Concept Scale.* Nashville, Tenn.: Counselor Recordings and Tests.

Harrow, A. J. 1972. *A taxonomy of the psychomotor domain.* New York: McKay.

Krathwohl, D. R., B. S. Bloom, and B. Masia. 1964. *Taxonomy of educational objectives, Handbook II: The affective domain.* New York: McKay.

Novack, Harry S., Elisa Bonaventura, and Peter S. Merenda. 1973. A scale for early detection of children with learning problems. *Exceptional Children* 40 (2): 98–106.

Nowicki, S., and B. Strickland. 1973. Nowicki-Strickland locus of Control. *Journal of Consulting and Clinical Psychology* 40:148–54.

Urban, W. H. 1963. *Draw-A-Person.* Los Angeles: Western Psychological Services.

Williams, H. G. 1974a. *Motor characteristics of perceptual motor development: Process descriptions and evaluations.* Toledo, Ohio: University of Toledo (mimeo).

————. 1974b. *Williams Gross Motor Coordination Test.* Toledo, Ohio: University of Toledo.

13

Factors that Affect Test Scores

Sometimes when students do not do well on a test, mutterings are heard about how nervous they were, how they ran out of time, or maybe how they had to bluff their way through the answer to an essay question. Some of these comments may be accurate, while others may just be "sour grapes."

Regardless, there has been enough concern about the factors that can affect test scores to cause researchers to look carefully at the problem. We do have a reasonably good understanding of the consequences of a variety of test-taking factors. In fact, some of these findings completely contradict what has always been considered "common knowledge." We have organized these factors into two major categories: (1) those factors that are characteristics of the individual examinee; and (2) those factors that are characteristics of the test setting, sometimes called administrative characteristics.

Characteristics of the Examinee

This category contains those factors that are controlled by the person taking the test. Namely, we must consider how the examinee handles the test situation and how he answers the questions. Not surprisingly, these are also the factors that most concern students.

Guessing

Whenever students have test items that require them to select the correct response from a list of possibilities, there is a chance of **guessing** the correct response. On a true-false item, the probability of guessing correctly is ½—one right answer out of two possible choices. The probability of guessing the right answer on a four-option multiple-choice question is ¼. Likewise, on a twenty-choice matching item, the probability of guessing the right answer is $\frac{1}{20}$. These probabilities of guessing correctly are based on the assumption that the student has no knowledge of the correct response.

The probability of guessing the correct answer on a selected response question is $1/K$, where K is the number of options.

Examiners are faced with a problem when students can merely guess the right answers to some of the test questions. How can we tell the difference between the answers of someone who is a random guesser and someone who is not guessing? All one can do is determine how many items can be answered by merely guessing and then make sure that the interpretable scores are significantly higher than that.

Fortunately, it is not difficult to estimate a guesser's score, because chance operates in an understood way. The chance score on a one hundred-item, four-option multiple-choice test is $100 \times ¼$, or 25. That is, each item has a ¼ probability of being guessed correctly; we would therefore expect ¼ of the 100 items to be correctly guessed. Of course, not all guessers will get exactly 25 out of 100 items correct. Some will do better, and some will do worse. Most will be near the score of 25, though. In fact, it is reasonable to assume that the guessers' scores will be normally distributed (following the bell-shaped curve) around the expected chance score of 25. The variance of this chance score distribution equals $N \times p \times q$, where N is the number of items on the test, p is the probability of guessing an item correctly, and q is the probability of guessing an item incorrectly.

The score of someone who guesses on all of the items on a test is:

$$N \times p,$$

where $N =$ the number of items and
$p =$ the probability of guessing an item correctly.

The standard deviation of a distribution of chance scores is:

$$\sqrt{N \times p \times q},$$

where $N =$ the number of items,
$p =$ the probability of guessing an item correctly, and
$q = 1 - p.$

Figure 13.1.
Distributions of Chance Scores on a True-False Test and a Multiple-Choice Test

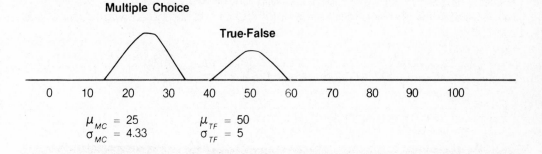

μ_{MC} = 25 μ_{TF} = 50
σ_{MC} = 4.33 σ_{TF} = 5

Figure 13.1 illustrates the distribution of chance scores (blind guesses) for a one hundred-item true-false test and a one hundred-item multiple-choice test that had four options per question. A score on the true-false above 60 is considered to be significantly above a blind-guess score. Similarly, a score of 34 or better is significantly above a guessing score on the multiple-choice test, since it is unlikely that a student could guess his way to a score two standard deviations above the expected chance score.

Corrections for Guessing

Some tests have a penalty or **correction for guessing.** The usual formula merely corrects for chance; it reduces an individual's score by the amount that one is expected to guess correctly.

$$\text{Corrected Score} = N_{\text{Right}} - \frac{N_{\text{Wrong}}}{K-1}$$

where K = the number of options.

For example, suppose Bob takes a one hundred-item multiple-choice test with four options per item. If he actually knows the answers to sixty questions but guesses on the other forty questions, we expect him to get a score of 70: the sixty that he knew plus ten of the forty items at which he guessed. Therefore, the score equals 70. Correcting the score for chance would do the following:

$$\text{Corrected Score} = 70 - \frac{30}{4-1} = 60.$$

The correction would bring Bob's score down to the number of answers that he really knew. This formula does not penalize Bob for guessing. In fact, if he could eliminate implausible options, he could guess at better than a one-fourth rate. Then he could improve his score, even when the correction for chance was used.

A penalty for guessing requires a weighting of the number of wrong responses, such as:

$$\text{Corrected Score} = N_{\text{Right}} - \frac{N_{\text{Wrong}} \times W}{K - 1}$$

where W is some weight, such as 2 or 3.

This way, the correction lowers the guesser's score a great deal from what it would have been had there been no guessing (that is, had unknown items been left unanswered). Thus, when a weighted correction is used, it is not to one's advantage to guess.

Suppose that the test that Bob took in the previous example had a weighting factor of three. Assuming again that Bob knows the answers to sixty of the one hundred items and guesses on the rest, his score will be:

$$\text{Corrected Score} = 70 - \frac{30 \times 3}{4 - 1} = 40 \, .$$

It is clearly against Bob's best interest to guess on a test that has such a penalty.

An individual's score may be corrected for guessing using this formula:

$$\text{Corrected Score} = N_{\text{Right}} - \frac{N_{\text{Wrong}}}{K - 1}$$

If an individual is to be penalized for guessing, a weight, W, greater than one may be included.

Changing Answers

Students believe strongly that one should rely on first impressions when answering multiple-choice questions. However, carefully done research studies have shown quite the opposite to be true.

Reiling and Taylor (1972) determined that more answers are changed from wrong to right during the course of a test than are changed from right to wrong. As a result, students who changed answers tended to improve their scores.

Positional Preference

Some poorly constructed tests repeatedly place the correct answer (or the incorrect answer) in the same position. For instance, some test constructors place the correct answer in position a and then develop the distracters in positions b, c, and d. A perceptive student will recognize such a pattern and choose (a) whenever in doubt.

Standardized tests have been carefully constructed so that this **positional preference** is not a factor. Essentially, correct responses are positioned at random, or at least not according to any discernible pattern. Classroom teachers can avoid this positional factor by ensuring that the correct responses are presented in an even and unsystematic manner.

Penmanship and Spelling

Although guessing and positional preference are limitations of objective tests, do not infer that essay tests are without similar problems. Research studies have established a number of factors that affect the scores on essay tests; two of the most important factors are the test taker's penmanship and spelling. (These factors were also discussed in chapter 8.)

Numerous studies, including Chase (1968) and Marshall and Powers (1969), have shown that students who have good penmanship receive higher grades on essay questions. When test responses are difficult to read, teachers award lower grades. Unfortunately, the quality of the handwriting may completely overshadow the quality of the response. *What* is written becomes secondary to *how* it is written.

Test scorers must make sure that they are not influenced by the student's penmanship, when penmanship is not being evaluated. Perhaps the easiest way to guard against this factor is to use a model answer or scoring guide. This strategy focuses the scorer's attention on the content of the response, rather than its appearance.

Spelling errors and punctuation errors have similar effects. Essay items laden with mistakes typically receive lower scores than technically proficient answers. This is appropriate if the test instructions make it clear that marks for spelling and penmanship will be included in the score. However, if the score is to reflect knowledge of the content only, incorporating other factors will change the meaning of the scores. To resolve this dilemma, some teachers give two scores: one for the content and one for mechanics, such as spelling, punctuation, and grammar.

> Spelling and punctuation should not influence the score on an essay item unless the student is informed beforehand that they will be considered in the scoring.

Bluffing

Just as some students guess their way through a test of objective items, so do others bluff a good response to an essay question. Bracht and Hopkins (1968) studied high school students and found that scores on essay tests are definitely related to the length of the response. Higher scores are given to students who write a great deal, regardless of the quality of their responses.

Some students are very adept at this **bluffing** strategy. For example, consider this student's response to the item, Explain in three hundred words or less how the American public's image of the Supreme Court has changed in the last twenty years:

> *Twenty years is a relatively short time in the entire history of the United States, but it is long enough for the attitudes and opinions of John Q. Public, the American common man, to change. Additionally, during these years there have been some changes in the persons who have served as justices on this highest court in the land. All of these factors have resulted in shifts in how the court and its decisions are viewed.*

This response does little more than restate the question. But even though it says nothing, it is written fairly well and does use seventy-six of the required three hundred words.

The way to guard against bluffing is to give very specific directions about what is expected in the response and to identify specific scoring criteria. Additionally, the use of a model answer containing the main points to be included in the response focuses the scorer's attention on the content of the response, rather than the general verbal ability of the examinee.

Reading Difficulty of Responses

The scores given to essay responses are also a function of the student's writing style. Writing characterized by simple, straightforward sentence structure tends to be given higher scores than answers that are difficult to read. Chase (1983) compared essay responses that had the same basic content but different levels of readability and found that the chore of reading the response influenced the grade it received. The more difficult the answer was to read and understand, the lower the grade it received.

Anxiety

The factors discussed above are basically mechanical factors that affect response. However, personality characteristics affect a student's test score, too.

Test anxiety is a commonly mentioned factor affecting test scores, regardless of the nature of the test. Numerous research studies (such as Chambers, Hopkins, and Hopkins 1972) have shown that there is a low, negative correlation between test anxiety and test performance. More specifically, students with high levels of test anxiety tend to score lower on cognitive tests. The relationship is not a particularly strong one, but it appears consistently in research literature.

Note that this relationship is strictly correlational and that correlations, by themselves, do *not* imply cause and effect. Regardless, students often say that they did poorly *because* of a high level of anxiety, and teachers often say that the students were anxious *because* they were not prepared to take the test. In addition, students who do poorly on the first items of the test become anxious and do even more poorly on the rest. Or perhaps upon completing the test and realizing they know little, students experience high anxiety.

Any or none of these explanations may be correct. The correlation does not indicate which explanation, if any, is correct. It merely indicates that an inverse relationship exists between the two variables, anxiety and performance. High scores are associated with low anxiety, but no direct cause-and-effect explanation can be made.

Teachers can help minimize the effects of anxiety by making testing situations as relaxed and stress-free as possible. The importance of the test and resulting scores should not be exaggerated. In fact, Jensen and Schmitt (1970) have shown that even the test title can induce a response set that affects the students' performance. Similarly, threatening, anxiety-producing instructions can cause some students to perform poorly. Teachers must consider all of these factors in constructing and administering a test.

Characteristics of the student's test taking behaviors that can affect test scores include:

- guessing
- positional preference
- changing answers
- anxiety

- penmanship
- spelling
- bluffing
- reading difficulty

Administrative Characteristics

Another set of factors has a direct impact on test scores, namely those characteristics of the testing situation that are under the control of the test administrator. Different testing procedures may be dictated by the age level of the students and the content area to be tested. For example, it is appropriate to test younger students in reading through samples of oral performance, while older children may be tested in mathematics through work sheets or problem sets. The knowledge of how the administrative factors of the test affect the scores is helpful in developing testing situations that are fair to all students and maximize the opportunities for students to perform well.

The Use of Separate Answer Sheets

Many teachers like to use **separate answer sheets** so that scoring can be done faster or that test copies can be reused. However, there is some concern about the appropriateness of separate answer sheets for younger children.

Research by Ramseyer and Cashen (1971) indicated that above-average first- and second-graders could not manage separate answer sheets, even when they were given practice sessions. Recording responses directly on the test paper resulted in significantly fewer errors.

By the end of third grade, and certainly by fourth grade, students are able to use separate answer sheets without any appreciable effect on their scores (Cashen and Ramseyer 1969). Since the use of separate answer sheets is so age related, they should not be used with students younger than third grade.

The Testing Arrangement

The physical make-up of the testing site—the **testing arrangement**—is of some concern. But as long as students are reasonably comfortable, physical conditions seem to have little effect. In a study with ninth-grade students, Ingle and DeAmico (1969) found that standardized achievement tests given in an auditorium with lap boards produced results quite similar to those of tests given in normal classroom situations.

The physical arrangements of most classrooms allow a great deal of flexibility in changing the test setting. Testing may be done in large groups, small groups, or individually. A part of the room may be designated as a testing center, or students may work at their desks. Whatever the arrangement, it should not affect the student's ability to perform.

The person who administers the test is also a factor in the testing arrangement. Hopkins, Lefever, and Hopkins (1967) found that student's scores were higher when their own classroom teacher administered the tests, instead of someone else. Furthermore, when teachers direct and monitor the testing situation, students feel that they are interested and concerned.

In general, students perform well on tests given in almost any physical arrangement, as long as control and rapport are established. Moderate variations in the physical make-up of the testing site affect scores negligibly. Thus, it seems that the test administrator is more important than the test location.

The Effect of Practice

Callenbach (1973) studied the effect of having second-grade students practice taking tests. He found that even when the content of the practice tests differed from the content of the criterion tests, the second-graders performed significantly better when they had been given practice sessions.

Perhaps the most important implication of the Callenbach study is that it is not unethical (in fact it helps) to teach students how to take tests. They are taught other study skills, so why not test taking? Students may score poorly on a test because they are awestruck or intimidated by the testing situation, not because they lack knowledge. It is the teacher's responsibility to make sure that every test is a valid measure of student competence, rather than student reaction to the testing situation.

> Practice appears to have a positive effect upon test performance, possibly by building a student's confidence in his ability to perform.

Group versus Individual Testing

A study by Niedermeyer and Sullivan (1972) has particular meaning for individualized programs. This study compared the effectiveness of individually administered constructed-response tests, an oral reading exercise, and group-administered multiple-choice tests used with first-graders. They found that the constructed-response and four-option multiple-choice tests worked well. Three-option multiple-choice items did not adequately identify the poor readers. Meetings with the participating first-grade teachers indicated that they preferred the individually administered constructed-response tests for the following reasons:

1. they are easier to administer;
2. they take less time if "on-the-spot" remediation is avoided;
3. they eliminate copying;
4. they give the teacher better knowledge of an individual child's skill level; and
5. they make the child feel good when he receives the individual attention of the teacher.

These reasons alone are important enough to justify the use of individualized testing programs at the primary level. The choice of item format seemed to affect how teachers thought the students felt about tests. However, it is quite possible that going over the responses to a multiple-choice test with individual students might also promote such desirable results. Again, we see the importance of promoting a one-to-one relationship between the teacher and the student.

Repeated Posttests

Individualized programs allow the possibility of some students taking the posttest for an objective repeatedly until the criterion level is attained. It is unwise to use the same posttest over and over again; students focus on the specific test items, not the domain that the items represent. Similarly, when only one form of the posttest is used, it is possible (indeed, likely) that students will discuss the test items. And since students take the posttests at different times, depending on their individual rates of progress, it is quite possible that students who have completed the posttest might share information about the test with their friends.

These problems can be lessened by using parallel forms of the posttests for repeated testings. This requires more teacher effort, but it solves the problem of using the same items for all students. Since students are not being compared to one another, it is not important that they respond to the same items. It is important, however, to make sure that all of the tests similarly represent the domain of items and that criterion levels are equivalent across the different forms of the test.

Constructing parallel forms can be facilitated by keeping an adequate file of test items. Teachers should construct or collect a relatively large number of test items for each of the instructional objectives. Then tests can be generated quite easily by selecting from the pool of items whenever a new form of the test is needed. Old items can be refined and additional items can regularly be added to the pool. A simple method is to write items on index cards and file them by objective. This procedure is much more satisfactory than starting from scratch whenever a new test is needed. Actually, creating parallel tests becomes quite simple.

Take-Home and Oral Exams

Perhaps the necessity of giving many tests prompts teachers to use creative testing strategies. For instance, in place of the more traditional forms of testing, take-home or oral examinations may be used. Of course, take-home examinations are not appropriate for younger children. In fact, the use of take-home tests with any group must address several limitations.

Take-home examinations have two major problems. First, there is no guarantee that the tests are taken independently. Since there is no control over the testing situation, it is possible that a variety of "human resources" might be used, including peers, parents, or siblings. Take-home tests may be given for instructional purposes, but not when the instruction involves evaluation, as well.

Another problem with take-home tests is that students spend different amounts of time in completing them. For instance, suppose a test is assigned Monday, to be due Tuesday; a student who has to work Monday night will be at a disadvantage to those who have the entire evening to work on the test. It would be fairer and more accurate to give the test in a controlled situation with reasonable time limits.

Oral tests present a different set of potential problems. The major difficulty is that the items and the scoring tend to be inconsistent from one instance to another. In fact, no two examinations may be alike.

For example, consider an oral test that asks the student to explain the water cycle. As the student progresses, the teacher has many chances to ask leading questions that prompt an expected answer. However, these questions, clues, and nonverbal feedback do much to shape the student's answer. Teachers may act quite differently, depending on the time of day or how many students they have already listened to; thus, the testing setting will not be consistent from one student to the next.

In addition, the scoring of oral examinations is quite unreliable. Whether criteria are met is often determined by who administers the test, rather than what the student says. Personal bias and other subjective factors may enter in, making objective measurement difficult.

Nonetheless, there are instances in which oral examinations are an appropriate form of measurement, such as in assessing whether a student can effectively use a foreign language. In these cases, standard directions and model answers help to reduce unreliability.

Teaching Students
How to Take Tests

Our discussion has shown that there are many influential factors that the student or test administrator can control. Certainly, students should be taught how to take tests so these factors affect all individuals equally. Only then can a test be an accurate measure of one's knowledge and ability, rather than a measure of how well he can take tests. Of course, the quality of the test also determines how much various factors influence scores, but some of this influence can be diminished when students know how to take tests.

Some people feel that if students are shown how to take tests, they are given an unfair advantage. Others argue that *testing* rather than the *learning* is emphasized. Overall, this line of reasoning is unfounded. There is a problem if the teacher covers only those things that will be on the test, simply giving answers to specific items. As a result, the student will learn what is on the test, but his knowledge will not be representative of some larger body of content.

Testing is intended to capture a sample of a student's maximum performance. However, if performance is heavily influenced by the testing situation or the kind of test items used, then the test is not a good assessment. The extent of this influence can be reduced by teaching the students how best to perform under the various testing conditions. The following suggestions will help students improve their test-taking skills.

Understanding Instructions

Students must understand test instructions in order to respond effectively. Factors such as time available, how much work to show, and penalties for guessing must be contained in the test directions. The instructions should also tell the student whether to select the *one best* answer or if several choices are allowed. On essay questions, the instructions must indicate how many parts are expected in the answer and whether the student has the freedom to state his opinion. Providing good instructions tells the student what is expected of him.

Practice in testlike settings will also help students feel more comfortable taking tests. If the practice sessions include questions with a variety of formats and instructions, the students will learn to read and follow instructions more carefully. Practice sessions also allow for discussion in which students can ask questions and share problems.

Answer Sheets

We have discussed the variety and number of tests available in education. It is thus not surprising to learn that a wide variety of answer sheets is also available. Some answer sheets number the items across rows, while others go down columns. Some allow stray marks, and others do not. Some have letter headings, some have number headings, and some have none at all. Finally, some answer sheets are machine scored (as presented in chapter 7), while some are scored by hand.

Students should know how to use many types of answer sheets so they will not be startled by an unfamiliar form. They must at least know how to use the particular answer sheet that they are given, including what kind of pencil to use and how to mark their responses correctly.

Speed

Most tests are not intended to be speeded tests. However, those designed to be completed within a class period may end up being affected by some speed factor.

Students have to be able to gauge their work speed so they have enough time to attempt all test items. These basic strategies are helpful:

1. Don't linger too long on any one item. If an answer does not come quickly, move on to another item, and return to the difficult one if time allows.
2. Allocate your time so enough is given to the items worth the most points. Pay attention to the item point values given on the test.
3. Always begin by looking over the whole test, so you have a rough idea of how much time should be allotted to each item or section of the test.

Checking

If the student has time left after completing the test, he should check his answers. *Checking* does not mean retaking the entire test, from start to finish. Instead, it means returning to those items about which there was some indecision or question. Accuracy of marking answers and performing computations can also be checked. This review process is made easier if students note troublesome items as they proceed through the test, using a checkmark or a circle around the item number. This way, one can refer back directly to those items that need more work.

Sleep and Food

Often the best advice that can be given to someone about to take an important test is to get a good night's sleep. There are many stories of people who studied all night and then slept through the test. Actually, it is better to study earlier and come into the test fully rested.

Some peoples' test performance is also affected by their nutritional habits. Taking a test right after a large meal is not recommended, nor is taking a test when you're very hungry. Either way, the student's mind is on food, not the test. Teachers obviously have little control over the sleeping and eating habits of their students, but suggestions should be made.

> Students should be taught how to take tests, just as they are taught other study skills. This approach to test taking not only makes students more knowledgeable, it also reduces some of the anxiety they feel.

SUMMARY

Many factors besides individual knowledge affect test scores. Characteristics of the student, test administrator, and testing location are all influential. Persons that construct tests must be aware of these factors and minimize their impact.

Student characteristics include those factors controlled by the test examinee—namely, how one handles the test situation and answers the test questions. We discussed the uses of guessing and bluffing, as well as the effects of mechanical factors, such as penmanship and spelling. We also addressed what is perhaps the greatest student concern: test anxiety.

Administrative factors that are part of the test setting were also described. The setting, type of answer sheet, and test giver all influence test scores. The purpose of explaining these factors is to help minimize their influence. A test score should be an accurate measure of student performance, not a measure of effects from extraneous factors.

Finally, we concluded that students should be taught how to take tests as a basic part of their academic skills. Some students are at a disadvantage in any testing situation, because they have poor test-taking skills. Providing instruction in those skills is not an unethical attempt to beat the system. Rather, it is an effort to make the test scores as accurate a measure of performance as possible.

KEY TERMS AND CONCEPTS

Correction for guessing   Separate answer sheets
Positional preference   Testing arrangement
Bluffing   Oral tests
Test anxiety

REVIEW ITEMS

1. A student who guesses on every test item will have the highest score on which kind of test? (Assume the tests have equal length.)
   a. true-false.
   b. multiple choice (four-option).
   c. multiple choice (five-option).
   d. fill-in-the-blank.

2. Generally, more test answers are changed from wrong to right than right to wrong.

   (T)   F

3. If a *correction* rather than a *penalty* for guessing is used on a multiple-choice test, students should be urged to:
   a. guess when they are unsure of an answer.

b. *not* guess when they are unsure of an answer.

c. guess only on items on which they have some partial knowledge.

4. Good penmanship and spelling tend to be positively correlated with the grades assigned to essay responses.

(T)   F

5. The relationship between test anxiety and test performance is generally:
   a. strong and positive.
   b. strong and negative.
   c. weak and positive.
   (d.) weak and negative.

6. Test anxiety causes poor test performance.
   a. true.
   b. false.
   (c.) not necessarily true or false.

7. Practice in test taking can raise test scores, especially for:
   (a) younger students.
   b. older students.
   c. essay tests.
   d. objective tests.

8. A major problem with oral examinations is that they tend to be:
   a. very time consuming.
   b. very anxiety producing.
   (c.) unreliable.
   d. formal rather than informal.

9. Students should be shown how to take tests so that the tests provide:
   a. enriched diagnostic information for future informational planning.
   b. information about the test setting, as well as the test content.
   c. information about wrong answers, as well as right answers.
   (d.) a more accurate picture of what the person is able to do.

10. Teaching students how to take tests will result in:

   a. more valid information from tests.
   b. higher test scores.
   c. more positive student attitudes toward tests.
   d. all of the above.

EXERCISES

13.1 Compare objective to essay items in terms of which student and administrative factors appear to affect each type of item. Does one type of item appear to be more susceptible to these extraneous factors?

13.2 What are the likely consequences of:

   a. guessing on a twenty-five-item true-false test?
   b. eliminating all d choices from consideration in a four-option multiple-choice test?
   c. changing completion responses after rereading the questions?

13.3 What are the likely consequences of:

   a. using separate answer sheets with second-graders?
   b. having a substitute teacher administer a test to the class?
   c. giving third-graders "practice" tests with different content before taking the actual test?

13.4 Suggest how a classroom teacher might minimize the consequences of:

   a. guessing on a true-false test.
   b. pupil anxiety in the testing situation.
   c. bluffing on an essay item.

13.5 Identify at least two potential influences on pupil performance for the following types of items:

   a. oral response items.
   b. take-home items.
   c. essay items.
   d. multiple-choice items.

13.6 For each of your answers to 13.5, suggest how the teacher might minimize the effects of these influences.

13.7 How might instruction on test taking be different for third-graders than for high school sophomores?

13.8 John knew the answers to seventy of the one hundred items on a five-option multiple-choice test and guessed on the remaining items.

   a. Find his score after correcting for guessing.
   b. Find his score after penalizing for guessing so that wrong answers are weighted twice the right answers.

REFERENCES

Bracht, G. H., and K. D. Hopkins. 1968. Comparative validities of essays and objective tests, Research Paper no. 20. Boulder, Colo.: Laboratory of Educational Research.

Callenbach, C. 1973. The effects of instruction and practice in content-independent test-taking technique upon the standardized reading test scores of selected second grade students. *Journal of Educational Measurement* 10:25–30.

Cashen, V. M., and G. C. Ramseyer. 1969. The use of separate answer sheets by primary age children. *Journal of Educational Measurement* 6:155–58.

Chambers, A. C., K. D. Hopkins, and B. R. Hopkins. 1972. Anxiety, physiologically and psychologically measured: Its effect on mental test performance. *Psychology in the Schools* 9:198–206.

Chase, C. I. 1968. The impact of some obvious variables on essay-test scores. *Journal of Educational Measurement* 5:315–18.

———. 1983. Essay test scores and reading difficulty. *Journal of Educational Measurement* 20:293–97.

Hopkins, K. D., D. W. Lefever, and B. R. Hopkins. 1967. TV vs. teacher administration of standardized tests: Comparability of scores. *Journal of Educational Measurement* 4:35–40.

Ingle, R. B., and G. DeAmico. 1969. The effect of physical conditions of the test room on standardized achievement test scores. *Journal of Educational Measurement* 6:237–40.

Jensen, J. A., and J. A. Schmitt. 1970. The influence of test title on test response. *Journal of Educational Measurement* 7:241–46.

Marshall, J. C., and J. M. Powers. 1969. Writing neatness, composition errors and essay grades. *Journal of Educational Measurement* 6:97–101.

Niedermeyer, F. C., and H. J. Sullivan. 1972. Differential effects of individualized and group testing strategies in an objectives-based instructional program. *Journal of Educational Measurement* 9:199–204.

Ramseyer, G. C., and V. M. Cashen. 1971. The effect of practice sessions on the use of separate answer sheets by first and second graders. *Journal of Educational Measurement* 8:177–81.

Reiling, E., and R. Taylor. 1972. A new approach to the problem of changing initial responses to multiple choice questions. *Journal of Educational Measurement* 8:177–81.

14

Current Issues
in Educational Testing

Since all who attend school—from kindergarten to college—are affected by testing, it is not surprising that testing causes some controversy. Many individual decisions, of various levels of importance, are based on test results. Testing also has social importance, which has prompted national and state legislation affecting testing in the schools.

In this final chapter, we will examine four of the most important current testing issues. We certainly will not exhaust all discussion of these issues in this chapter, nor this text. Instead, our purpose is to provide an informative overview for the classroom teacher.

Test Bias

The issue of **test bias** is argued quite regularly in popular newspapers and magazines, as well as professional literature. Stories tell of individuals or groups of people who feel they have been discriminated against because of how they scored on a particular test. Charges leveled against tests often suggest that racism or sexism is at the heart of the problem, which becomes a rallying point for test critics. Such emotional overtones often accompany charges of test bias.

Flaugher (1978) has pointed out that test bias has many different meanings and aspects. This information generates considerable confusion about test bias, its meaning and implications. For this reason, we feel it is important that test users understand the logical and statistical meaning of test bias. Perhaps this more objective foundation will enable teachers to address charges in unemotional, technically accurate terms.

What is a Biased Test?

Osterlind (1983) defines *bias* as

> *a systematic error in the measurement process.... The term is conceptually distinct and operationally different from the concepts of fairness, equality, prejudice, or preference or any of the other connotations sometimes associated with its use in popular speech. (1983, 10)*

A test or even a single test item is biased if its scores are consistently too high or too low for an individual or group. This is different from random measurement error, which is unsystematic, increasing and decreasing at random.

Performance Bias

Performance bias is probably the most commonly considered form of test bias. It occurs when one or more groups consistently misrepresent (either by overestimating or underestimating) whatever is being measured.

Suppose, for example, that an employer uses a test to predict how well applicants for a particular job are likely to do once they are hired. The initial test results predict that a specific group—say, single men between 25 and 30—will not be reliable employees. However, previous experience has shown these men to be quite dependable. This difference between what is *predicted* and what *actually happens* is due to performance bias. This particular test is biased against single men between 25 and 30, because it underestimates their level of performance. Thus, the use of this test as a selection tool is inappropriate, since its predictive ability is questionable, at best. If the test were used, no single men between 25 and 30 would be hired, when, in fact, they would most likely perform quite well.

A similar kind of test bias exists when a test overpredicts for a certain group. In this case, the test would predict successful performance on the criterion task, but actual performance would be much lower.

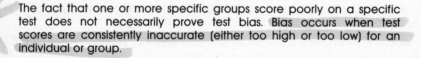

> The fact that one or more specific groups score poorly on a specific test does not necessarily prove test bias. Bias occurs when test scores are consistently inaccurate (either too high or too low) for an individual or group.

A second way to look at bias is to focus on individual test items. A single item may be biased if some groups of examinees are drawn to certain distracters, such as incorrect responses on a multiple-choice test. When students from different groups have the same pattern of responses across the distracters, the item would be unbiased.

The Test versus the Use of the Test. Over the past decade, numerous studies have shown how various groups—racial, ethnic, and otherwise—perform on achievement tests, aptitude tests, and interest inventories. The focus of such studies has been on differences in performance and what causes them. Not surprisingly, the blame is often placed on test bias.

Undoubtedly, many tests are biased. In addition, the extent of bias varies across tests and groups taking tests. Test users must be able to distinguish between bias in the *test itself* and bias in the *use made of the test results.*

Statistics and illustrations can be found to support just about any position, no matter how bizarre. Likewise, test scores can be used to perpetuate racist or sexist practices, even though the test itself is not biased. Suppose, for example, that a cognitive aptitude test is used to screen individuals for entry into a training program for carpenters. The test measures memorization skills and accurately differentiates individuals on this skill. Suppose that individuals from a particular minority group consistently score low on the cognitive aptitude test, and, therefore, are denied entry into the carpentry training program. The cognitive aptitude test itself is not biased in that it accurately measures memorization skills. However, memorization skills have little to do with success as a carpenter. The use of these test results is biased in that it prevents a certain group from entering the occupation. It is the responsibility of those people knowledgeable about testing to separate the technical, measurement aspects of test bias from the inappropriate interpretations of test scores.

> There is a distinction between a test being biased and using test results in a biased manner. This difference is important in getting at the source of the problem.

Content Bias

The above discussion of bias focuses on bias related to test performance. There is also another form, called **content bias.** It can be introduced through (1) disproportionate representation (for example, males versus females); and (2) stereotyping (for example, sexual and racial). The detection of content bias requires a content analysis of the test items.

> Content bias is introduced if there is disproportionate representation or stereotyping of certain groups in the test items.

Research on achievement tests and vocational interest inventories has revealed considerable content bias. For example, in an assessment of two interest inventories, Becker (1975) found that occupations were categorized by sex and that occupations designated for females had lower status and lower pay. Tittle (1974) found that achievement tests contained both disproportionate representation and stereotyping. For instance, reference to males was more frequent and increased with the grade level of the test. Females, on the other hand, were often pictured in traditional occupations, playing more passive and inactive roles.

Most of the examination of bias in intelligence tests has centered on performance, but there has been some consideration of content bias. Zoref and Williams (1980) conducted a content analysis of the items in six intelligence tests and found considerable evidence of content bias, including both disproportionate representation and stereotyping. The following conclusions were drawn:

1. Male representation is greater than female representation, even though the 1970 census showed the total population to be 47 percent male and 53 percent female. All tests had disproportionate representation; in one case, 87 percent of the items discussed males, and only 13 percent discussed females.
2. In most of the tests analyzed, race was disproportionately represented such that whites were overrepresented. Although the 1970 census showed total population to be 14 percent nonwhite, two of the tests had no items dealing with nonwhites.
3. Stereotyping by sex was found in most tests analyzed, and most stereotyped items were due to role. Characteristics of male stereotyping were strength, rigor, ruggedness, historic contribution, and mechanical aptitude. Those of female stereotyping included domesticity, passivity, and general inactivity.
4. Whites were stereotyped consistently, but since most tests have few items dealing with nonwhites, the low percentages of nonwhite stereotyping may be misleading. (Zoref and Williams 1980, 315–19)

What difference does it make if achievement and intelligence tests are content biased? Most obviously, biased items and tests foster inappropriate and inaccurate perceptions, endorsing stereotypes and discrimination. Also, content bias may affect performance by introducing concepts that are more familiar to some groups than to others. This charge has been made against standardized tests that assume a "typical" socioeconomic background, such as white, middle class.

What Has Been Done about Bias?

The testing community is sensitive to concerns about test bias. Test publishers try to eliminate bias through a number of procedures. For example, the Educational Testing Service (ETS) looked closely at whether the Scholastic Aptitude Test (SAT) was valid for deaf persons. They found that "the SAT underpredicted performances for the deaf students. Their first-year college grades were higher than the grades predicted" (ETS 1982, 9). However, when the SAT was used in combination with high school grade point average (which overpredicted performance), the predictions were as accurate for deaf as for hearing students. The following conclusion was drawn:

> We at ETS must be very careful when our tests are used for deaf individuals. We must try to assure that these students are not deprived of an education because of low scores, when with support services they could do very well. (ETS 1982, 9)

A second example of test publishers' efforts deals with achievement tests, rather than aptitude tests. A section of the *Iowa Test of Basic Skills, Manual for School Administrators* (1982) describes the procedures used to minimize any cultural bias, including:

1. employing contributing test authors with diverse cultural backgrounds;
2. selecting materials that reflect the varied interests of pupils from a wide range of cultural backgrounds and experiences;
3. reviewing materials at all stages of development for lack of relevance or unfairness for diverse groups;
4. conducting research on relationships between cultural background and such factors as academic aptitude, achievement, social acceptance, persistence, and extracurricular participation; and
5. conducting research on educational and testing needs for different groups. (Hieronymous, Lindquist, and Hoover 1982, 114)

Such thorough and time-consuming efforts are evidence that test publishers are concerned with charges about biased tests and are making efforts to solve existing problems.

Teacher-constructed tests are usually achievement tests. Test scores indicate how successfully the student responded to the test items under given test conditions. But we have seen that any number of factors may cause students to get low scores, from test anxiety to poor handwriting. If, in fact, these external factors cause low scores, is it the fault of the test? Certainly not, and it cannot be concluded that the test is biased.

Intelligence tests—tests of general ability—have a greater likelihood of being biased than achievement tests. Scores on such tests are supposed to indicate an individual's inherent ability to learn many different kinds of content and skills, based on having learned a few such things. If all individuals taking the test have had about the same intellectual opportunities, the test will be a good indicator of intelligence. But if this is not the case, the test will probably yield biased indicators of intelligence.

So, what can we conclude about test bias? A test is not necessarily biased because certain individuals or groups consistently score low or high. The test may be measuring accurately the achievement of a particular group; the score thus reflects individual deficiencies in the area being tested. If external factors from any source cause low scores, it is not the test that is biased. The test is biased, however, if it contains a systematic error and misinterpretations are made of the results. In practice this occurs less frequently than testing critics would have us believe.

Ethical Considerations and
Acceptable Procedures for Test Use

Test results are used for a variety of specific purposes by people with different professional roles and interests; hence, proper test use certainly merits concern. Use of test results, especially for admission and screening purposes, has received considerable attention within recent years, not only in professional circles, but also in the courts.

Several professional publications and articles deal with the ethical and appropriate use of tests. In addition, *Standards for Educational and Psychological Tests* (1974), published by the American Psychological Association, contains a straightforward discussion of the topic. In this section, we will review basic procedural considerations that apply to classroom teachers, guidance counselors, and other educators.

Test Use

Although tests are used for many specific purposes, two general uses can be established: *decision making* and *description.* Decision making involves the use of test results for screening purposes, such as who will be admitted to a specific college or who will be hired for a particular job. Decisions may also be made about the quality of programs, such as evaluating elementary curriculum using achievement test scores of third-grade students.

Description focuses on test information that aids in understanding the test taker. Using test results to diagnose a student's academic weaknesses or strengths is an example of this application. A psychologist's clinical review of test results is another descriptive example, since the test results are used to describe the individual test taker.

Classroom test results are used for both general purposes, decision making and description. Teachers make decisions about factors such as grades based at least partially on test results. On the other hand, test results are used to describe student needs, values, and attitudes. The use of tests for description is more flexible than for decision making, which may affect the application of standards for test use. As described in *Standards for Educational and Psychological Tests:*

*The standards of test use may not have to be so rigidly followed when the pur-
pose of testing is the understanding of an individual. . . . In short, exploration of an
individual case is different from standardized testing. (1974, 57)*

What are the standards of acceptable test use? Basically, they concern (1) the
skills and knowledge of the test user; (2) characteristics of the test; and
(3) procedures for using the test and its results. The relative importance of these factors depends upon the specific situation.

Skills and Knowledge of the Test User.   A test user must be competent to administer
and evaluate the test under consideration. This statement seems straightforward
enough, but it implies more than knowing testing procedures. Knowledge of measurement theory and information relevant to the testing area are also necessary.
Moreover, adequate technical knowledge is required to understand information
given in the test manual (such as reliability and validity data) and to conduct a
qualified evaluation of the test. Most importantly, one clearly must understand the
educational measurement and research relevant to the test before deciding how
the test and its results will be used. In summary, competent test users know their tests
and all relevant measurement principles.

Characteristics of the Test.   Test users must have goals and objectives that identify
what is to be accomplished through testing. Tests should be used for their intended
purposes, as dictated by the goals and objectives of the testing. We have seen that
tests designed for one purpose may not be appropriate for another; certainly, a
diagnostic test would not be used for selection purposes.
  Published tests provide extensive information in the accompanying test manual,
including detailed descriptions of test administration and use. Technical information
pertaining to validity and reliability is also provided. (However, remember that there
are no established standards for reliability and validity.)
  The test user must also be knowledgeable of the subject so that the test's appropriateness may be evaluated. If a test manual omits relevant topics or is vague on
technical points, the adequacy of the test is probably questionable.

Procedures for Using a Test.   The standardized procedures for administering a test,
as described in the manual, must be followed carefully. Appropriate and consistent
conditions must be maintained to enable the persons being tested to give their best
performance. The test user is also responsible for all scoring, coding, and recording
of test data, which must be accurate.

> The test user is responsible for selecting an appropriate and ade-
> quate test for the specific purposes of testing. He must also ensure
> that the test is administered in a consistent and fair manner.

Many published tests are **secure tests,** meaning that the test items do not circulate. In order for a test to remain secure, all copies must be retained after the test has been administered. Moreover, while the test is being used, test administrators must guard against any reproduction of items. Proper security must be maintained and enforced with appropriate corrective action.

Use of Test Results

The interpretation of test results is at the heart of much controversy. The legitimacy of any interpretation depends upon the purpose for which the test was given: Was it legitimate? For example, suppose teachers select a standardized achievement test for use in an elementary school. It is the teachers' responsibility to provide adequate information to parents and others about factors such as test reliability and validity. The teachers must be able to support and defend their choice. In addition, the persons doing the interpretation must be qualified.

To whom should test data be released? Quite obviously, the individuals responsible for interpreting the results must have access to the data. The individual tested, as well as his agent, parent, or guardian, also have the right to know the test scores and interpretations. In some instances, the examinee even has the right to know scores on individual test items.

The issue of access to information is addressed by federal legislation in the **Buckley Amendment.** This legislation gives students and their parents the right of access to test scores; it also limits the disclosure of such information without written consent of the examinees or their parents. Certain individuals are exempted from written consent, including

> other school officials, including teachers, within the educational institution or local educational agency who have been determined by the agency or institution to have legitimate educational interests or, under certain restrictions, to officials of another school in which the student intends to enroll. (Federal Register 1976, 24673)

Essentially, this means that only qualified educators within the examinee's school or agency (or one in which the examinee intends to enroll) may be given test data without written consent. **Informed consent** means that the examinee knows what test scores will be released and how they will be used.

Test scores and their interpretations should be treated as confidential information. Psychologists and counselors are usually quite sensitive about maintaining confidentiality; this should also be a concern of teachers. Information should be transmitted only to those people who have a legal right to it. The information transmitted should be as objective as possible; any subjective judgments should be clearly identified as such. Confidentiality must also be maintained in the storage and disposal of test results and interpretations. Records should be stored in a secure, limited-access area; when results are disposed of, they should be shredded or burned.

> Teachers and school officials must ensure that confidentiality is maintained in the use, storage, and disposal of test scores and interpretations.

Other Considerations

Teachers, counselors, and any others using test results should make every effort to promote the welfare and best interests of their students. Tests should not be used to badger or intimidate students. Rather, they should be recognized for the information they contain.

Teachers who have adequate understanding of educational measurement realize that measurement is imperfect. Measurement error exists in any testing. This degree of error must be acknowledged so it does not affect the use of test results. For example, a low score on an IQ test should not generate teacher expectations that the student will do poorly in all academic subjects.

Tests that are used regularly should be reviewed and evaluated from time to time. Programs and objectives change; tests that were appropriate at one time may no longer be relevant, or they may not be the best tests available. Teachers should be involved in the review of any tests related to instructional programs.

Obsolete test information should be deleted from student records. Generally, objective test scores remain useful over longer periods than subjective interpretations. When updated information becomes available, it should take precedent over older results.

Teachers are primarily concerned with testing in subjects and skills areas. Basically, the concept of test fairness infers that students are to be tested on what is taught in their classes. This concept has been reinforced by the courts whenever issues have been raised about test content. Fincher (1979) has summarized this point:

> The courts have clearly preferred concepts of achievement or accomplishment that can be seen as a logical expectation from the training or instruction students receive. (1979, 6)

Thus, teachers must make certain that the tests they give cover the content they teach.

In summary, ethical considerations and procedures for test use are based on common sense. Educators that use tests should know what they are doing: They must understand the complete purpose and process of testing, from administration to interpretation. Educators are responsible for the proper use of test results, whether the scores are from a teacher-constructed test or a published test. Confidentiality should be ensured, and written, informed consent must be obtained when necessary. Only when these standards are met can the welfare of the student be respected and protected, fairly and legally.

Competency Testing

The issue of competency testing has received much recent attention in educational measurement. Practically all states have approached this issue, in some cases actually passing legislation that specifies test content and performance levels.

When performance standards are introduced into competency testing, we have **minimum competency testing,** indicating a level of performance required for promotion or graduation. Such testing is not limited to education; numerous professions have certification or licensure requirements that are based on test performance. However, for the purpose of this discussion, we will limit our comments to competency testing at elementary and secondary school levels.

Why should competency testing be an issue in the schools? Isn't it reasonable to expect that students be competent in academic and skills areas before they are promoted or graduated? After all, we do not want an unqualified doctor or an incompetent teacher to be certified. Why should it be any different for students as they advance through school?

On the surface, the issue of competency testing seems quite straightforward. But it is, in fact, a very complex subject. Hopefully, the following discussion will help clarify some of these issues.

The Meaning
of Minimum Competency Testing

Minimum competency testing is defined a number of different ways in educational measurement literature. Some include rather elaborate descriptions of what is to be involved in the process, while others stress desired results and effects. One of the most useful definitions of minimum competency testing is given by Miller:

Minimum competency tests are constructed to measure the acquisition of competence or skills to or beyond a certain, defined standard. (1978, 6)

In order for a school system to implement a program of minimum competency testing, it is necessary to identify the skills to be tested. Should this include school skills, life skills, or both? Will testing be limited to reading, mathematics, and other so-called "basic" skills, or should it include skills in areas such as art, music, and foreign language?

The dichotomy between *school skills* and *life skills* may not be very distinctive, but since schools are in the business of developing school skills, these should take priority. There also should be some rationale for establishing promotional standards for the school skills. As Glass (1978) indicated, setting meaningful standards is a difficult if not impossible task. What minimum levels are necessary for success in life? By whose standards?

If a student falls below a certain level of math necessary for performing simple calculations, we do not remove him from society. Nor is it likely that this individual will go through life unable to obtain a checking account because of his low performance. There is basically no way to set minimum standards for life skills, however these skills may be defined.

> Minimum competency testing should focus on school skills. The inclusion of life skills is very tenuous and does not lend itself to setting standards and definitions.

It has been suggested that simulated situations be used in minimum competency testing (see, for example, Brickell 1978). Simulation may be used for performance testing in vocational areas, as discussed earlier. But simulation of real life situations does not appear to be feasible at the large-scale level testing required by most minimum competency testing programs. Paper-and-pencil tests are used extensively and will most likely continue to be. Because of time limitations, both for taking and scoring tests, objective items are often used. It is not likely that work samples, other than test performance, will be a part of minimum competency testing, due to the time required for scoring and the possible lack of control of work done in a nontesting situation.

Minimum competency tests can be obtained from several outside agencies, including test publishers and government offices, such as the state department of education. If teachers construct competency tests for local schools, there is an intuitive feeling that validity is enhanced. On the other hand, constructing such tests may be an excessive burden to individual teachers. Moreover, there may be an undesirable diversity among school systems as to levels of difficulty and acceptable standards of performance. Whether or not students are judged competent may then become more a function of the specific school systems in which they are enrolled than actual levels of performance.

> Most minimum competency testing involves the use of paper-and-pencil tests, constructed locally or obtained directly from a test publisher or government agency.

Rationale and Benefits
of Minimum Competency Testing

The development and implementation of minimum competency testing programs is a large task. It is hoped that the benefits that accrue from such programs make the effort extended worthwhile.

Much of the motivation for minimum competency testing—especially in states where it has been legislated—comes from attempts to correct perceived deficiencies in the schools. This attitude is unfortunate for two reasons. First, in many situations, minimum competency testing is advocated by people outside of education. Although they may mean well, these individuals are often not well informed about the complexities of the issue and, quite frankly, are not qualified to deal with the problem.

In addition, there is considerable confusion about the types of deficiencies minimum competency testing can address. For example, it is argued that minimum competency testing is needed because Scholastic Aptitude Test (SAT) scores have been declining over the years. The majority of students that take the SAT would have no difficulty passing a minimum competency test. However, doing so would not likely raise their SAT scores. Such competency programs are not designed specifically to increase performance on the SAT, and it is unlikely that they will do so, even indirectly. The rationale for minimum competency testing must include a consideration of realistic benefits.

General Rationale. Logically, minimum competency testing is a reasonable procedure: Students should master certain content and skills at various levels as they advance through the educational system; certainly, upon graduation it is reasonable to require specified levels of performance.

Educators who develop and implement programs should know what can be expected of students at various points. For example, for promotion to ninth grade, a student should have mastery of the basic arithmetic operations that are prerequisite for high school mathematics. Intuitively, we feel that it is not fair to award advancement or graduation to all students who have simply "put in their time," regardless of performance levels. It is unfair to those who have excelled, and it is also unfair to those who have real problems that need attention.

Perceived Benefits. Advocates of minimum competency testing argue for numerous benefits, most of them general, long-range effects. For instance, if minimum competency testing is required for high school graduation, the diploma will attain greater credibility. In essence, the diploma acquires meaning beyond course credits and specified time in school. Thus, minimum competency testing enhances public confidence in the schools, which is certainly beneficial.

Minimum competency testing is believed to produce several benefits:

1. It results in the establishment of meaningful standards in the schools;
2. It causes a school and even a community to be more specific about its educational goals;
3. It makes the public better informed about educational outcomes; and
4. It provides a basis for educational accountability.

Again, these are certainly beneficial outcomes. However, keep in mind that there may be little real data to support them.

For students, minimum competency testing may result in more individualized instruction, especially for those who need remedial work in order to meet performance standards. Students who have the greatest educational needs receive adequate help. It is also implied that basic skills—such as writing, reading, and math—will receive increased emphasis, as these are usually the skills tested for competency. Generally, the student's perceived benefit is an improved education, one that emphasizes *product,* not merely *process.*

> The perceived benefits of minimum competency testing are numerous and varied, ranging from improvement of the school's image and programs to specific attention to individual student needs.

Perceived Drawbacks of Minimum Competency Testing

Definite disadvantages are also associated with minimum competency testing. One practical disadvantage is the cost of developing and implementing a minimum competency testing program. A lot of time, money, and effort is needed to produce such a program.

The matter of test control is also important. Some people believe that "those who control the tests, control the curriculum." Thus, teachers teach for the test, especially if any teacher accountability is associated with the testing program.

In some states, efforts have been made to keep control at the local level to allow for diversity. But basically, diversity is not compatible with attaining standards, unless standards are to be flexible, which is somewhat of a contradiction in terms. Moreover, if a student is judged by such inconsistent standards, his score may be a function of where he was tested, not how he performed.

Establishing standards and identifying levels of performance proficiency is a complex and controversial task. Glass (1978) concluded that it is impossible to base mastery or competence levels on statistical procedures, since setting standards is arbitrary and subjective. Procedures for establishing standards have been developed (see, for example, Angoff 1971), but all involve some type of subjective judgment. This does not mean that educators should abandon all attempts at setting standards, but it is important to recognize the subjectivity involved.

> All standard-setting procedures involve subjectivity. No psychological or statistical procedures can generate standards without including some arbitrary decisions.

Minimum competency testing has other implied disadvantages, as well. Gifted students may be ignored and mediocrity may be encouraged, as resources and efforts are concentrated on maximizing the number of students that attain minimum competency. In addition, students who persistently fail may be more inclined to drop out of school.

Minimum competency testing may also promote bias against certain groups of students, especially those with special needs. Students may become labeled unfairly when they do not attain minimum competency levels.

There is presently no empirical evidence that all of these perceived effects will come about. However, they do represent the kinds of undesirable effects that have been cited by opponents of minimum competency testing.

> Minimum competency testing is costly in terms of money, resources, and time. Not only is the testing program itself expensive; remedial programs are costly, as well.

Responsibilities:
State and Local Levels

State departments of education and local school systems assume varying responsibilities among states that have implemented minimum competency testing. In some states, the departments of education have essentially passed on the entire responsibility to school systems. In other states, the department of education plays a more participatory role, generating tests or items, designing recordkeeping systems, and providing technical assistance to the schools. Regardless of who does specific tasks, certain responsibilities have emerged, as listed below:

1. To develop a very specific definition of the domain to be tested.
2. To widely publicize the domain.
3. To ensure that good test development procedures are followed.

4. To determine that the test is a fair measure of what is taught.
5. To design a standard recordkeeping system.
6. To conduct criterion-related validity studies of the tests used.
7. To analyze item-response patterns.
8. To plan and conduct small-scale evaluations on the impact of the program on the curriculum and tracking.
9. To set up procedures by which students may question the accuracy of their scores and see their test, answer sheet, and the answer key. (Madaus 1982, 12)

Whether the department of education or the local school system assumes these responsibilities depends upon the particular state. If the department of education has a lot of control, it may assume all responsibility. More commonly, the responsibility is divided between the department of education and the local school district.

Publicizing the domain to be tested may include circulating sample tests among parents, students, and the community, which requires local effort. If common tests are used by all schools in the state, the department of education should conduct the tasks associated with numbers 6, 7, and 8. Local data are needed to correlate test scores with other measures of similar skills and knowledge. Item-response patterns should be analyzed by school system, region, ethnic background, type of curriculum, and the like to determine if there are any significant patterns and biases. If local tests are used, item-response studies should be conducted at that level.

> Responsibilities for minimum competency testing are usually assumed cooperatively by the state department of education and local school system.

**Legal Principles
of Minimum Competency Testing**

Not surprisingly, minimum competency testing has considerable legal ramifications due to its potential impact on the quality of education. A number of testing programs and applications have already been challenged in the courts.

Citron (1982) has identified and summarized five principles based on such legal action, including:

1. *Appropriate use of competency tests is constitutional.*
2. *There must be adequate notice.*
3. *Competency tests may not carry forward the effects of past racial discrimination.*
4. *A graduation test must reflect material taught.*

5. *Section 540 [of the Rehabilitation Act of 1973] does not prohibit requiring handicapped students to meet valid test requirements in order to receive a regular diploma. (1982, 11)*

Most states in which minimum competency testing has been legislated also require remedial instruction provisions for students not attaining minimum competency. Of course, remedial instruction must be provided at the local level. Indeed, one of the contending issues of minimum competency testing is who should fund remedial instruction, the state or the local school district.

Minimum competency testing reflects the extent of learning that takes place; namely, it reflects directly what occurs in the classroom. For this reason, the teacher's role is at the center of the issue. It is not likely that many teachers will be among legislators passing state laws, but they can have significant influence. Teachers should be involved in all tasks, not only administering tests, but determining the domains to be tested and developing or selecting appropriate items and tests. Teachers should not perform technical tasks that require specialized training. Such assistance should be provided by state departments of education or districtwide consultants. However, teachers should have input whenever local standards are being developed.

Competency testing is a complex issue. Educators are responsible for developing and implementing testing programs, which is an extensive task. However, minimum competency testing is a public issue—it is not internal to education.

Although their concern is genuine, most people (including legislators) are generally not aware of the extensive problems associated with competency testing, which causes considerable pressure. Feelings are strong, for and against. Therefore, competency testing will remain controversial and continue to demand substantial attention from the education profession.

Public Law 94-142: Its Impact on Testing

The impact of **Public Law 94-142 (P.L. 94-142), The Education of All Handicapped Children Act,** has been felt in all areas of education. Specifically, this Act is intended

> *to assure that all handicapped children have available to them ... a free appropriate public education which emphasizes special education and related services to meet their unique needs, ... to assist states and localities to provide for the education of all handicapped children, and to assess and assure the effectiveness of efforts to educate all handicapped children. (Pelosi and Hocutt 1977, 3)*

The effect of P.L. 94-142 on testing has been to increase its use in screening handicapped children and diagnosing their educational needs so that appropriate instruction can be provided.

P.L. 94-142, The Education of All Handicapped Children Act, was passed in 1975. Actually, it did not establish a new set of ideas but reinforced decisions that had been made in the courts over many years. Most of these court decisions were concerned with providing free public education for handicapped children.

Bersoff and Veltman (1979) explain that the basis for many cases was the Fourteenth Amendment, which guarantees "any person within its jurisdiction the equal protection of the laws." In part, this right has been interpreted as the right to an equal education (1979, 11).

A second legal basis was the due process clause, which prohibits states from depriving "any person of life, liberty, or property, without due process of law." It was argued that property and liberty interests are involved when schools determine the type of education to be given to handicapped children (1979, 11).

Even though P.L. 94-142 reinforced existing rights rather than expand the rights of handicapped children, it did directly mandate free public education for all handicapped children. In addition, it established requirements of what educational agencies must do and the procedures that they must use in order to receive funds under the Act. Overall, P.L. 94-142 brought some degree of uniformity to the identification of handicapped children and the procedures to be used in establishing appropriate educational programs.

Major Components of P.L. 94-142

The major components of P.L. 94-142 are shown in Figure 14.1. A brief description of these components is given here, and then a number of the specific ramifications of the Act on tests and testing programs are described. Although Figure 14.1 consists of components, it also represents a process model, since the components are processes. These processes are sequenced in the figure.

Screening and Identification. P.L. 94-142 provides that state departments of education are responsible for identifying, locating, and evaluating *all* handicapped children in their respective states. Of course, most of the actual testing of children who are thought to be handicapped is done at the local level by school districts and community agencies. The law requires that screening be done for persons up to the age of 21. However, the provision of educational services is only required for school-aged children. And in some states, educational services are not mandated for preschool and postsecondary students.

A major goal of screening is to provide an accurate count of the numbers of

Figure 14.1.
Major Components of Public Law 94-142

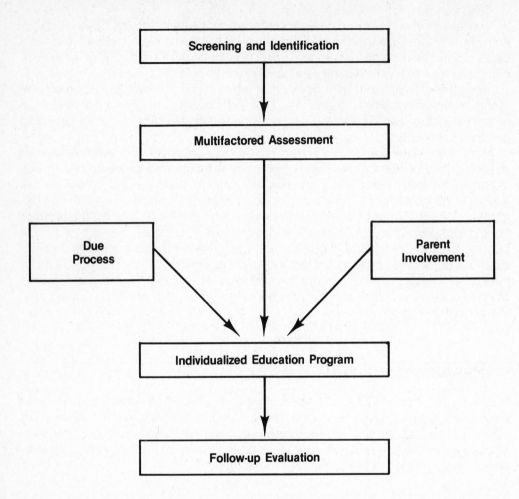

children with various handicapping conditions. To do so, we must first define *hand-icapped children:*

> Under Public Law 94-142, the term "handicapped children" denotes those children diagnosed as mentally retarded, hearing impaired, speech impaired, visually handicapped, seriously emotionally disturbed, orthopedically impaired, or otherwise health impaired, multihandicapped, and those with specific learning disabilities. (Brown 1980, 356)

Clearly, this thorough list of handicaps suggests that an effective screening program would require a testing staff capable of administering a wide variety of tests and measures. Moreover, the importance of complete identification of all handicapped children is reinforced because federal funds are dispersed in accordance with the number of handicapped children found; that is, the amount of money distributed is directly proportional to the number of children identified. Thus, from a financial standpoint, as well as an educational one, it is important to locate *all* handicapped children.

Multifactored Assessment. Once a handicapped child has been identified, it is necessary to conduct a comprehensive, **multifactored assessment** of his disability, evaluating all areas related to the suspected handicap. For example, a child with delayed language development should also be tested for possible hearing loss and psychological status, as well as communication development, since these areas may be related to the handicap. Measures of fine and gross motor development might also be given to determine whether the delay is only language-related or involves some motor deficiency.

The importance of comprehensive, multifactored testing is clear; however, it poses one practical concern: No single test, such as an intelligence test, can serve as the sole basis for decisions about educational programming. Another implication is that the training necessary for administering the necessary variety of tests and physiological measures is extensive. In fact, a number of professionals is needed, including psychologists, audiologists, teachers, speech therapists, and other such specialists.

Despite its cost and complexity, multifactored assessment remains a major component of handicapped education. For an appropriate educational program cannot be developed unless individual needs are assessed.

Parent Involvement. An emphasis on parental involvement runs throughout P.L. 94-142. The initial concern was the right of parents to gain free public education for their handicapped children. In addition, other provisions were made. For instance, if school-aged children are referred for services, their parents must be so notified in writing. On the other hand, parents must give written permission for assessments to identify a possible handicap. Parents also have the right to participate in the assessment and in subsequent meetings about the child's educational program. Moreover, they can secure independent evaluations, and this information must also be considered by school officials. And as discussed earlier, parents have access to all school records concerning their child's screening, assessment, and placement.

Detailed procedures are described to ensure the parents' rights in each of these activities. Overall, the purpose of stipulated parent involvement is to bring parents and families into the decision-making process. Quite clearly, parents must understand before they can become involved in their child's education.

Individualized Educational Program. P.L. 94-142 provides that an **Individualized Educational Program (IEP)** meeting must take place within thirty days after it has been determined that a child is eligible for special services. This meeting is attended by the parents and school personnel, often the principal, special education teacher, and school psychologist. Others designated by the parents or school may also attend.

The purpose of the IEP meeting is to develop a specific program for the child.

> *The IEP must contain a description of the level of the child's present performance, annual and short-term instructional objectives and objective criteria and evaluation procedures for determining whether instructional objectives are being met. (Bersoff and Veltman 1979, 19)*

The IEP also recommends placement for the student, which can range from a regular classroom, to a special education program, to an institution. Ideally, the placement setting should be as close to a regular classroom as possible, given the child's handicapping condition. The term **least restrictive environment** describes this setting as the least restrictive (or most "normal") educational environment in which the handicapped child can function successfully. This term has sometimes been interpreted to mean that all handicapped children should be placed in regular classrooms. This is not a realistic interpretation, nor was it the intent of the legislation.

The IEP is not limited to in-class educational activities. Related services include

> *transportation and such developmental, corrective, and other supportive services including speech pathology and audiology, psychological services, physical and occupational therapy, recreation, and medical and counseling services . . . as may be required to assist a handicapped child to benefit from special education. (Brown 1980, 357)*

IEP meetings are held annually to monitor the child's progress and establish new objectives. If parents and school people cannot agree on an IEP, there are provisions for due process hearings or, ultimately, civil suits.

Follow-Up Evaluation. The follow-up evaluation reviews end-of-the-year posttest scores that document the child's progress and serve as the basis for revising the IEP for the coming year. The follow-up may also address the appropriateness of the present placement and suggest revisions, if needed.

A second use of the follow-up is to identify those practices that were successful. Such an evaluation of the educational program provides managerial accountability and documents the efficiency of services.

Concerns about Testing

The extensive use of tests in screening and multifactored assessments requires that tests be as accurate and fair as possible. P.L. 94-142 contains these requirements for the testing program:

1. The tests and the administration of the tests must be in the child's language.
2. The tests must have been validated for the specific purpose for which they are used.
3. The tests are administered by trained personnel.
4. No *single* procedure can be used.
5. The evaluation is done by an interdisciplinary team, at least one member of which has knowledge in the area of the suspected disability.
6. The child is assessed in *all* areas related to the suspected disability.

The enactment of P.L. 94-142 has caused the testing program for handicapped children to be examined and, in most cases, revised to comply with requirements of the law. For instance, the stipulation that testing be done in the child's native language has made it necessary for school districts to purchase tests printed in several languages and to locate multilingual people in the community who can serve as interpreters or be trained to administer tests.

Tests for handicapped individuals have been validated for the specific purposes for which they are used; thus, more general tests, such as IQ tests, are no longer appropriate. Instead, the tests must focus on all specific facets of the child's handicapping condition. This requirement has caused some concern, because it necessitates the review of many, many tests to develop a sound, comprehensive testing program adequate for a wide range of handicapping conditions.

The requirement that tests be administered by trained personnel according to the instructions in the test manuals should not be a problem, since this requirement must be met in any testing program. However, since testing now requires an interdisciplinary team, school districts must put more people, time, and money into the testing program. The screening and identification phase can thus be costly, because it requires the services of school psychologists, audiologists, and other specially trained people. The interdisciplinary team is seen as an asset, though, because it ensures that a complete understanding of the child's handicap will be obtained. This information can then be used to plan the most appropriate educational program for that individual.

The stipulation that no single form of measurement can be used enhances the multifactored nature of the assessment. The child should be assessed on both educational and psychological factors. In addition, the measures should provide a number of item types so the child can demonstrate his full range of abilities.

Testing the child in all areas related to the disability requires more than one might expect. P.L. 94-142 states that this could include health, vision, hearing, social and emotional status, general intelligence, academic performance, communication status, and motor abilities. Of course, not all children have to be tested in all areas. Only those areas related to a specific disability need be included.

Summary Comments about P.L. 94-142

P.L. 94-142 has had a substantial effect on many testing practices. It has legally required certain practices and procedures that have, in turn, required more people, time, and resources from the schools. The result has been to have more accurate and complete data about each child than was possible before. And the usefulness of these data in establishing IEPs and in monitoring the child's progress has certainly been worth the additional costs.

How does P.L. 94-142 specifically affect the classroom teacher? Clearly, classroom teachers may encounter handicapped students in their classes—certainly not severely handicapped children, but children who can function in the regular classroom, despite their handicaps. This will require attitude changes on the part of some teachers, along with possible instructional adjustments in order to accommodate the handicapped student

As far as testing is concerned, the teacher should be knowledgeable about the process and participate in the interpretation of test results. Classroom teachers are not expected to become experts in psychological or handicapped testing, but they should understand the implications of their students' test results. Discussions with specialists such as school psychologists and participation in the relevant processes contained in Figure 14.1 will help the classroom teacher understand and accept the handicapped student.

SUMMARY

This chapter has provided overviews of four current issues in educational testing: test bias, ethical considerations, competency testing, and P.L. 94-142. Although these issues may not have an immediate impact, it is important that teachers be well informed. Sooner or later, in one way or another, teachers will be affected by these issues.

Teachers cannot be testing experts in all areas. In fact, the testing and measurement that will always concern most teachers is that done while conducting instruction. However, it is naive to think that other testing issues are irrelevant.

Whenever decisions are made at state or local levels, teachers must be informed. And to the extent that they can participate, teachers must have input. Teachers should be represented in any decision-making groups so there will be no surprises when decisions are implemented. The key is active participation at all levels of the educational process.

KEY TERMS AND CONCEPTS

Test bias
Performance bias
Content bias
Secure tests
Buckley Amendment
Informed consent
Minimum competency
   testing
Public Law 94-142
   (P.L. 94-142), The
   Education of
   All Handicapped
   Children Act

Multifactored
   assessment
Individualized
   Educational Program
   (IEP)
Least restrictive
   environment

REVIEW ITEMS

1. Which situation is an example of test bias?
   a. third-grade boys consistently score lower than third-grade girls on a reading test.
   b. women consistently score higher than men on a test used to predict success in a specific profession.
   c. all of the above.
   d. none of the above.

2. A specific test item is biased if one or more groups:
   a. consistently respond incorrectly to the item.
   b. have lower scores than other groups on the item.
   c. are differentially attracted to the distracters of the item.
   d. are unable to read the item with understanding.

3. In an analysis of content bias of intelligence tests, it was found that:
   a. females tended to be overrepresented.
   b. males tended to be overrepresented.
   c. nonwhites tended to be overrepresented.
   d. essentially no content bias was found.

4. If a published test is "secure," it means that:
   a. the test items do not circulate.
   b. only a publisher's representative can administer the test.
   c. results of the test are released only through the school or agency using the test.
   d. the test results are confidential.

5. Access to test information—that is, the persons having a right to know test scores of others—is addressed by:
   a. federal legislation through P.L. 94-142.
   b. state legislation.
   c. federal legislation through the Dole and Baker Amendment.
   d. federal legislation through the Buckley Amendment.

6. The concept of achievement test fairness, as interpreted in court cases, basically means that:
   a. students tested are scored in a consistent manner.
   b. students are tested on what is taught in their classes.
   c. no ethnic groups consistently score lower (or higher) than other groups.
   d. test administration be standardized for all groups taking the test.

7. Identify a benefit that would *not* likely be a result of a minimum competency testing program:
   a. basic skills receive increased attention.
   b. programs for gifted students are implemented.
   c. required skills and knowledge are more specifically defined.
   d. individualized instruction is provided for slow learners.

8. The responsibilities of minimum competency testing are usually shared by state and local agencies. Which of the duties must be assumed, at least in part, at the local level?
   a. designing a standard recordkeeping system.
   b. publicizing the domain to be tested.
   c. determining that the test is measuring what is taught.
   d. analyzing item-response patterns.

9. Public Law 94-142 is the:
   (a) Education of All Handicapped Children Act.
   b. Equal Rights for Handicapped Children Act.
   c. Classroom Education Handicapped Children Act.
   d. Public Schools and Handicapped Children Act.

10. Individualized Educational Programs (IEPs) should be reviewed _____ to monitor the child's progress and establish new objectives.
    a. every 30 days.
    b. quarterly (every three months).
    c. semiannually (every six months).
    (d) annually.

11. One effect of P.L. 94-142 on testing programs for handicapped students is that:
    a. more general tests, such as those measuring academic ability, are used.
    (b) more specific-purpose tests are used.
    c. more locally constructed tests of all types are used.
    d. more published attitude inventories are used.

12. Test bias (or bias in the scores of a test) occurs if there is random error in the measurement.

        T   (F)

13. Achievement tests in academic and skills areas have less likelihood of being biased than intelligence tests or general ability tests.

        (T)   F

14. If a test continually presents women performing lower-status, service-type tasks, the test is performance biased.

        T   (F)

15. Clinical use of test results by a school psychologist attempting to diagnose a specific student's weaknesses and strengths is an example of a decision-making use of test results.

        (T)   (F)

16. The difference between competency testing and minimum competency testing is the application of standards for the latter.

          T   F

17. If a minimum competency testing program is implemented in a high school, the testing should focus on life skills.

          T   F

18. One benefit of minimum competency testing at the secondary level is that it will substantially increase the numbers of students passing aptitude tests, such as the Scholastic Aptitude Test (SAT).

          T   F

19. The most acceptable approach to establishing standards for a minimum competency testing program is to base standards on statistical procedures.

          T   F

20. If scores on tests of minimum competency were correlated with scores on tests measuring similar skills and knowledge, high correlations would be evidence of test validity.

          T   F

21. P.L. 94-142 prohibits the use of minimum competency testing as part of high school graduation requirements for handicapped students.

          T   F

22. P.L. 94-142 specifies that educational services for the handicapped must be provided for all persons up to the age of 21.

          T   F

23. The dispersion of federal funds to individual states under P.L. 94-142 is based on the number of school-aged children in each state.

          T   F

24. The intent of the term *least restrictive environment* relative to placement is eventually to have all handicapped children educated in regular classrooms.

          T   F

EXERCISES

14.1 Discuss a testing issue of particular interest and write a short paper of 8–10 double-spaced pages. Identify any controversy in the issue—pros and cons, if they exist—and discuss implications for teaching. (Some of the references at the end of this chapter may be helpful if you select one of the issues already discussed.)

14.2 Take a position either for or against minimum competency testing and prepare a short position paper (not over twelve double-spaced pages) on the topic.

14.3 Conduct library research or contact the department of education in your state to determine the status of legislation and implementation guidelines concerning competency testing. Summarize the present status and identify the implications for teachers.

14.4 Choose a teaching area of interest and identify or develop an example of possible test bias. Also develop an example situation in which test bias may be incorrectly inferred.

REFERENCES

Angoff, W. H. 1971. Scales, norms, and equivalent scores. In *Educational measurement,* 2d ed., ed. R. L. Thorndike. Washington, D.C.: American Council on Education.

Becker, R. L. 1975. *Reading-free vocational interest inventory.* Final Report. U.S. Office of Education Research Project 452227. Washington, D.C.: American Association on Mental Deficiency.

Bersoff, Donald N., and E. S. Veltman. 1979. Public Law 94-142: Legal implications for the education of handicapped children. *Journal of Research and Development in Education* 12:10–22.

Brickell, H. M. 1978. Seven key notes on minimum competency testing. *Phi Delta Kappan* 59, no. 9 (May): 589–91.

Brown, F. G. 1980. *Guidelines for test use: A commentary on the standards for educational and psychological tests.* Washington, D.C.: National Council on Measurement in Education.

Brown, R. T. 1980. A closer examination of the Education for All Handicapped Children Act: A guide for the 1980s. *Psychology in the Schools* 17:355–60.

Citron, C. H. 1982. Competency testing: Emerging principles. *Educational Measurement: Issues and Practice* 1, no. 4 (Winter): 10–11.

Educational Testing Service. 1982. SAT: Is it valid for the deaf? *ETS Developments* 28 (Winter): 8–9.

1977. *Ethical standards for psychologists.* Rev. ed. Washington, D.C.: American Psychological Association.

1976. *Federal Register.* 41, no. 118 (June 17): 24673.

Fincher, C. 1979. Using tests constructively in an era of controversy. *The College Board Review* no. 113 (Fall): 2–7.

Flaugher, R. L. 1978. The many definitions of test bias. *American Psychologist* 33: 671–79.

Glass, G. V. 1978. Standards and criteria. *Journal of Educational Measurement* 15, no. 4 (Winter): 237–61.

Hieronymous, A. M., E. F. Lindquist, and H. D. Hoover. 1982. *Iowa Test of Basic Skills, manual for school administrators.* Chicago: Riverside Publishing.

Madaus, G. F. 1982. Competency testing: State and local level responsibilities. *Educational Measurement: Issues and Practice* 1, no. 4 (Winter): 12.

Miller, B. S., ed. 1978. *Minimum competency testing: A report of four regional conferences.* St. Louis, Mo.: CEMREL.

Osterlind, S. J. 1983. *Test item bias.* Beverly Hills, Calif: Sage Publication.

Pelosi, J., and A. Hocutt. 1977. *The Education of All Handicapped Children Act.* Chapel Hill, N.C.: Graham Child Development Center, University of North Carolina.

1974. *Standards for educational and psychological tests.* Washington, D.C.: American Psychological Association.

Tittle, C. K. 1974. Sex bias in education measurement: Fact or fiction? *Measurement and Evaluation In Guidance* 6:219–26.

Zoref, L., and P. Williams. 1980. A look at content bias in IQ tests. *Journal of Educational Measurement* 17, no. 4 (Winter): 313–22.

Appendix 1:
The Use of
Microcomputers
in Classroom Testing
and Recordkeeping

The microcomputer has become a highly visible teaching aid at all levels of education. It has extensive capabilities for instruction, and, since measurement and testing are a part of instruction that often involves quantification, the microcomputer is certainly applicable in these areas.

In this appendix, we provide an overview of how microcomputers may be used in classroom testing and recordkeeping. A number of microcomputers and many software programs related to measurement are available to computer users of all skill levels. Our discussion will remain general, since specific applications depend on the equipment and software available, as well as a common level of computer knowledge. Then, too, the field of computer technology is changing so rapidly that new materials are developed continually.

Microcomputer Terminology

The subject of computers has generated a body of related terminology. To provide a common background, we will first define commonly used terms. Do not consider this as a comprehensive glossary of computer terms. Only those terms used in this introduction to microcomputers will be defined.

Address: An identifier that designates a particular location for the data in storage.

Cassette: A plastic box, about 4½ × 2 inches, containing a magnetic tape on which programs and data can be recorded.

Central Processing Unit (CPU): The major hardware component of a computer system, including the control unit, memory, and related facilities.

Computer: A data processing machine capable of conducting substantial mathematical, computational, logical, and repetitious operations; it contains the necessary equipment, including the console, cables, screen, and so forth.

Diskette: A circular, mylar-coated disk on which programs and data may be stored.

Documentation: Information in printed form that explains the nature and use of software, including its functions, applications, and limitations.

Hardware: The physical equipment of the computer, including facilities such as the CPU and printer.

Memory: The area of the computer in which programs and data are stored.

Microcomputer: A compact and complete computer system.

On-Line: A descriptor indicating that the process or equipment is connected directly to the computer. For example, *on-line testing* means that the testing is connected to the computer, and the computer performs its functions while the testing is being done.

Printer: An equipment component that provides information such as data or analysis results in written form.

Program: A set of instructions, written in a specified format, that directs the computer about what it is to do and the order in which tasks (or operations) are to be done.

Programming: The process of writing instructions for the computer; the preparation of software.

Random Access: A procedure for retrieving data based on its address.

Sequential Access: A procedure for retrieving data according to a specified order.

Software: The instructions that direct the computer to perform designated functions. Software may consist of one or more programs.

Terminal: The equipment (hardware) for transmitting input to the computer and then receiving output from it. The terminal typically includes a screen or video display on which information appears.

User-friendly: A term used to indicate the extent to which a computer is relatively easy to use without knowing the technical language and procedures.

Process of Using a Microcomputer

A microcomputer user typically sits at a terminal and, through a keyboard very much like that of a typewriter, enters data and commands into the computer. The computer keyboard usually has more keys than a regular typewriter keyboard. These extra keys are used to issue commands for commonly used operations.

Using a microcomputer involves three primary steps: (1) transmitting input; (2) processing data; and (3) receiving output. These steps are described in Figure A.1, along with an illustration of the overall sequence, as indicated by the arrows.

Transmitting input consists of putting data, such as student test scores, into the computer. However, data by themselves do not cause anything to happen; the computer must be told how to format the data and what to do with it. Format is specified through the program, which may be an available software component. If software is not available, actual programming is necessary. Obviously, this must be done by someone who knows how to program that specific computer to do a specific task.

The second step is the processing step, which consists of analyzing the data using the software specified. Processing requires very little time, usually not more than a few seconds. It may take a little longer if the computer is being asked to do several things at once; then a sort of waiting line, a queue, forms and tasks are completed one by one, in the order in which they were received. If there is an error of some type in transmitting input—such as data entered improperly or a program not specified adequately—an error message will appear on the video display and indicate what is wrong.

After the data are processed, another message will appear on the video display indicating that the operation has been completed. The user can then receive the output, either on the video display or through the printer. A command is usually required to route the output to the printer. Output may first be viewed on the video display until it is decided whether all or part of it should be printed. Printed copy is easier to read and provides a more useful written record. But even after it's been printed, the output is retained in the computer's memory. This way, one can go back and make changes or additions without having to start completely over.

Output for measurement and testing may take a number of forms, including student records such as grades, test items, statistics generated from a distribution of test scores, objectives, and item analyses. In addition, the computer could assemble an entire test if an item bank was included in its memory. Different types of output are mentioned in the following section dealing with application.

Figure A.1.
Steps in the Process of Using a Microcomputer

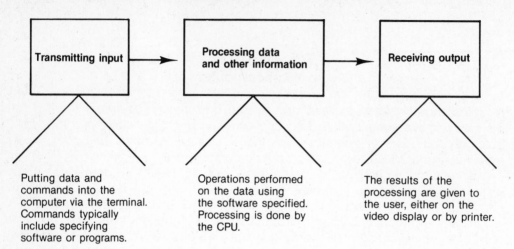

This discussion of the process of using a microcomputer is quite general. More specific instructions must correspond to the type of microcomputer being used. Such instructions for microcomputers and software are provided by their respective manuals, which outline specific operations in detail. Moreover, computer manufacturers often provide training sessions for their customers, involving several hours over a period of one or more weeks.

Microcomputer Applications in Measurement

Hsu and Nitko (1983) identify three major capabilities of microcomputers that make them applicable to classroom measurement and testing:

1. *The capacity for storing large amounts of information.*
2. *The ability to retrieve information and to make calculations quickly.*
3. *The capability of repeatedly performing the same task an unlimited number of times without fatigue or loss of efficiency. (1983, 16)*

These capabilities are related in that they complement each other for the completion of various tasks.

Many aspects of classroom measurement and testing can be done or supported by microcomputers. Hsu and Nitko (1983) identify seventeen specific tasks, called *applications,* which can be grouped into larger categories. Several categories of applications are listed and described below. However, in any specific situation, the extent of the application will depend on the available hardware and software.

1. *Recordkeeping.* With its capacity for storing information, the computer can be used for keeping a variety of data about students: test scores, grades, aptitude data, and so on. The computer can be used as a sophisticated gradebook and for storing student records.

2. *Test Preparation.* Computers can store objectives files for instructional units or courses and corresponding test items related to objectives. Objectives can be used for the selection of items, which should enhance the content validity of the test. The computer can select a specified number of items for the test and assemble them into a test format. If desirable, conditions can be specified for the selection of items, such as a range for difficulty level.

3. *Analysis of Test Data.* The potential computer use for tasks in this category seems almost unlimited. Of course, computers can be used for scoring the test, if the test consists of objectively scored items. Scoring of essay items can also be done, but this has not become a widely accepted practice. The computer can also provide statistical information about a group of test scores, such as mean and standard deviation, and information about individual items, such as difficulty levels and discrimination indexes. Reliability coefficients for the test can also be determined. In short, the computer provides the opportunity of generating results that were not obtained in the past because teachers simply did not have the time to perform the calculations.

4. *Test Data Interpretation.* The computer can provide comparisons of individual test performance with that of a group, such as a normative group. Local norms can be compared with state or national norms if these are available for a published test. Grade distribution for a single test or a combination of measures can be generated, as well. Group performance may be interpreted relative to some established level of performance.

5. *Test Revision.* The computer can provide detailed information about items that can be used in test revision. For example, counting the number of times that distracters (incorrect responses) are selected on a specific multiple-choice item may indicate that one or more of the distracters are never selected. Such an item is deficient in that at least some of its distracters clearly are not plausible. Of course, any item analysis data can be used for test revision.

6. *Test Administration.* Unless a classroom has as many microcomputers or terminals as students, a test for an entire class would not likely be administered by computer. However, individual tests (such as diagnostic tests) can be administered

by computer if appropriate software is available. Also, a make-up test can be assembled by the computer and then administered. Such test administration by computer is an example of on-line testing.

This description of applications certainly does not exhaust the possible uses of the microcomputer in the classroom, but it does provide an overview of major categories.

It is not likely that many teachers will do the programming necessary to perform specific tasks. Instead, they will select from the very large number of software programs available in the testing and measurement field. The next section will provide background information to aid teachers in this selection.

Criteria for the Selection of Software

A primary criterion for the selection of software is that it must be compatible with the available hardware. More specifically, the software must be for use on your particular computer. Most software is available in a number of formats, corresponding to a number of different computers. However, software for one microcomputer will not necessarily work for another. Therefore, you must know what is applicable for your specific computer.

Various forms have been proposed for evaluating software. For example, Bitter (1984) poses a list of questions that can be used for evaluating educational software designed for testing and related purposes. Here is a useful listing of the types of information necessary in evaluating software.

Background Information

Title:

Publisher:
  Publisher's Address:
  Service Telephone Number:

Hardware requirements:

Will the program run on present equipment?   Yes   No

Cost:

Check all materials provided with the program:
    _____ Technical manual   _____ User's manual
    _____ Cassette   _____ Diskette
Other _____

Check all potential users of the program:

_____ Teachers

_____ Students

_____ Aides

_____ Principal

_____ Other school administrators

Check all grade levels for which the program applies:

_____ K/primary

_____ Intermediate

_____ Middle school

_____ Junior high school

_____ Senior high school

If the program is subject or skill specific (for instance, history, reading), list where applicable.

_____

Applications Information

Check all applications for which the program may be used:

_____ Test item file. If checked, list:

Types of items available _____

Skills and subject areas _____

Capacity (number of items) _____

Can teacher-constructed items be added?   Yes   No

Can tests be assembled by computer   Yes   No

_____ Test administration

Can the student self-administer a test?   Yes   No

Can tests from other sources be used?   Yes   No

    If yes, list types _____

_____ Test scoring

_____ Test data analysis. If checked, indicate available information:

_____ Descriptive statistics, such as means and variance for a group of students.

_____ Reliability estimates.

_____ Individual score comparisons with group scores.

_____ Individual or group scores compared with normative group scores.

_____ Item analysis.

_____ Graphics, such as distribution of scores.

_____ Recordkeeping. If checked, indicate available information:

_____ Individual student records may be accumulated.

_____ Other data than test scores may be included.

_____ Maximum number of scores per student.

_____ Maximum number of students.

_____ Grade assignment capability.

Evaluation of Content Characteristics

Rate all that apply:

	Very good	Adequate	Unacceptable
1. Item construction	_____	_____	_____
2. Item comprehensiveness	_____	_____	_____
3. Item difficulty levels	_____	_____	_____
4. Item validity	_____	_____	_____
5. Comprehensiveness of test statistics available	_____	_____	_____
6. Comprehensiveness of item analysis statistics	_____	_____	_____
7. Procedures for estimating reliability	_____	_____	_____
8. Appropriateness of norms	_____	_____	_____
9. Comprehensiveness of recordkeeping	_____	_____	_____
10. Grading capabilities	_____	_____	_____

Evaluation of Technical Characteristics

Rate all that apply:

	Very good	Adequate	Unacceptable
1. Clarify of the display	_____	_____	_____
2. Printer capacity	_____	_____	_____
3. Information storage capacity	_____	_____	_____
4. Ease of data entry	_____	_____	_____
5. Retrieval and/or feedback time	_____	_____	_____
6. Ease of detecting errors	_____	_____	_____
7. Ease of correcting errors	_____	_____	_____
8. Documentation	_____	_____	_____
9. Ease of operation	_____	_____	_____
10. Flexibility of data input	_____	_____	_____

This evaluation form is helpful in examining potential software packages. Teachers might also want to supplement this form or combine the parts differently to evaluate software in a specific situation. For instance, ten examples each were given for content characteristics and technical characteristics. In a specific situation, one may want to rate additional or different characteristics. Nonetheless, the above listing does provide an adequate base of criteria for teachers as they consider the evaluation of available software.

Sources for Software

A number of directories and catalogs list available computer software, including programs for measurement and testing. Such directories give brief descriptions of the software, including information about the specific computers for which it is applicable.

One example of a directory of computer software is published in cooperation with *Classroom Computer Learning,* a periodical. The directory is entitled *Classroom Computer Learning Directory of New Educational Computer Software* (1983–84). Two entries from a recent issue of this directory are described below.

The Classroom Answer: Reading

Management kits designed for use with the Houghton-Mifflin reading program. They help teachers manage instruction for up to 35 students per class by machine-scoring tests, maintaining student records and producing informative reports. Grades 1–8. (1983–84, 131)

This description is followed by a review of the program disks available and their costs, along with a listing of applicable computers.

Testing Basic Math Skills 1 and 2

Two programs correlated to the Society for Visual Education's Development of Basic Math Skills series. Each provides an assessment of student mastery at the appropriate grade level and stores the results of the last ten tests for each of 50 students. Grades 2–8. (1983–84, 58)

Again, the available disks and applicable equipment are given following the description.

SUMMARY

Computer technology is changing and expanding so rapidly that nothing remains current very long. Thus, whenever a teacher is reviewing computer sources, it is important that the material be as up-to-date as possible. In addition, once a particular piece of software has been selected, the teacher should contact the publisher for a detailed description, possibly even a sales call. At this point, a software evaluation form is a very useful tool.

The use of computers in the classroom has expanded greatly over the past several years and will certainly continue to do so in the future. Thus, teachers should expect that they will use computers in their classes, for many purposes, including testing. To do so, teachers must be familiar with the use and application of computers.

Our discussion in this appendix is only an overview of basic information. To achieve competence in this area, teachers must learn about computers and apply this knowledge regularly in their work. The benefits of computer knowledge will surely surpass the effort needed to learn.

REFERENCES

Bitter, Gary G. 1984. *Computers in today's world*. New York: John Wiley and Sons.

1983–84. *Classroom computer learning directory of new educational computer software*. Winter. Belmont, Calif.: Pitman Learning.

Hsu, Tse-chi, and Anthony J. Nitko. 1983. Microcomputing testing software teachers can use. *Educational Measurement, Issues and Practice* 2, no. 4 (Winter): 15–18, 23–30.

SUGGESTED READING

Brzezinski, Evelyn J., and Michael D. Hiscox, eds. 1984. *Educational Measurement: Issues and Practice* 3 (2).

Appendix 2:
Answers
to Review Items

Chapter 1

1. c
2. d
3. b
4. c
5. a
6. a
7. b
8. b
9. d
10. F
11. F
12. T
13. F
14. T
15. F
16. F
17. diagonistic
18. a. S   b. F
    c. F   d. S   e. F

Chapter 2

1. T
2. F
3. c
4. b
5. F
6. d
7. b
8. T

Chapter 3

1. b
2. c
3. c
4. T
5. b
6. c
7. d
8. a
9. T
10. d

Chapter 4

1. a
2. a
3. d
4. d
5. a
6. c
7. b
8. a
9. a
10. c
11. a
12. c
13. a
14. b
15. d
16. c
17. b
18. c
19. b
20. c
21. d
22. c
23. c
24. b
25. a
26. b
27. b
28. a
29. d
30. c
31. d
32. b
33. d
34. c
35. b
36. b
37. c
38. T
39. T
40. T
41. F

Chapter 5

1. c
2. a
3. d
4. c
5. d
6. a
7. d
8. b
9. a
10. d
11. c
12. c
13. b
14. b

15. a
16. d
17. a

18. c
19. c
20. b

Chapter 6

1. b
2. c
3. a
4. T
5. a

6. T
7. F
8. d
9. F
10. a

Chapter 7

1. c
2. d
3. d
4. b
5. d
6. b
7. b
8. d
9. c
10. d
11. c

12. b
13. a
14. F
15. T
16. F
17. F
18. F
19. F
20. F
21. premises
22. five, eight

Chapter 8

1. b
2. a
3. b
4. a
5. c
6. d
7. a
8. a
9. c
10. c

11. b
12. a
13. F
14. T
15. T
16. F
17. T
18. T
19. F
20. T

Chapter 9

1. d
2. b
3. F
4. b
5. a

6. d
7. a
8. F
9. d
10. d

Chapter 10

1. c
2. b
3. d
4. c
5. c
6. a
7. a

8. F
9. W, W, P, T, W,
   W, T, P, T, P
10. Codes, local or state;
    Accepted practice;
    Instructor's criteria;
    Manufacturer's recommendations

Chapter 11

1. d
2. T
3. d
4. a
5. T

6. b
7. b
8. a
9. b
10. F

Chapter 12

1. b
2. a
3. F
4. b
5. F

6. T
7. d
8. d
9. b
10. c

Chapter 13

1. a
2. T
3. a
4. T
5. d

6. c
7. a
8. c
9. d
10. d

Chapter 14

1. d
2. c
3. b
4. a
5. d
6. b
7. b
8. c
9. a
10. d
11. b
12. F

13. T
14. F
15. F
16. T
17. F
18. F
19. F
20. T
21. F
22. F
23. F
24. F

Appendix 3:
Solutions
to Chapter Exercises

Note: Solutions are not provided for exercises that (1) direct the reader to some type of extended activity, such as reading a journal article, or (2) indicate considerable discussion or description.

Chapter 1

1.2
 a. No.
 b. Yes.
 c. Yes.
 d. Yes.
 e. No.

1.5
 a. instructional.
 b. guidance and counseling.
 c. administration.
 d. instructional.
 e. guidance and counseling.

1.7
 a. norm-referenced.
 b. norm-referenced.
 c. criterion-referenced.

d. criterion-referenced.
e. norm-referenced.

Chapter 2

2.1
a. 4, 6, 4, 8, 2, 4, 3, 5, 8, 6.
b. $\bar{X} = 5$, Median $= 4.5$, Mode $= 4$.
c. 6.
d. $s^2 = 3.6$, $s = 1.9$.
e. Diane, John.
f. 1.00, 0.70.
g. using top and bottom 3, 0.33, 0.33.
h. 0.69.

2.2
a. 16.83 (or 17).
b. 17.
c. 17.5.
d. 5.

2.4
a.

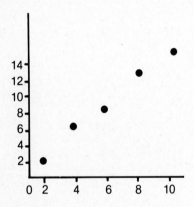

b. strong and positive.
c. 0.98.

Chapter 3

3.4
a. 3.
b. 16.
c. 85.

3.5
41 to 60; 97 to 99.

3.6
Short quizzes may not be so reliable as to warrant any greater precision in the scores that are reported.

3.7
1.07.

3.8
Percentiles may be the easiest to explain, since even nonstatistical audiences understand percentages. Standard scores and stanines require some understanding of distributions and standard deviations and would probably require more explanation and charts than percentiles.

3.9
Norm groups are not relevant to criterion-referenced tests.

3.10
Grades might reflect effort and ability, as well as actual performance.

Chapter 4

4.1
Different sources of error exist between stability reliability and equivalence reliability. In stability reliability, sources are associated with changes over time in what is being measured, such as instability in a trait. In equivalence reliability, sources are associated with a lack of equivalence between two forms of the test.

4.2
a. 0.70.
b. The new test would require 83 items, so 38 items would need to be added.

4.3
0.79.

4.4
0.64.

4.5
0.68.

4.6
Using KR-21, 0.65.

4.7
Use the KR-20 formula; proportions of students passing and failing each item would need to be determined, along with the sum of the products of those proportions and the variance of the total scores.

4.8
There would be very little variance in the test scores, which would keep the reliability coefficient low, even if measurement were consistent.

4.9
  a. True variance is 230: $r_{11} = 0.85$.
  b. Test A has the higher reliability, 0.89; Test B has 0.83.
  c. $s_o^2 = 268$; $s_e = 8.18$.

4.10
The true variance would be zero and the reliability would be zero.

4.11
0.50.

4.12
Since reliability can be conceptualized as the ratio of s_t^2 / s_o^2 and s_t^2 is part of s_o^2, reliability cannot be greater than 1.0. Variance cannot take on negative values, so neither can reliability coefficients.

4.13
7.15.

4.14
The ratio of s_e/number of items is 4.4 percent; since this is less than 5 percent, the test has high consistency.

4.15

Stability reliability is being estimated, and apparently the cognitive skill was not stable over the three-month period.

4.16

$s_e = 7.5$. The probability that Jack would have obtained the 90 if his true score is 100 is 0.092; if his true score is 95, 0.251; if his true score is 90, 0.500.

Chapter 5

5.3

0.83. Sources of variance contained in the proportion of variance not common with the criterion test are those specific to the original test.

5.5

The proportion of the valid variance is 0.54 and the validity coefficient is 0.73.

5.6

If creativity is a single trait, we would expect one general factor with all tests loading on that factor. If creativity consists of four constructs, we would expect four factors. A possible pattern of factor loadings would be at least one test loading on each factor and no test loading on more than one factor. This pattern would provide a mixture of group and specific factors.

Chapter 6

6.3

— Almost all major league catchers are right-handed.

— The number of books in the school library is:
  a. more than 4,000.
  b. 3,001 to 4,000.
  c. 2,001 to 3,000.
  d. less than 2,000.

— Middle-class flight refers to:
  a. middle-class businessmen using air travel.
  b. certain staircases.
  c. the middle-class exodus from the city to the suburbs.
  d. the middle-class exodus from the snowbelt to the sunbelt.

6.5

Using only one item format might limit the nature of the questions asked and the thought processes required of the examinees. The examinees, however, might appreciate not being disrupted by switching from one format to another.

6.6

Anything that makes scores inconsistent from one occasion to the next lowers the reliability of the test. Fluctuating standards or sloppy marking would have such an effect. A test with adequate content sampling will have a reasonable number of items over all of the important topics of a class. Thus, there will be good content validity. True-false and multiple-choice tests are reliably scored, and because each item requires little testing time, they have very good levels of content sampling.

6.8

The strength of this suggestion is that the tester would have four times as many bits of information on each examinee. The weakness is that each bit of information would be more susceptible to guessing and probably not be nearly as discriminating as the information from the multiple-choice test.

Chapter 7

7.1

There is less likelihood of guessing the correct responses of matching items, certainly with respect to true-false items. With respect to multiple choice, matching items do not require the construction of plausible distracters, which can be difficult and time consuming.

7.2

The item is far too long and contains the same number of premises and responses.

7.4

a. The blank is placed near the beginning of the item.
b. It contains a grammatical clue (an).
c. "Swiss cheese item," too many blanks; the intent of the item is obscure.
d. The blanks are placed near the beginning of the item, and the intent of the item is not clear.

7.7

A power test is one on which the students would show little if any improvement in performance if given additional time. A speeded test has a specified time limit, so at least some students would do better given more time. Teacher-constructed tests are usually power tests, because speed of performance is seldom measured.

7.8

Separate answer sheets are usually designed to speed the scoring, which is worthwhile if large numbers of students are tested. A disadvantage of separate answer sheets is that there may be confusion and procedural errors in their use, especially with younger children.

Chapter 8

8.1
  a. Item is too broad and lacks direction.
  b. Stem requires low-level learning outcomes, which are measured more efficiently with another item format.
  c. Item lacks direction, and the response is not restricted.
  d. The response cannot be scored with the direction "write all you know." Also, the item is too broad and lacks direction.
  e. The item lacks direction.

8.4

Students generally are not able to select those items on which they will do best; items will tend to be of unequal difficulty; good students will be penalized because they may tend to select the more challenging items; scoring difficulties are introduced because students are, in effect, taking different tests.

8.5
0.67

Chapter 9

9.2

The student's performance was very near the national average but somewhat below the local average. The local average must be above the national average.

9.3

Teachers use the detailed information criterion-referenced tests provide in planning instruction for individual students. School principals are more interested in how average performance in a particular school compares with the performance of other schools in the district, a norm-referenced interpretation.

9.5

Most people will easily understand the graphs but will use the narrative to get a more specific understanding of the results. Only audiences with some statistical background will want more information, such as that provided by percentiles and stanines.

9.6
A test that is unique to a school is likely to have an excellent match between the test items and the school's objectives. However, the basis of comparison with other schools may be quite limited.

Chapter 10

The exercises in this chapter require quite extensive responses; for some, the response depends upon the specific curriculum materials selected by the reader.

Chapter 11

11.2
Tests that assess scholastic aptitude are likely to be very verbally oriented. There will be a great overlap between intelligence and scholastic aptitude tests, though, because they will share components such as memory, spatial relations, and deductive reasoning.

11.3
Achievement tests are concerned with content validity, a logical process. Aptitude tests are concerned with predictive validity, a statistical process in which test scores are correlated with subsequent levels of performance.

11.4
Although scholastic aptitude tests (such as the SAT) are sometimes described as measures of achievement in our high schools, they have not served this purpose well. Those who take the test are a unique subset of students; thus, the content of the test is not representative of high school curricula. (There are also other answers to this exercise.)

11.8
Two children might receive the same score on an aptitude test at an early age yet have different long-range expectations based on factors such as parents' socioeconomic level and degree of involvement with their child. These factors clearly affect the quality of educational opportunities available to the child.

11.9
— For younger children, a biased test might place them in a slow-learner group. It

might then be difficult to get that child out of this inappropriate placement, which would be damaging.

— A high school student might enter a career field with an unrealistic expectation of success if the decision to enter that field was based on a biased test.

Chapter 12

12.2
Cognitive tests measure maximum performance; students can fake low scores, but not high ones. Affective measures are concerned with typical performance, so role playing and faking are real problems.

12.3
Both internal consistency and stability reliability coefficients can be used to estimate reliability of measures of depression. The test scores would also have to correlate with clinical diagnoses of depression.

12.4
Many of the limitations on psychomotor and affective performance are caused by factors not affected by instruction. Thus, it is difficult to base grades on things that are beyond the teacher's influence.

12.8
The greater the amount of inference required of the observer, the greater the probability of inconsistency in scores. Thus, reliability is lower for checklists that require large inferences.

12.9
There is more disagreement about the definitions of psychological constructs, attitudes, and beliefs than about psychomotor variables. An item writer would have an easier task matching items to the definition for the psychomotor measures.

Chapter 13

13.1
Guessing—Objective
Positional preference—Objective
Bluffing—Essay
Changing answers—Objective
Separate answer sheets—Objective

13.2

a. Guessing correctly on about half the items.
b. It depends on whether the test creator has a positional preference.
c. This would probably increase one's score.

13.3

a. Second-graders would have difficulty with separate answer sheets.
b. The scores would probably be lower than if the regular teacher administered the tests.
c. Practice tests would probably raise the scores on the actual test.

13.4

a. Have students explain why false statements are false.
b. Establish rapport and explain how the scores will be used.
c. Compare answers to a model answer.

13.5

a. Nonverbal cues and general level of poise.
b. Help from others and large investment of time.
c. Bluffing and penmanship.
d. Guessing and positional preference.

13.6

a. Standard questions for all examinees.
b. Test in class.
c. Model answers.
d. Use many questions; randomly order correct responses.

13.7

Young children need instruction on following directions and marking answer sheets. Older students may look for grammatical clues, longest response, and other indications of the answer.

13.8

a. 70.
b. 64.

Chapter 14

The exercises in this chapter require extended activities or responses.

Appendix 4:
Table of the Normal Curve

$\frac{x}{\sigma}$	Area	Ordinate	$\frac{x}{\sigma}$	Area	Ordinate	$\frac{x}{\sigma}$	Area	Ordinate	$\frac{x}{\sigma}$	Area	Ordinate
.00	.0000	.3989	.23	.0910	.3885	.46	.1772	.3589	.69	.2549	.3144
.01	.0040	.3989	.24	.0948	.3876	.47	.1808	.3572	.70	.2580	.3123
.02	.0080	.3989	.25	.0987	.3867	.48	.1844	.3555	.71	.2611	.3101
.03	.0120	.3988	.26	.1026	.3857	.49	.1879	.3538	.72	.2642	.3079
.04	.0160	.3986	.27	.1064	.3847	.50	.1915	.3521	.73	.2673	.3056
.05	.0199	.3984	.28	.1103	.3836	.51	.1950	.3503	.74	.2703	.3034
.06	.0239	.3982	.29	.1141	.3825	.52	.1985	.3485	.75	.2734	.3011
.07	.0279	.3980	.30	.1179	.3814	.53	.2019	.3467	.76	.2764	.2989
.08	.0319	.3977	.31	.1217	.3802	.54	.2054	.3448	.77	.2794	.2966
.09	.0359	.3973	.32	.1255	.3790	.55	.2088	.3429	.78	.2823	.2943
.10	.0398	.3970	.33	.1293	.3778	.56	.2123	.3410	.79	.2852	.2920
.11	.0438	.3965	.34	.1331	.3765	.57	.2157	.3391	.80	.2881	.2897
.12	.0478	.3961	.35	.1368	.3752	.58	.2190	.3372	.81	.2910	.2874
.13	.0517	.3956	.36	.1406	.3739	.59	.2224	.3352	.82	.2939	.2850
.14	.0557	.3951	.37	.1443	.3725	.60	.2257	.3332	.83	.2967	.2827
.15	.0596	.3945	.38	.1480	.3712	.61	.2291	.3312	.84	.2995	.2803
.16	.0636	.3939	.39	.1517	.3697	.62	.2324	.3292	.85	.3023	.2780
.17	.0675	.3932	.40	.1554	.3683	.63	.2357	.3271	.86	.3051	.2756
.18	.0714	.3925	.41	.1591	.3668	.64	.2389	.3251	.87	.3078	.2732
.19	.0753	.3918	.42	.1628	.3653	.65	.2422	.3230	.88	.3106	.2709
.20	.0793	.3910	.43	.1664	.3637	.66	.2454	.3209	.89	.3133	.2685
.21	.0832	.3902	.44	.1700	.3621	.67	.2486	.3187	.90	.3159	.2661
.22	.0871	.3894	.45	.1736	.3605	.68	.2517	.3166	.91	.3186	.2637

$\frac{x}{\sigma}$	Area	Ordinate	$\frac{x}{\sigma}$	Area	Ordinate	$\frac{x}{\sigma}$	Area	Ordinate	$\frac{x}{\sigma}$	Area	Ordinate
.92	.3212	.2613	1.30	.4032	.1714	1.68	.4535	.0973	2.05	.4798	.0488
.93	.3238	.2589	1.31	.4049	.1691	1.69	.4545	.0957	2.06	.4803	.0478
.94	.3264	.2565	1.32	.4066	.1669	1.70	.4554	.0940	2.07	.4808	.0468
.95	.3289	.2541	1.33	.4082	.1647	1.71	.4564	.0925	2.08	.4812	.0459
.96	.3315	.2516	1.34	.4099	.1626	1.72	.4573	.0909	2.09	.4817	.0449
.97	.3340	.2492	1.35	.4115	.1604	1.73	.4582	.0893	2.10	.4821	.0440
.98	.3365	.2468	1.36	.4131	.1582	1.74	.4591	.0878	2.11	.4826	.0431
.99	.3389	.2444	1.37	.4147	.1561	1.75	.4599	.0863	2.12	.4830	.0422
1.00	.3413	.2420	1.38	.4162	.1539	1.76	.4608	.0848	2.13	.4834	.0413
1.01	.3438	.2396	1.39	.4177	.1518	1.77	.4616	.0833	2.14	.4838	.0404
1.02	.3461	.2371	1.40	.4192	.1497	1.78	.4625	.0818	2.15	.4842	.0395
1.03	.3485	.2347	1.41	.4207	.1476	1.79	.4633	.0804	2.16	.4846	.0387
1.04	.3508	.2323	1.42	.4222	.1456	1.80	.4641	.0790	2.17	.4850	.0379
1.05	.3531	.2299	1.43	.4236	.1435	1.81	.4649	.0775	2.18	.4854	.0371
1.06	.3554	.2275	1.44	.4251	.1415	1.82	.4656	.0761	2.19	.4857	.0363
1.07	.3577	.2251	1.45	.4265	.1394	1.83	.4664	.0748	2.20	.4861	.0355
1.08	.3599	.2227	1.46	.4279	.1374	1.84	.4671	.0734	2.21	.4864	.0347
1.09	.3621	.2203	1.47	.4292	.1354	1.85	.4678	.0721	2.22	.4868	.0339
1.10	.3643	.2179	1.48	.4306	.1334	1.86	.4686	.0707	2.23	.4871	.0332
1.11	.3665	.2155	1.49	.4319	.1315	1.87	.4693	.0694	2.24	.4875	.0325
1.12	.3686	.2131	1.50	.4332	.1295	1.88	.4699	.0681	2.25	.4878	.0317
1.13	.3708	.2107	1.51	.4345	.1276	1.89	.4706	.0669	2.26	.4881	.0310
1.14	.3729	.2083	1.52	.4357	.1257	1.90	.4713	.0656	2.27	.4884	.0303
1.15	.3749	.2059	1.53	.4370	.1238	1.91	.4719	.0644	2.28	.4887	.0297
1.16	.3770	.2036	1.54	.4382	.1219	1.92	.4726	.0632	2.29	.4890	.0290
1.17	.3790	.2012	1.55	.4394	.1200	1.93	.4732	.0620	2.30	.4893	.0283
1.18	.3810	.1989	1.56	.4406	.1182	1.94	.4738	.0608	2.31	.4896	.0277
1.19	.3830	.1965	1.57	.4418	.1163	1.95	.4744	.0596	2.32	.4898	.0270
1.20	.3849	.1942	1.58	.4429	.1145	1.96	.4750	.0584	2.33	.4901	.0264
1.21	.3869	.1919	1.59	.4441	.1127	1.97	.4756	.0573	2.34	.4904	.0258
1.22	.3888	.1895	1.60	.4452	.1109	1.98	.4761	.0562	2.35	.4906	.0252
1.23	.3907	.1872	1.61	.4463	.1092	1.99	.4767	.0551	2.36	.4909	.0246
1.24	.3925	.1849	1.62	.4474	.1074	2.00	.4772	.0540	2.37	.4911	.0241
1.25	.3944	.1826	1.63	.4484	.1057	2.01	.4778	.0529	2.38	.4913	.0235
1.26	.3962	.1804	1.64	.4495	.1040	2.02	.4783	.0519	2.39	.4916	.0229
1.27	.3980	.1781	1.65	.4505	.1023	2.03	.4788	.0508	2.40	.4918	.0224
1.28	.3997	.1758	1.66	.4515	.1006	2.04	.4793	.0498	2.41	.4920	.0219
1.29	.4015	.1736	1.67	.4525	.0989				2.42	.4922	.0213

$\frac{x}{\sigma}$	Area	Ordinate	$\frac{x}{\sigma}$	Area	Ordinate	$\frac{x}{\sigma}$	Area	Ordinate	$\frac{x}{\sigma}$	Area	Ordinate
2.43	.4925	.0208	2.58	.4951	.0143	2.73	.4968	.0096	2.88	.4980	.0063
2.44	.4927	.0203	2.59	.4952	.0139	2.74	.4969	.0093	2.89	.4981	.0061
2.45	.4929	.0198	2.60	.4953	.0136	2.75	.4970	.0091	2.90	.4981	.0060
2.46	.4931	.0194	2.61	.4955	.0132	2.76	.4971	.0088	2.91	.4982	.0058
2.47	.4932	.0189	2.62	.4956	.0129	2.77	.4972	.0086	2.92	.4982	.0056
2.48	.4934	.0184	2.63	.4957	.0126	2.78	.4973	.0084	2.93	.4983	.0055
2.49	.4936	.0180	2.64	.4959	.0122	2.79	.4974	.0081	2.94	.4984	.0053
2.50	.4938	.0175	2.65	.4960	.0119	2.80	.4974	.0079	2.95	.4984	.0051
2.51	.4940	.0171	2.66	.4961	.0116	2.81	.4975	.0077	2.96	.4985	.0050
2.52	.4941	.0167	2.67	.4962	.0113	2.82	.4976	.0075	2.97	.4985	.0048
2.53	.4943	.0163	2.68	.4963	.0110	2.83	.4977	.0073	2.98	.4986	.0047
2.54	.4945	.0158	2.69	.4964	.0107	2.84	.4977	.0071	2.99	.4986	.0046
2.55	.4946	.0154	2.70	.4965	.0104	2.85	.4978	.0069	3.00	.4987	.0044
2.56	.4948	.0151	2.71	.4966	.0101	2.86	.4979	.0067			
2.57	.4949	.0147	2.72	.4967	.0099	2.87	.4979	.0065			

Glossary
of Key Terms
and Concepts

Achievement test: a measure of knowledge and skills in a content area.

Acquiescence set: the tendency to agree with statements on a test or affective measure.

Affective: having to do with attitudes, beliefs, and values.

Affective taxonomy: a system for classifying different levels of internalization of an attitude or value.

Agree-Disagree format: an item style that asks one to report the extent of agreement with statements; also called Likert scales (see definition of Likert scales).

Analytic scoring: a method of scoring essay items in which specific points of the correct response are identified and scored individually.

Anecdotal record: a more-or-less subjective record of an observed event.

Aptitude: a natural talent or ability.

Aptitude test: a measure of natural ability used to predict subsequent performance.

Assessment: collecting data in the context of conducting measurement.

Association form: a short-answer item format in which the student is given a set of words or phrases and must supply corresponding words or phrases according to a defined basis.

Attitude test: a measure of one's feelings toward a person or thing.

Bluffing: a strategy for responding to essay questions; providing an answer that may not directly address the question.

Buckley Amendment: legislation that gives students and their parents access to information about themselves, including test scores.

Central tendency: an average or middle value for a distribution of scores.

Checklist: a measure of the presence or absence of listed attributes.

Coefficient of determination: the square of the correlation coefficient; the percentage of the variance in one variable that is predictable from another variable.

Cognitive: having to do with knowing or understanding.

Cognitive taxonomy: a system for classifying different levels of understanding.

Completion form: a short-answer item format in which the student is to supply the missing word or words in a given item.

Concurrent validity: a form of criterion validity based on the correlation of test scores with those on a criterion measure obtained at about the same time.

Construct: a psychological trait, attribute, or quality.

Construct validity: the extent to which a test measures certain psychological traits.

Content bias: disproportionate representation of topics and terms within test items.

Content sampling: the extent to which the items on a test represent the entire domain of possible items in a content area.

Content validity: the extent to which a test or measure is representative of a defined body of knowledge.

Correction for guessing: a mathematical adjustment that brings the score to zero for someone who guessed on each item.

Correlation: a measure of the strength and direction of the association between two sets of scores.

Covariation: variance that two or more tests have in common.

Criterion-referenced measurement: measurement in which an individual's score is interpreted by being referenced to a defined body of learner behaviors or to some specified level of performance.

Criterion validity: validity based on the correlation between test scores and scores on some measure representing an identified criterion.

Cronbach alpha procedure: a procedure for estimating internal consistency reliability, based on parts of a test.

Cross-validation: related to predictive validity; using results from one sample of individuals to determine if validity coefficients will remain stable for another sample.

Descriptive statistics: summary characteristics of distributions, such as shape, average, and dispersion.

Diagnostic test: a test used to measure a student's strengths and weaknesses in a given area.

Difficulty: the percentage of persons who correctly answered a test item.

Discrimination: the ability of a test item to separate high and low scores on a total test.

Dispersion: the spread among scores in a distribution.

Distracter: one of the incorrect options or possible responses on a multiple-choice item.

Equivalence reliability: the extent to which measurement on two or more forms of a test is consistent.

Equivalent (parallel) forms: two or more forms of a test covering the same content whose item difficulty levels are similar.

Error component: the part of an individual's test score that is due to unsystematic factors, such as scoring errors.

Essay item: an item format that requires the student to structure a rather long written response, up to several paragraphs.

Evaluation: the process of making a value judgment based on information from one or more sources.

Factor analysis: an analytical procedure that can be used for identifying the number and nature of constructs underlying a set of measures.

Factor loading: from factor analysis; a correlation between a factor and a test score.

Formative testing: testing done to monitor student progress over a period of time.

Frequency distribution: a listing of scores and the number of persons receiving each score.

g-factor: a general intelligence trait that Charles Spearman theorized was common to all intellectual tasks.

General factor: from factor analysis; a factor that has substantial loading with all measures or tests.

Global-quality scaling: a method of scoring an essay item; also called holistic scoring; scoring based on the general impression of overall adequacy and quality of the response.

Grade equivalent scores: norm-referenced scores that report performance in terms of grade and month (such as 4.6—fourth grade, sixth month).

Grading: the process of evaluating performance and assigning a mark of performance level; commonly associated with assigning letters, A, B, C, D, and F—A being of better or higher performance than B and so on.

Grammatical clue: a flaw in objective items in which the wording or punctuation directs the examinee to the correct answer.

Group factor: from factor analysis; a factor that has high loadings with two or more but not all measures or tests.

Grouped frequency distribution: a frequency distribution that categorizes scores by intervals.

Guessing: a conjecture, often random, that is made when the correct answer to a question is not known.

Halo effect: an effect that can enter into the scoring of essay items; the tendency to give high scores to students known to be good students and vice versa, independent of the quality of the response.

Histogram: a bar graph that describes a distribution of scores.

Individualized Educational Program (IEP): a written plan of instruction that includes current achievement levels, annual goals, short-term objectives, specific services, dates when services begin, and methods of evaluation; a requirement of P.L. 94-142.

Information processing model: a theory of intellectual performance that includes perception, short- and long-term memory, and controlling processes.

Informed consent: giving approval for certain procedures after indicating an understanding of those procedures; for instance, giving consent to disclose test scores for a specified purpose.

Intelligence: the capacity for reasoning and understanding.

Intelligence quotient (IQ): the ratio of mental age to chronological age multiplied by 100 $(100 \times [MA/CA])$; one whose mental age is average for his chronological age group has an IQ of 100.

Internal consistency reliability: the extent to which parts of a test are consistent in measurement.

Interval: a defined distance on a scale of measurement.

Interval measurement: measurements that classify, order, and have equal distances between points on the scales.

Item bank: a set of items from which tests can be created to match a school's or district's objectives.

Item statistics: summary descriptions of a group's performance on a particular test item.

Item-total correlation: the coefficient that describes the association between the scores on a particular item and the scores on the entire test.

Kuder-Richardson Formula 20 procedure (KR-20): a split-half approach to estimating reliability that provides the mean of all possible split-half reliability coefficients for a test.

Kuder-Richardson Formula 21 procedure (KR-21): a split-half approach to estimating reliability that may be substituted for the KR-20 procedure if item difficulty levels are similar.

Labeling: to designate or describe an individual with a term or title.

Least restrictive environment: the placement in which a handicapped person can learn most successfully that is as similar to the placement of nonhandicapped persons as possible; the "most normal" setting in which a handicapped person can learn successfully.

Likert scales: a method of affective measurement in which people rate the intensity of their agreement to given statements.

Local norm: the average test performance in some city or region.

Matching item: an item consisting of a two-column format—premises and responses—that requires the student to make a correspondence between the two.

Mean: the arithmetic average of a set of scores.

Measurement: the assignment of numerals to objects or events according to rules such that the numeral conveys quantitative meaning.

Measurement scales: classifications of measures based on the amount of information contained in each score.

Median: the midpoint in a distribution; the fiftieth percentile.

Mental age: the average intellectual functioning of normal persons at a given age, usually expressed in months.

Minimum competency testing: testing designed to measure the acquisition of competence or skills to or beyond a defined standard.

Mode: the score that occurs most frequently in a set of scores.

Multifactored assessment: assessment that usually includes the physical, cognitive, psychological, and social factors that are believed to affect learning.

Multiple-choice item: a test format in which the examinee selects the correct answer from a list of possible options.

National norm: the average performance of a sample selected to be representative of the entire country.

Negative skewness: asymmetry in which most of the scores in a distribution are at the high end.

Nominal measurement: measurement that classifies elements into mutually exclusive and exhaustive categories.

Norm groups: samples used as the basis for interpreting test scores.

Norm-referenced measurement: measurement in which an individual's score is interpreted by comparing it to the scores of a defined group.

Normal distribution: a family of bell-shaped, symmetrical distributions whose curve is described mathematically by a general equation called the Laplace-Gaussian normal probability function.

Norms: the test scores (also possibly statistics generated from scores) of one or more defined groups considered to be representative.

Objective items: items that can be objectively scored; items on which persons select a response from a list of options.

Objectivity (in scoring): the extent to which equally competent scorers obtain the same result.

Options: the choices a respondent has in answering a forced-choice test item, such as a multiple-choice question.

Oral tests: examinations in which both the questioning and answering are done aloud.

Ordinal measurement: measurement that classifies and orders along a continuum.

Parallel forms: two or more forms of a test covering the same content whose item difficulty levels are similar.

Penalty for guessing: a mathematical procedure for lowering scores as a function of the number of incorrect answers.

Percentiles: norm-referenced scores that indicate the percentage of a norm group that a particular score exceeded.

Performance bias: bias introduced when individuals are not able to perform on a test because they have not had the opportunity to learn the test content.

Performance test: non-paper-and-pencil tests that require the student to engage in some type of process, produce a product, or both.

Positional preference: the regular placement of the correct response in a particular position; for instance, always in choice c.

Positive skewness: asymmetry in which most of the scores in a distribution are low.

Power test: a test in which time does not affect quality of performance; that is, students would not perform better if given additional time.

Practice effect: the consequences of taking similar tests or testlike exercises.

Predictive validity: a form of criterion validity based on the correlation of test scores with scores on a criterion measure obtained at some later time.

Premises: in a matching item, the column of words consisting of item stems.

Prescriptive test: a test designed to identify student deficiencies, weaknesses, or problems and to suggest corrective learning activities.

Primary mental abilities: intellectual performance factors that are theorized to be independent, such as number facility, verbal meaning, inductive reasoning, perceptual speed, spatial relations, memory, and verbal fluency.

Psychomotor: having to do with movement or motor skills.

Psychomotor taxonomy: a system for classifying psychomotor behaviors in terms of the amount of concentration required.

Public Law 94-142 (P.L. 94-142), The Education of All Handicapped Children Act: legislation passed in 1975 that assures a free and appropriate public education for identified handicapped children.

Question form: a short-answer item format in which the student is required to construct a brief response to a question asked in the item stem.

Range: the difference between the highest and lowest scores in a distribution.

Rating scale: a measure that contains one's estimate of the value of a person or thing.

Ratio measurement: measurement that classifies, orders, has equal units, and a true zero point.

Reading difficulty: the level of reading ability required to understand test questions.

Relevance: the match between test items and the definition of what is to be measured; the match between test items and the content area to be assessed.

Reliability: consistency of measurement; the extent to which a test is consistent in measuring whatever it measures.

Reliability coefficient: a numerical index of reliability based on a correlation coefficient; theoretically, the index can range from zero to $+1.0$.

Role playing: the act of assuming a pose or role when responding to affective questions.

Scatterplot: a two-dimensional graph of the relationship between two sets of scores.

Scholastic aptitude: one's ability to do well on school-related tasks.

Scorer reliability: the consistency with which two or more individuals would score the same response to a test item.

Secure test: a test (often commercially published) that is not circulated so it can be used repeatedly.

Semantic differential: a method of affective measurement that uses bipolar adjectives.

Separate answer sheets: forms provided for item response that are not attached to nor contained in the test copy; many can be electronically scored.

Short-answer item: a test item for which the student supplies a brief response, usually consisting of a word or phrase.

Skewness: the asymmetrical shape of a distribution.

Socially acceptable response: an answer to a question that may be inaccurate but conforms to desired social norms.

Spearman-Brown formula: a formula for estimating reliability if test length is changed.

Specific determiners: terms such as *always, never, every,* and *all* that provide clues to correct answers.

Specific factor: from factor analysis; a factor that has a high loading with only one measure or test.

Speeded test: a test administered so that students are required to complete the exam within a specified amount of time.

Split-half method: a procedure for estimating test reliability by which a test is divided into two comparable halves and the scores on the halves are then correlated.

Stability reliability: the extent to which measurement on the same test is consistent over time.

Standard deviation: a measure of dispersion in a distribution that is the positive square root of the variance.

Standard error of measurement: the standard deviation of the distribution of error scores.

Standard score: a norm-referenced measurement that indicates how many standard deviations a score is above or below the mean.

Standardized achievement test: an achievement test given under standard directions and conditions.

Standardized test: a test administered under standard conditions to extend the basis for score interpretation beyond that particular setting.

Stanines: norm-referenced scores that can range from 1 to 9; they have a mean of 5 and a standard deviation of 2.

Statistics: descriptive characteristics of a distribution of scores; also, that area of mathematics dealing with the collection, organization, and interpretation of numerical data.

Stem: the introductory part of an objective test item.

Summative testing: testing done at the conclusion of a course or some larger instructional period.

Take-home test: a test that a student completes outside of class, usually in an uncontrolled setting.

Technical adequacy: the level of test reliability and validity necessary before the test can be recommended for use.

Test: a set of items or questions presented to one or more individuals under specified conditions for purposes of measurement.

Test anxiety: a psychological state of stress caused by a testing situation.

Test bias: a systematic error in the measurement process.

Test-Retest method: a procedure for estimating test reliability by which the same test is administered twice to the same individuals and the scores on the two administrations are then correlated.

Testing: the process of administering and taking a test.

Testing arrangement: the setting in which a test is administered.

Transformed standard scores: z-scores that have been converted to a distribution with a prespecified mean and standard deviation.

True component: the part of an individual's score that is nonerror; the score if the test were perfectly reliable.

True-false item: a test format in which examinees indicate whether given statements are correct (true) or incorrect (false).

Usability: the practical factors that must be considered in test selection: cost, testing time, administrative background, and so on.

Validity: the extent to which a test measures what it is intended to measure.

Validity coefficient: a numerical index of test validity that theoretically can take on values from zero to +1.0, inclusive.

Variance: a measure of dispersion.

Weighted scores: the composite scores that are weighted combinations of two or more separate scores.

Work sample: a nontest measurement of student learning.

Yes-No format: an item style that merely seeks the endorsement of statements.

Glossary
of
Statistical Symbols and Formulas

This glossary contains commonly used statistical symbols and formulas. The notation used is consistent with that in the text, which is consistent with that of most books on measurement and statistics.

Corrected score: A score corrected for chance guessing.

$$\text{corrected score} = N_{\text{right}} - \frac{N_{\text{wrong}}}{K - 1}$$

Correlation coefficient:

$$r = \frac{N \Sigma XY - \Sigma X \, \Sigma Y}{\sqrt{(N \Sigma X^2 - (\Sigma X)^2)(N \Sigma Y^2 - (\Sigma X)^2)}}$$

Difficulty index: p, the percentage who answered an item correctly.

Discrimination index: D, a measure of how an item separates high and low scores on a test.

$$D = pH - pL$$

Mean:

$$X = \frac{\Sigma X}{N} \quad \text{or} \quad \frac{\Sigma f X_{mdpt}}{N}$$

If a subscript is included, it identifies specifically the distribution for which the mean is being considered: for example:

$\bar{X}_t$ = mean of the distribution of true scores, and

$\bar{X}_{chance}$ = Np, the mean of a distribution of chance (guessing) scores.

Reliability coefficient: r_{11}; other subscripts are used as follows, depending on the formula used for estimating reliability.

Cronbach Alpha Formula

$$r_\alpha = \frac{J}{J - 1}\left(1 - \frac{\Sigma s_j^2}{s^2}\right)$$

Kuder-Richardson Formula 20 (KR-20)

$$r_{20} = \frac{n}{n - 1}\left(1 - \frac{\Sigma pq}{s^2}\right)$$

Kuder-Richardson Formula 21 (KR-21)

$$r_{21} = \frac{n}{n - 1}\left(1 - \frac{\bar{X}(n - \bar{X})}{ns^2}\right)$$

Total test reliability

For example, when estimating reliability using the split-half procedure:

$$r_t = \frac{2r_{11}}{1 + r_{11}}$$

Spearman-Brown formula: A formula for estimating the reliability of a longer or shorter test.

$$r'_{11} = \frac{Kr_{11}}{1 + (K - 1)r_{11}}$$

Standard deviation: s, a measure of dispersion in the same metric as the scores.

$$s = \sqrt{\frac{\Sigma(X - \bar{X})^2}{N}}$$

$$S_{chance} = \sqrt{Npq},$$ the standard deviation of a distribution of chance scores.

Standard error of measurement:

$$S_e = s_o \sqrt{1 - r_{11}}$$

Standard score: z, a score expressed as the difference between the observed score and the mean in standard deviation units.

$$z = \frac{X - \bar{X}}{s}$$

Summation sign: Σ, a mathematical operation indicating to sum whatever is represented by the symbol that follows. For example,

$$\sum_{i=1}^{5} X_i$$

indicates to sum the first five X-values.

Transformed standard score:

$$X' = \bar{X}' + s'z$$

Variance: s^2, a measure of dispersion in squared scores.

$$s^2 = \frac{\Sigma(X - \bar{X})^2}{N}$$

If a subscript is included, it identifies specifically the variance; for example:

$$s_o^2 = \textit{variance of the observed distribution.}$$

Weighted score:

$$z' = \frac{\Sigma w_i z_i}{\Sigma w_i}$$

Subject Index

Validity coefficient, 98, 103, 187, 195
Valuing, 249
Variance, 32–34, 42, 43
  computational formula, 32
  definition of, 32
Vocational-Technical Consortium of States
    (V-TECS), 213–14

*Wechsler Intelligence Scale for Children,
  Revised (WISC-R)*, 237

Weighted scores, 58
Wide Range Achievement Test, 199
Work sample, 4, 207, 220–23, 225–27
  definition of, 221
  reliability of, 225
  validity of, 225–26

Yes-no format, 251, 260

z-scores, 52